74.95

BookClub
ROTARY CLUB OF EVANSTON LIGHTHOUSE

Presented in Honor of

Dave D. Davis

February 19, 2019

Rotary Club
of Evanston Lighthouse

Sustainable Solutions: University–Community Partnerships

UNIVERSITY–COMMUNITY PARTNERSHIPS

EDITED BY **B.D. WORTHAM-GALVIN, JENNIFER H. ALLEN**
AND **JACOB D.B. SHERMAN**

Greenleaf
PUBLISHING

© 2016 Greenleaf Publishing Limited

Published by Greenleaf Publishing Limited
Aizlewood's Mill
Nursery Street
Sheffield S3 8GG
UK
www.greenleaf-publishing.com

The right of B.D. Wortham-Galvin, Jennifer Allen and Jacob Sherman to be identified as Editors of this Work has been asserted by them in accordance with sections 77 and 78 of the Copyright, Designs and Patents Act 1988.

Cover by LaliAbril.com.
Printed and bound by Printondemand-worldwide.com, UK.

British Library Cataloguing in Publication Data:
   A catalogue record for this book is available from the British Library.

   ISBN-13: 978-1-78353-570-5 [hardback]
   ISBN-13: 978-1-78353-572-9 [PDF ebook]
   ISBN-13: 978-1-78353-571-2 [ePub ebook]

Contents

Foreword: The 21st-century, community-engaged university

Thomas Fisher

Director, Metropolitan Design Center and Dayton Hudson Chair in Urban Design, University of Minnesota

The essays in this volume show higher education in the process of reinventing itself. That reinvention has happened to universities before, often in the face of social, economic, and technological upheavals. In response to the Industrial Revolution of the 19th century, with its mechanization of hand labor, universities added professional education and the teaching of the "mechanical arts" to the traditional liberal arts curriculum, and in reaction to the technological revolution of the 20th century, with its focus on mass production and mass consumption, universities increased their research output and made post-secondary education available to a much larger percentage of the population.

With the emergence of the 21st-century digital revolution, however, universities seem once again faced with a dire need to change. Students now have a much wider range of options in terms of how to gain knowledge and where to earn a degree, and a much faster way of accessing information than the traditional lecture can provide. And universities' traditional sources of support—tuition-paying parents, government agencies, state legislatures—have become less dependable or able to pay at the same time.

Which makes the content of this book so significant. Through the publicly engaged work documented here, universities can help create a more sustainable future not only for communities, but also for the institution itself. In the digital age, universities need to focus on what cannot get turned into an app, and of those options, service-learning in community settings remains one of the most immersive and irreducible to software. Paradoxically, by getting students off campus, working in communities, universities have one of the most compelling reasons why students should come to a campus.

The digital age has shifted not only how students access information, but also what they do with it. The division of knowledge into disciplines, which fit the mechanization and mass-production mind-sets of the 19th and 20th centuries, seems increasingly misaligned with the 21st century, in which the scale and complexity of the challenges facing communities demand a more integrated, interdisciplinary approach. Community engagement offers one way of accomplishing this, fostering the interaction of disciplinary knowledge and relating it to the problems of particular places and groups of people.

Universities, even those internationally known for their community engagement such as Portland State University, still tend to marginalize community-based work, in part because of the apparent lack of funding to support it. But that, too, seems about to change. Financial capital dominated the economies of the last two centuries, but in the 21st century, with the emergence of a sharing or collaborative economy, real wealth lies with those places that have the greatest social capital.

All of the work described in these pages has leveraged an amazing amount of social capital, and this book documents the impact it has had in terms of improving the quality of people's lives, the productivity of the workforce, and the sustainability of these communities. In the face of budgetary cuts for higher education among state legislatures and federal agencies, universities need a new economic model, one based on the value they create in the communities they serve and the equity stake they have in the future of their regions. And who can make the case for that better than publicly engaged research universities?

Governments have a lot to gain from this. As various authors show here, community engagement can help improve the effectiveness of government programs, boost local economies, and improve the conditions in which employees work and students learn. Community engagement provides one of the most effective ways that governments can increase the social, cultural, environmental, and financial capital of their citizens, by leveraging the stores of intellectual capital that universities represent.

Such engagement also remains one of the best ways for college students to learn. As the chapters in this book demonstrate, students learn best when applying their knowledge to real situations, when teaching others about what they have learned, and when recognizing the importance of cultural and contextual differences in the process. Working with community members allows students to see the relevance of what they have learned and to remember it better because of the lasting effect it has had on them and their community partners.

This work has its challenges, as this book also recounts. In addition to having little incentive or support to engage in it, faculty members often have little training or institutional help in making community connections, something that Portland State University has done more than most to address. Many students also have relatively little preparation before getting involved in community projects, a problem that many of these authors have successfully addressed in their classes and curricula. Furthermore, communities can feel like research subjects or the victims of the academic equivalent of a hit-and-run if the engagement occurs in too superficial or short-term a way, as several chapters here warn. The legalities of intellectual property, the liabilities of students venturing off campus, and the logistics of accessing communities also create challenges that institutions need to address if they want to sustain this work and sustain themselves in the process.

No volume that I know of does a better job of conveying what to do—and what not to do—when doing community work than the book before you. Its authors convey the engagement of faculty, students, and communities in a number of remarkably rewarding experiences, and these writers do so in a thoroughly engaging way, producing a book that is a pleasure to read. That in itself speaks to the change required of higher education in the 21st century. Universities need to see everyone—not just each pupil, but every member of the public—as their students and to see everything they do, in the community as well as in the classroom, as an educational activity. The 21st-century university now exists everywhere and the chapters of this book show the great good that can happen when these invaluable institutions recognize that fact, and act on it.

Introduction: University–community relationships and the call to action

B.D. Wortham-Galvin, Jennifer H. Allen, and Jacob D.B. Sherman

The role of the university

In the cinema, the scholar at work is most often portrayed alone in the bowels of a library or archives, surrounded by a multitude of dusty tomes, disheveled, and unaware of the time of day, other people, and the outside world. Their work is solitary in terms of both process and product. This archetype reinforces assumptions made within the academy. Despite the emphasis on the oft-repeated trinity upon hire, today's scholar is most often evaluated not on teaching or service but primarily through the metric of research—typically defined as a systematic inquiry leading to verifiable (and highly vetted) conclusions. This idea of research is ubiquitous in colleges and universities within virtually all disciplines. The academy has forgotten that this has not always been the case, nor is it the only current or future available model.

Ernest Boyer (1990) describes the current state of academia as the third phase in a varied trajectory. The first stage has also been captured on the silver screen, mostly in the venue of all-boys prep schools (often set in the 1950s or 1960s) with the professor as heroic mentor who holistically enriches his students' lives; here, teaching is the primary mission of the professor as protagonist.[1] Based on a British paradigm, this first stage in the mission of the professoriate—associated with the colonial college—focused primarily on building character, with education understood less under the rubric of science and more under morality.

---

1 Exemplars are Robin Williams as John Keating in *Dead Poets Society* or Kevin Kline as William Hundert in *The Emperor's Club*.

Boyer associates the second chapter in the development of academia with the establishment of the land grant institutions.[2] Land grant universities, with their concentration on promoting technological innovation in agriculture, shifted the emphasis to service, applied knowledge, and promoted the "idea of education as a democratic function to serve the common good" (Boyer, 1990, p. 5). In this case, service was understood broadly as not only the serving of society but also the reshaping of it. One can also point to the launching of the first city college in the United States, contemporaneous with the establishment of the land grant institutions, as emphasizing knowledge production based on a service mission. The distinction between the two institutions was the sociocultural and economic production that diverged in the rural and urban settings. Thus, when established during a time of urbanization, industrialization, and mass immigration, the first city college in New York—originally called the Free Academy—focused on "whether an institution can be successfully controlled by the popular will, not by the privileged few."[3]

Today's professoriate has inherited the final phase from the influence of German universities and their pursuit of research—introduced in the United States at the turn of the 20th century and firmly taking hold after World War II.[4] Here, the primary mission of the academy is research, with research being circumscribed within a scientific paradigm which values gathering observable, empirical, measurable evidence, subject to principles of quantification and objective rationality with the intent of reducing biased interpretation.

Knowledge production

It is an overstatement to claim that the American university has oppressed the professoriate, but the circumscription of research continues to embrace the precepts of the "Enlightenment Project" to the detriment of both individual scholars and scholarship as whole.[5] Research practices, nevertheless, are culturally

2 The Morrill Act of 1862 led to the development of many institutions that are present today as flagship universities for their states. While their original mission focused on the scientification of agriculture, today these institutions engage a diverse set of disciplines including architecture.

3 This is part of a speech made by Dr. Horace Webster (https://www.ccny.cuny.edu/about/history), the first president of the Free Academy (today known as the City College of New York) at the opening of the institution on 21 January 1849.

4 Boyer (1990, p. 9) notes that Johns Hopkins University was the first institution founded upon this conception of research as the primary mission of the university.

5 Habermas (1983) introduces the term "Enlightenment Project" in "Modernity: An incomplete project"; it is also discussed at length in Wortham (2007). See also Adorno and Horkheimer (1972).

conditioned.[6] The Enlightenment Project is a set of ideas advanced by the discourse of modernity in the 18th, 19th, and 20th centuries which seeks to promote the values of the Enlightenment—equality, liberty, faith in human knowledge, universal reason, freedom, and democracy—in order to establish a universal culture which is secular, rational, humanitarian, and progressive. The Enlightenment Project follows along the axiom that for any given inquiry there is only one possible right answer. From this, it follows that a controlled and rational picture of the world can be represented. In the university system of the 20th and 21st centuries, it is the cultural memory of the Enlightenment Project that still holds fast in describing what the work of the scholar should be. John O'Toole makes a similar argument noting that the academy validates its mandate based on scholarship derived from the intellectual constructs of Logos ("the passing on of the laws through the word of the masters") and Logic ("the process of systematically establishing and validating fixed objective truths about natural laws").[7] He argues that the fixation on Logos and Logic pushes certain disciplines and their processes and products outside of the academy, necessitating the plea to be (re)considered as equals to their academic peers. Because research is artifice, it can be reconstructed. The argument is not to abandon scientific methods of research, but to make them one of many ways of pursuing knowledge so that scholarship does not sacrifice connection and interaction at the altar of rationality. The collection of work in this volume establishes that the production of knowledge should not be confined to a narrow dictionary or scientific definition that delimits the province of knowing to "the facts, information and skills acquired by a person" or to "what is known in a particular field," which by its narrow circumscription necessarily leaves gaping holes in such production and/or what we mean by knowledge.[8]

Knowledge should remain under the auspices of philosophy. In his dialogues, Aristotle defined three types of knowledge: the theoretical, the poetical, and the practical (Barnes, 1984).[9] For him, these modes of knowledge were all necessary constituents to praxis related to human activities that were the means to the ends of truth, production in action. In other words, the concept of knowledge

---

6 When historian Raymond Williams (1976) critiques the Oxford English Dictionary (OED) as a sociocultural invention and reminds us that words are not just defined by their philological and etymological past but also by their cultural history, he makes transparent the notion that research is a construct. The limitation of unquestioningly relying upon a source like the OED is that the user is limited to meaning based only on the origin of words that, while providing range and variation, sacrifices connection and interaction; it does not render the context legible.

7 Tess Brady's work led the authors to John O'Toole's discussion of research and the arts. Both discuss the uneasy relationship between the creative and the traditional academic discourses relative to higher education in Australia in Brady (2000) and O'Toole (1998).

8 These definitions represent parts i and iii of the Oxford English Dictionary's definition of knowledge (http://www.oed.com).

9 For a more detailed discussion of Aristotle's comments on knowledge, see Barnes's introduction.

was writ larger than a reliance upon verifiable facts. As Ivan Illich (1973) asserts, "…the nature of knowledge, whether scientific or ontological, consists in reconciling meaning and being." This less narrow view of "knowledge," therefore, includes the open-ended, the unprovable, the speculative, not limited to scientific knowledge.

Scientific knowledge and methods, transformed from Aristotle's delineation by the Enlightenment and again by modernization, continue to dominate contemporary academic discourse. The incorporation of technology beyond a narrow use as a tool for specific tasks and/or the content of discrete inquiries had expanded in the United States to serve as a societal frame for almost all human activity.[10] In spite of the technologically determined shape of research expectations, anthropologist Clifford Geertz (1980, pp. 165-166) notes that tight disciplinary circumscriptions have begun to loosen over the past century:

> Something is happening to the way we think about the way we think… [P]hilosophical inquiries looking like literary criticism (think of Stanley Cavell on Beckett or Thoreau, Sartre on Flaubert) … baroque fantasies presented as deadpan empirical observations (Borges, Barthelme), … documentaries that read like true confessions (Mailer), parables posing as ethnographies (Castaneda), theoretical treatises set out as travelogues (Levi-Strauss), ideological arguments cast as historiographical inquiries (Edward Said)…

The unnecessary nature of this disciplinary boundary crossing is precisely why it should be necessary, and not deemed subsidiary, within the academy. Knowledge production depends on the transdisciplinary, on identifying larger patterns, and on hermeneutics as much as it does on facts, hypotheses and reproducible results.[11] This means moving speculative and inventive inquiry from the margins to the center of what is deemed significant work.

10 This is, in part, the premise of Illich's *Tools for Conviviality*. In the first chapter, he discusses the transition of the medical profession in the 20th century from science as a tool in the advancement of the field to a totalizing constraint on practice (both moments to which he refers as watersheds). Illich (1973, p. 7) believes that this applies to all parts of society, not just the medical profession: "Other … institutions have passed through the same two watersheds. This is certainly true for the major social agencies that have reorganized according to scientific criteria during the last 150 years. Education … social work, transportation, and even civil engineering have followed this evolution. At first, new knowledge is applied to the solution of a clearly stated problem and scientific measuring sticks are applied to account for the new efficiency. But at a second point, the progress demonstrated in a previous achievement is used as a rationale for the exploitation of society as a whole in the service of a value which is determined and constantly revised by an element of society, by one of its self-certifying professional elites" (ibid.).

11 The word hermeneutics is derived from the Greek word for interpreter and is related to the name of the Greek God Hermes who served as the interpreter of the messages of the Gods. In classical antiquity (see Aristotle's treatise, *De Interpretatione*), hermeneutics derived out of the study of literature and the expectation that texts be coherent, consistent in grammar and style. In a contemporary setting, hermeneutics is often narrowly defined as the interpretation of texts or artifacts of the arts and architecture.

All disciplinary inquiry can benefit from exploration into the meaning and import of phenomena observed as well as things imagined. Martin Heidegger (1962) endorsed this broadening of hermeneutics from discrete interpretation to existential understanding, so that being in the world is just as important as knowing about the world. Advocates of this unrestrained approach claim that not everything can be studied or understood via scientific methods and that hermeneutics does not have to come after knowledge but can produce knowledge.[12] Thus, in a community-based knowledge production schema, it is not just the product that is of consequence. The process itself, the search, the inquiry, can be as substantial, if not more so, than the rendering of conclusions.

In basing its definition on the scientific method, the *Oxford English Dictionary* reminds us that research is defined not only as the search for knowledge but also as a repeated search.[13] It is the searching part of scholarship that could also benefit from a community-based methodology. At their best, community-based methods are not linear but circle back upon issues, principles, and information multiple times, often utilizing different methods during the (re)search. The intellectual work of an academic should not be to publish and then teach what has been published. Theory should lead to practice as practice to theory; teaching should lead to theory, as theory can lead to teaching. The capaciousness of community-based methods illustrates that practice, theory, and teaching should not be held as mutually exclusive, nor in a hierarchal relationship but as equal elements that at any moment can serve as the generator for the others. The public nature of these investigations allows knowledge to be disseminated, challenged, and developed in a collective and comprehensive way with the community itself. This is the foundational premise of Portland State University's (PSU) mission—to "let knowledge serve the city." Community-based methods have remained at the heart of the teaching, research, and service praxis of the members of this institution since its inception. What has changed is how PSU has applied those values and methodologies of knowledge production based on community partnerships under the rubric of sustainability (Allen and Ervin, 2016).

Types of university–community partnerships

Essential foundations for university–community partnerships are trust and communication. Hugh Sockett's philosophical analysis of those levels of trust provides a useful tool for being self-aware and making transparent the partnership needs

12 Sociologist Max Weber advocates the use of hermeneutics as a means for understanding the social context of texts (broadly defined) and for understanding the experiences of the author engaged in the text. This type of knowledge becomes as important as the (factual) knowledge found objectively in the text (Mommsen, 1992, p. 327).

13 "research, v. 2. To search again or repeatedly" (http://www.oed.com).

and/or desires for a given project (Sockett, 1998). Sockett describes the four types of partnerships as: Service, Exchange, Cooperative, and Systemic and Transformative. This categorization allows both the university and the community partner to understand how to construct an effective partnership by making transparent differing resources, expertise, power, and/or agendas. What follows in this book is a series of case studies by PSU faculty that utilize differing relationships within Sockett's rubric. It should be made clear that there is no implied hierarchy or value judgment to the relationships established or used. The case studies are meant to be a tool by which others can evaluate and transform for their own pursuits. The usefulness of Sockett's establishment of categorization of inter-institutional relationships is in fact for transparency, self-awareness, and hopefully thoughtful consideration of the desired outcomes for both parties and their relative capacities to achieve those outcomes.

A Service relationship under Sockett's schema is one in which the university unit (faculty, students, or some combination thereof) offers support (either volunteer or through paid contract) for a community institution's existing functions or programs. Simple examples might be students volunteering for a neighborhood's cleanup effort (that was scheduled and organized by the neighborhood organization); or students being paid (through a nonprofit) to help bilingual kids, who might not have English-speaking households, with their homework.

In Exchange partnerships, both the university unit and the community organization "exchange resources for their mutual benefit" in order to achieve a mutually determined outcome (Sockett, 1998, p. 77). One example could be the university's members providing training for community leaders in best practices for whatever topic or skills are the focus of their mission.

Cooperative relationships involve shared responsibilities between the university and community organizations. Within this schema, a project is usually clearly defined and does not continue beyond its specific circumscription. Curriculum development by the university for implementation by the community organization at their behest is one example of such a relationship.

The final category of Systemic and Transformative partnerships not only involves comprehensive shared responsibilities (e.g. planning, decision-making, funding, operations, evaluations) for the activities, but also includes the transformation of *both* parties in the relationship. This often leads to a revision of the relationship's desired activities and can be cyclical and longer term.

Within this volume, the case studies present a variety of paths to establish Exchange, Cooperation, and/or Systemic and Transformative partnerships. A few of the chapters even highlight how projects may move between and include more than one relationship type. Notably missing in this volume are relationships based on Service. One can only speculate as to why PSU's faculty are not documenting the performance of this level of partnership. One potential explanation is that the Service category is often an entry level relationship for someone beginning to experiment with university–community partnerships. Given that community engagement has been at the heart of PSU's mission since the 1990s under the leadership of Judith Ramaley, it is possible that the faculty have moved beyond this level as they have matured as educators and scholars, and are focusing on the other three levels because they represent a more sustained and developed set of relationships.[14] It could also be that faculty are more interested in documenting the latter three as part of their scholarly agenda rather than the first, which might seem to be merely volunteerism.

PSU case studies in university–community partnerships

The Exchange relationships established by PSU faculty demonstrate the plurality of this type of endeavor. The testing and extension of pedagogical boundaries in favor of expressly building students' and faculties' civic capacities is discussed in the chapter by Kevin Kecskes *et al.*, as a way to understand how university–community partnerships bring different outcomes and build various capacities for multiple stakeholders throughout the endeavor. By contrast, Brad Melaugh and Thea Kindschuh look at the contributing theories, features, and outcomes of two waste reduction programs, and how their perspectives on community engagement can be effectively integrated into a campus's academic and community identity. Their discussion of the Reuse Room and the Waste Audit Living Lab Experience reveals how both projects aim to engage the student body and greater PSU community in waste reduction efforts from different perspectives. Moving from ecological sustainability discourses into sociocultural ones, Per Henningsgaard illustrates the relationship between cultural sustainability and the classroom publishing methodology. His discussion of a particular university–community partnership focuses on PSU students and faculty training several dozen Roosevelt High School students in editing, design, production, and marketing, as well as helping develop a curriculum that empowers high school students and increases their sense of agency by giving them control of their own publishing house.

Two case studies bridge between Exchange and Cooperative partnerships. PSU has a record of more than ten years of transformational program work on the ground in Vietnam, playing a leading role in shaping Vietnam's sustainability agenda since 2003 that established a clear series of exchange relationships. Shpresa Halimi *et al.* focus on PSU's story in shaping the future of the coastal city of Hoi An by approaching sustainable development processes and practices through a collaborative, solutions-seeking journey taken together with Vietnamese partners that moves that international work into the realm of the Cooperative partnership. Whereas PSU's university–community work in Vietnam falls more under the auspices of economic and ecological sustainability discourses, Deborah Smith

---

14 A more comprehensive version of PSU's story can be found in Volume 1, Chapter 1 of the Sustainable Solutions Series, authored by Jennifer Allen and David Ervin (Wortham-Galvin *et al.*, 2016).

Arthur broadens the discussion to remind us who is oft left out of the sustainabil-ity dialogue through a case study that examines issues of mass incarceration and ex-offender reintegration into PSU's sustainability portfolio. Her chapter examines three Capstone courses that partner with correctional facilities and allow univer-sity students to engage directly with people experiencing incarceration, thereby contributing to community reintegration and overall community sustainability.

University–community partnerships that demonstrate Cooperative planning and sharing of responsibilities can include community-based research and documenta-tion, research on problems identified by communities, and grant-supported projects that end when funding is exhausted, just to name a few. Five chapters within this volume squarely focus on developing those types of relationships. First, Catherine McNeur's case study shows ways that public humanities courses can not only be used to help a city agency focused on greening the city get more attention and sup-port, but also develop innovative ways to make Portlanders more aware of the history of their city through the trees that have silently witnessed so much of it. The project opens up social questions about why certain trees have been preserved over others and why most of the preserved trees are in wealthier neighborhoods. Next, designing a research method that is replicable is at the center of Hunter Shobe and Gwyneth Manser's investigation of food accessibility and affordability. Their methodology intrinsically links research, student-centered pedagogies, and addressing the needs of the community partner around a topic that serves as a poignant reminder of the deep disparities between rich and poor, white populations and people of color: food. Further discussion of the intersection of economics and sustainability is explored by Charles Heying and Stephen Marotta. Heying and Marotta examine "localness" and its manifestations within Portland's artisans and makers, acknowledging their research does not just observe but also shapes the community. Their chapter provides a narrative of the process by which important research partnerships develop, and how these relationships yield valuable lessons that inform evolving research meth-odologies as well as blur the line between "successful" and "failed" research. Also leveraging business relationships as a means to a more sustainable future, Marga-rette Leite discusses the SAGE green modular class project: an ongoing community-engaged teaching and research-based initiative that uses industry and community partnerships to develop, promote, and disseminate a healthier modular classroom for children in Oregon and across the country. She highlights how SAGE serves as a model for effective action in the marketplace that positively impacts communities in need. Finally, Jack Corbett *et al.* return us to the international realm to remind us that good intentions do not automatically assure productive collaboration, and effective internationalization requires development of frameworks and resources facilitating institutional practice. Their chapter demonstrates that doing so requires an ability to move beyond agreements in principle or formal statements of mutual interest to a more nuanced appreciation of practice; that is, to addressing challenges to the viability of potentially fragile inter-institutional relationships.

The final case studies in this volume cross the boundaries between Cooperative, Systematic and Transformative relationships. Renée Bogin Curtis and Nelda Reyes

Garcia review Community Environmental Services' (CES) evaluation research conducted through strong, local partnerships to inform culturally specific, inclusive methods of sustainability planning and outreach in Latino communities. The research finds culturally framed knowledge and concerns, and identified opportunities to impact individual environmental attitudes and community norms through the development of culturally specific campaigns to raise recycling awareness. These opportunities and limits pushed CES to develop and adapt tools to meet partner needs, while implementing culturally specific and inclusive planning and outreach strategies; thus moving what began as a Cooperative relationship into a Systematic and Transformative one. In the chapter that follows, public or applied history collaboration with Native American peoples is grounded in unique historical, cultural, and political circumstances, which continue to reverberate with cultural injury to indigenous peoples. Katrine Barber and Donna Sinclair address the notion that indigenous–university partnerships require a relational process that attends to the past, generates reciprocity, and creates outcomes that benefit native communities. They, too, move between two partnership types in their quest to support native peoples leading in their own relationship to sustainable praxis. Finally, Alma Trinidad *et al.* highlight the use of Critical Indigenous Pedagogy of Place (CIPP) in interdisciplinary teaching, mentoring, and research, *in collaboration with*, and *for* community-based organizations promoting social sustainability, equity, and change. CIPP is a method and approach that is deeply informed by context with a specific focus on rootedness of place, and makes empowerment ecologically valid and credible to cultural groups, their histories, and unique knowledge bases. This approach is used to bridge community-based learning projects and facilitate university–community partnerships that acknowledge shared responsibility, leadership, and transformation in the pursuit of a more equitable and sustainable future.

In the final chapter of the volume, Wortham-Galvin returns to the four relationship types through the disciplinary lens of architecture in order to offer a critical evaluation of public interest design praxis.

Conclusion

> There goes in the world a notion, that the scholar should be a recluse ... Action is with the scholar ... essential... Without it, thought can never ripen into truth... The preamble of thought, the transition through which it passes from the unconscious to the conscious, is action... But the final value of action, like that of books, and better than books, is, that it is a resource (Emerson, 1981, p. 33).[15]

15 Emerson's essay was originally given as a speech in 1837 to the Phi Beta Kappa Society in Cambridge, Massachusetts. His speech inspired the title of the society's literary quarterly, *The American Scholar*, established in 1932.

Paraphrasing, in part, Aristotle's definition of praxis, Ralph Waldo Emerson uttered these words prior to the development of the land grant universities, when service was elevated as the primary objective of the professoriate. Emerson's speech asserted that the scholar's pursuits should be threefold: (1) the investigation and understanding of nature, not only external but inclusive of the scholar's own mind and person; (2) to study "the mind of the Past" to gain alternative perspectives and to attempt to "get at the truth"; and (3) to take action. As Emerson exhorted 180 years ago, research should not remain in the realm of facts and observations but include experience. The cases studies presented in this volume are exemplars of research and knowledge as action.

References

Adorno, T. & Horkheimer, M. (1972). *The Dialectics of Enlightenment*. New York: Herder & Herder.

Allen, J. & Ervin, D. (2016). Building sustainable scholarship: lessons from Portland State University. In B.D. Wortham-Galvin, J.H. Allen & J.D.B. Sherman (Eds.), *Let Knowledge Serve the City*, Sustainable Solutions Series. Sheffield, UK: Greenleaf Publishing.

Barnes, J. (Ed.) (1984). *The Complete Works of Aristotle*. Princeton, NJ: Princeton University Press.

Boyer, E. (1990). *Scholarship Reconsidered: Priorities of the Professorate*. New York: The Carnegie Foundation for the Advancement of Teaching.

Brady, T. (2000). A question of genre: De-mystifying the exegesis. *TEXT*, 4(1). Retrieved from http://www.textjournal.com.au/april00/brady.htm

Emerson, R.W. (1981). The American scholar. In E.F. Irey (Ed.), *A Concordance to Five Essays of Ralph Waldo Emerson*. New York: Garland Publishing.

Geertz, C. (1980). Blurred genres: The refiguration of social thought. *The American Scholar*, 49(2), 165-179.

Habermas, J. (1983). Modernity: An incomplete project. In H. Foster (Ed.), *The Anti-aesthetic: Essays on Postmodern Culture*. Port Townsend, WA: Bay Press.

Heidegger, M. (1962). *Being and Time* (J. Macquarrie, Trans.). New York: Harper & Row. (Original work published 1927)

Illich, I. (1973). *Tools for Conviviality*. New York: Harper & Row Publishers.

Mommsen, W.J. (1992). *The Political and Social Theory of Max Weber*. Chicago, IL: University of Chicago Press.

O'Toole, J. (1998). Logos and logic under siege: Performance and research in the performing, visual and creative arts. *TEXT*, 2(1), 56.

Sockett, H. (1998). Levels of partnership. *Metropolitan Universities*, 8(4), 75-82.

Williams, R. (1976). *Keywords: A Vocabulary of Culture and Society*. London: Croom Helm.

Wortham, B.D. (2007). The way we think about the way we think: Architecture is a paradigm for reconsidering research. *Journal of Architectural Education*, 61(1), 44-53.

Wortham-Galvin, B.D., Allen, J. & Sherman, J. (2016) *Let Knowledge Serve the City*, Sustainable Solutions Series. Sheffield, UK: Greenleaf Publishing.

1

A year-long journey in the orchard

Growing community amid the brambles

Kevin Kecskes, Rita Sumner, Erin Elliott, and Adriane Ackerman

It was a grey and chilly Saturday morning in February. About 35 people gathered at a non-descript street corner at 10 a.m. in Outer East Portland, Oregon. Most were students in a junior-year level public administration course focused on civic engagement; others included the instructor, a few neighbors, some volunteer staff members from a local nonprofit, and an AmeriCorp member. It was drizzling. People shuffled around, mostly to keep warm but also because they were nervous. The class assembled that day to assist a local nonprofit organization conduct door-to-door surveys in order to canvass the neighborhood about the idea of removing blackberry brambles and garbage from a nearby vacant lot owned by the City of Portland. We received instructions, clipboards, pens and maps; students paired off and headed out on foot. One student, Martina (pseudonym), arrived late and was paired with one of the instructors. After about an hour of somewhat successful door knocking, Martina told the instructor she was a police cadet in training. They spoke casually about her interests, experiences, and dreams. Eventually, she told the instructor that this class and especially this canvassing community-based learning (CBL) activity really "opened her eyes about leadership." In particular, she mentioned that it seemed to her like much of her police cadet training puts officers in a defensive posture (assuming and preparing for the worst). She noted that the public tended to react to police officers in very formal ways, often with fear. She noticed that the inviting tone of our interactions while canvassing seemed to elicit a very different, more open and casual response from people. She shared that the class is showing her that there are many ways to lead. Finally, she mentioned that she would never view the police cadet training in the same way again and that she would try to bring this new leadership approach to her fellow cadets.

Martina was one student in one winter-term course. Yet she was part of something much larger: 1) an experiment to intentionally bring an academic program within the department closer through a year-long, coordinated CBL project as part of a budding community–university partnership; 2) an effort to build capacity and positive outcomes with a neighborhood-level nonprofit; 3) a commitment to our university's social sustainability efforts in coordination with targeted neighborhoods; and, finally, 4) an opportunity to test and extend our own pedagogical boundaries in favor of expressly building students' and our own civic capacities.

In this chapter, we will tell and reflect on a story set in this emerging era of hyper-complex, or wicked problems (Rittel and Webber, 1973; Conklin, 2005). Our case expressly involves the building of a robust community–university partnership; our implementation strategy is a year-long CBL/community building effort involving three university instructors, support staff from Portland State University's (PSU) Institute for Sustainable Solutions (ISS), a fledgling neighborhood-based nonprofit and approximately one hundred undergraduate students. We are guided theoretically by inchoate interest in a "collective impact" model (Kania and Kramer, 2011). Our overarching goal—first and foremost as members of the professional educational community—is to extend students' and our own civic commitment and civic muscle. Concurrently, we are driven to align this process with the larger university context of engaging with the local community through partnerships.

Guiding theoretical frameworks

University transformation

University of Pennsylvania historian Ira Harkavy (2015) succinctly illustrates the changing nature of higher education and summarizes the essence of why civic work is critically important for post-secondary institutions today:

> [A] higher education democratic civic and community engagement movement has developed across the United States and around the world to better educate students for democratic citizenship and to improve schooling and the quality of life… Over the past two and a half decades, the academic benefits of community engagement have also been illustrated in practice—and the intellectual case for engagement effectively made by leading scholars and educators… That case can be briefly summarized as follows: When institutions of higher education

give very high priority to actively solving real-world problems…that are manifested in their local communities (such as poverty, poor schooling, inadequate healthcare), institutions of higher education will generate knowledge that is both nationally and globally significant and be better able to realize their primary mission of contributing to a healthy, democratic society.

American Association of Colleges and Universities (AACU) President Carol Geary-Schneider (2015) deepens Harkavy's argument with a specific focus on distinct, new global century learning outcomes for liberal education. The evidence-based strategies she, and many others, suggest are encapsulated in AACU's "high impact practices". [1] Further, Geary-Schneider argues that students need to be regularly confronted with "unscripted problems," provided with significant opportunities to address them, and afforded occasions to demonstrate their responses in significant and public ways that count.

[A]ll college students need to prepare to contribute in a world marked by open or unscripted problems—problems where the right answer is far from known and where solutions are necessarily created under conditions of uncertainty. These are the kinds of…problems we face both in the global community and in our own diverse and deeply divided democracy… The fact is that our graduates are entering a world of extraordinary complexity and uncertainty. The solutions they create will hold lasting consequence for our shared future (Geary-Schneider, 2015).

System leadership and co-production

What kind of "shared future" will emerge? And, what clues do disciplinary scholars provide about pathways to get there? Senge *et al.* (2015) suggest that a systems leadership approach that focuses on establishing and creatively managing organizational tension is needed. Main techniques they suggest include taking a broad view of the environment, asking good questions, and listening. New public governance theory (Morgan and Cook, 2014; Pestoff *et al.*, 2012) calls for boundary-spanning leadership that requires actors to work among undefined structures with loosely coupled groups of participants, assist them in creating a sense of shared meaning, and support them in maintaining direction. Adopting a co-production (Ostrom, 1996) approach where collective space is established for key civil society actors— especially citizens—to create new approaches to address entrenched community challenges is an essential implementation strategy (Block, 2009; Boyte, 2004; Fung, 2015; Nabatchi and Leighninger, 2015). Adaptive leadership that instills confidence in groups and individuals closest to the challenge (e.g., community members and others directly impacted by social challenges) is what is needed to productively

1 For further information, please see www.aacu.org/resources/high-impact-practices

engage a broad public to develop new approaches and accelerate substantive change (Heifetz *et al.*, 2009).

Social sustainability

These key concepts connect closely to issues of sustainability, especially social sustainability, the main focus of this book. McKenzie (2004, p. 21) suggests "social sustainability occurs when the formal and informal processes, systems, structures, and relationship actively support the capacity of current and future generations to create healthy and livable communities." Social sustainability is closely associated with the more actionable concept of social capital (Messer and Kecskes, 2008). Social capital is commonly understood to be composed of norms of reciprocity[2] and mutual trust focusing on relations between and among actors (Coleman, 1988). Putnam (1993, pp. 35-36) further develops the conceptualization of social capital as "features of social organization that facilitate coordination and cooperation for mutual benefit. Social capital enhances the benefits of investment in physical and human capital." Social capital is conceived as the currency of social organization that, through processes of coordination and trust, results in achievable products or goods for those in the organization and the community. Social capital is an expression of shared expectations that leads to cooperative behavior that produces mutual benefits.

How, then, is social sustainability increased? Or, germane to our topic as educators, how does one equip students with knowledge, skills, and attitudes to build and enact social sustainability agendas? The response, in short, is to regularly put students in environments where they can learn by doing. Specifically, students need opportunities to actively learn in communities where they can add value to cooperative energy that is being generated toward positive collective ends (Geary-Schneider, 2015; Kecskes *et al.*, 2014). Indeed, a desire to institutionalize the exploration of these topics and build effective leaders spawned the creation of an academic program focused specifically on civic leadership by PSU's Division of Public Administration in the Hatfield School of Government nearly a decade ago. Intentionally, CBL is the main pedagogical strategy employed in all core courses in the program (Nishishiba and Kecskes, 2012).

Collective impact and faculty context

Lastly, before exploring the orchard case study, we turn to the two foundational theory frames that originally inspired our work: collective impact and department-level engagement. The collective impact framework establishes the need for social actors to combine efforts and work in unison toward common goals. Sweeping *collective* impact strategies and outcomes are juxtaposed to the more common *isolated*

---

2 The norm of reciprocity is the expectation that people will respond favorably to each other by returning benefits for benefits, and responding with either indifference or hostility to harms (Putnam, 1993).

impact approach used by well-meaning civil society actors today (Kania and Kramer, 2011; Senge *et al.*, 2015). Similar to this philosophy, the engaged department framework emphasizes a collective action orientation for members of the academic unit (Kecskes, 2013; Battistoni *et al.*, 2003). In the case of the orchard, PSU's ISS acted as the "backbone organization"—a key role in the collective impact framework[3] —to strategically connect the university with specific members of a targeted neighborhood community as well as to support communication and multiple reinforcing activities. While members of the entire Division of Public Administration were not involved, core faculty affiliated with the undergraduate civic leadership program embedded within the Division were; the authors intentionally joined efforts in this year-long experiment. From the outset, participants in this initiative adopted an attitude of curious inquiry and set forth an action research agenda. Our overarching research strategy was simple as participant-observers: document and interpret what happens over the year with particular focus on students, community members, the nonprofit organization in the neighborhood, ISS, and the faculty. In the following sections of this chapter we will briefly introduce the case for our study, discuss our research methodology, present and analyze our findings, consider areas for further investigation, and share concluding thoughts.

Case design: Green Lents and the community orchard project

In 2013, ISS launched the Sustainable Neighborhoods Initiative (SNI) that aims to connect PSU students and faculty with community partners to advance sustainability efforts on a neighborhood scale (SNI, 2015), exemplifying PSU's motto of "Let Knowledge Serve the City." Through this initiative, ISS acts as a convener to align university and community partner goals to provide meaningful service-learning experiences for students and increased capacity for partners serving neighborhoods in the Portland area (SNI, 2015). As three faculty teaching the same course (PA 311—Introduction to Civic Engagement) over the academic year within the Civic Leadership minor, faculty proposed the idea of increasing capacity for both students and partners if we engaged in a year-long project in lieu of disconnected, short-term, quarter-long projects.

---

3 The five conditions for collective success are: 1) common agenda, 2) shared management systems, 3) mutually reinforcing activities, 4) continuous communication, and 5) backbone support organization (Kania and Kramer, 2011).

Figure 1.1 **This heuristic places the public work—the orchard case study—at the center. Informing the work are theories and action focused on civic leadership and social sustainability in the pedagogical context of community-based learning**

Source: Pond and Ackerman (2015)

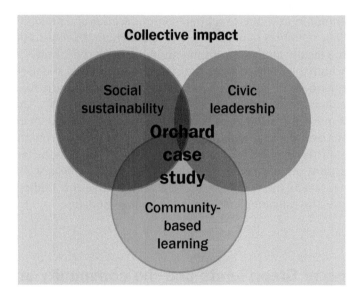

PA 311 provides an introduction to the key concepts related to civic engagement with opportunities to apply guided classroom learning and civic skills relating to real-world issues that occur within a community of interest (see Fig. 1.1). The course explores the view that civic leadership and renewal focuses on creating opportunities for ordinary citizens to come together, deliberate, and take action collectively to address public problems or issues that citizens themselves define as important and in ways that citizens themselves decide are appropriate and/or needed (Gibson, 2006).

For the project, we aimed to engage students in a big picture, long-term, connected project that embodied the spirit of collaboration needed for addressing "unscripted problems" within a community in Portland, Ore. We challenged ISS to think beyond a ten-week term and imagine an integrated academic year-long project that was developmental by design. This would increase student engagement capacity for a partner project from 25–35 students (one class, one term only) to nearly 100. As we discussed the potential of a connected project, a nascent local nonprofit named Green Lents (GL) emerged as a partner that could utilize our proposed protracted model. GL mission is to "provide volunteer, education, and leadership opportunities in and around Lents" in southeast Portland and to "build local resilience and promote environmental stewardship to benefit plants, animals, and people" (Green Lents, 2015a). The GL mission distinctly embodied the aims of sustainability and increasing social capital.

The Malden Court Community Orchard

At the time of the planning meetings, GL was in the early phases of planning for the development of the Malden Court Community Orchard, which was described as a group of neighbors and organizations in Lents working to create and maintain a community orchard that reflects the dreams and needs of its diverse community (Green Lents, 2015b). The orchard project is coordinated by a team of local neighbors and organizations committed to stewardship of a vacant city site, to create and maintain a community orchard. The project strives to "create inclusive space for growing food and harvesting, building community and collaboration, creating learning and building opportunities, improving watershed health, and sharing abundance" (Green Lents, 2015c). The purpose of our collaboration was to increase the capacity of the all-volunteer GL leadership team tasked with: 1) coordinating the construction of the orchard; and, more importantly, 2) building neighbor/local citizen-level commitment to the initiative. The action strategy was to reach out to more community members for input than would otherwise be possible. This would be accomplished through a series of student-led canvassing events and community design meetings throughout the year.

Student teams in each ten-week iteration of the course spent two 2-hour canvassing sessions in the neighborhood, going door-to-door, gathering community input regarding community development ideas for the orchard space. For each consecutive term the canvassing questions built directly on data gathered by students during the previous term; this created a communication feedback loop between community members and GL. For example, in fall term the students asked questions to better understand the importance of the orchard to community members (neighbors) such as how likely they were to be involved, to rank the goals of the orchard by importance, what kind of foods they wanted to see planted, what concerns they would like to share, and so on. These questions were then reiterated and more qualitatively explored in the community design meetings. In winter term, after initial feedback from fall term, a new set of students canvassed again to garner further information about how community members might use the space, as well as information on more logistical aspects of physical design. Spring term was the culminating canvassing event where GL focused on applying data collected from the two previous terms. The canvassing focused on gathering final input from neighbors on orchard design and initial construction details. Each term built upon the social capital that had been established with the previous round of students and organizers.

A second component of the project was to promote attendance and help to facilitate a series of community design meetings where neighbors could illustrate, map out, and discuss visions for the orchard in real-time with other community members. These spaces facilitated community conversations around issues as practical as where entrances should be located and what kinds of trees should be planted, as well as more qualitative inquiry including shared visions of the orchard through storytelling and envisioning processes. In spring term the nearly complete graphic design of the orchard was publicly shared; however, GL remained flexible by inviting neighbors to continue to add comments and preferences (see Fig. 1.2). Not only did students take notes and help with set up and break down at these meetings, but they also had an integral representative role, sharing community input garnered from community members during student canvassing rotations. Student deliverables for both course requirements and tangible items for partner review included a formally written report on their canvassing experience as well as in-class debriefs with GL staff that included open dialogue and discussion, the compilation of survey and meeting data, and a final written common assignment integrating students' service experience with theories of civic engagement and social sustainability.

Figure 1.2 **Design and style ideas for the orchard's education-focused building. Sample photographic images were provided for canvassing to gather community members' preferences**

Source: Adriane Ackerman, with special thanks to Audrey Pond, PSU undergraduate student and ISS Fellow, for permission to use her images.

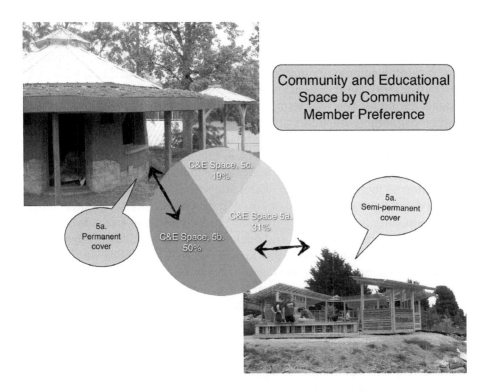

ISS Fellowships: increasing leadership capacity

After the first (fall) term, ISS piloted a new "ISS Fellow" program designed to increase the community engagement and practical leadership experience of select, promising students as well as to directly build additional capacity for all involved in the initiative. Two undergraduate student "Fellows" were recruited for winter term to assist the project by facilitating communication and planning between the community partners, neighbors, and university faculty and staff (Pond and Ackerman, 2015). The addition of the two Fellows added significant value to the project. For example, the second iteration of the course in winter term was able to gain input from 104 community members, nearly doubling the input from the previous term. In spring term, the ISS Fellows created an opportunity for bi-and multi-lingual students to amplify GL capacity by reaching out to residents who had only rudimentary abilities to communicate in English. Guided by the co-production and collective impact models and working iteratively we thus refined the roles of ISS as convener and the Fellows as co-learners, co-researchers, mediators, and peer mentors.

Research methods

Trajectory for interpreting the orchard project

In an effort to reconstruct the arrangement of pedagogical conditions, processes, and contexts in the Malden Court Orchard CBL project, we followed Yin's (2003) guidance in positioning the research inquiry. For this case, we pursued the inquiry directed toward *how* a course in public administration at a university has enabled an educational trajectory that demonstrates both transformation toward community-based learning strategies at Portland State University (Messer and Kecskes, 2008) and holistic preparation of undergraduate students to ethically and thoughtfully "enter a world of extraordinary complexity and uncertainty"…and to create solutions that "will hold lasting consequence for our shared future" (Geary-Schneider, 2015).

Case design for the Malden Court Orchard

To illuminate details of this descriptive case study, we have relied on Reason and Bradbury's action research orientation that seeks to create "participative communities of inquiry in which qualities of engagement, curiosity, and question posing are brought to bear on significant social issues" (Reason and Bradbury, 2008, p. 1). This orientation brings together action and reflection, theory and practice. This action research CBL course sought to address a key social issue as identified by our community partner—developing community capacity to create and sustain local space to include a community orchard and community gathering and learning place. En route to problem-solving and filling the capacity void, the social complexity and challenges from larger contextual factors became evident to students as well as to all actors involved. Thus, careful attention to progressively strengthening student understanding was necessary to scaffold student learning, in other words, to ensure that students' insights were successfully transferred from one term to the next. Concurrently, dialogue was ongoing among faculty, Fellows, and community partners to identify needed adjustments in content areas for additional emphasis in the classroom.

Case propositions

The case propositions direct our attention to concepts relevant to analyzing and describing this case (Yin, 2003). At the highest level of view, the case demonstrates the intersection of social sustainability, civic leadership, and CBL as intended at the outset (see Fig. 1.1). For viewing this pedagogical intersection, to reiterate, we strived to plan and act toward the philosophical shift within higher education supportive of Harkavy's (2015) and other scholars' argument on the criticality of civic engagement in universities along with Geary-Schneider's (2015) description of student preparatory immersion in "high impact practices" to enhance their ability to confront "unscripted problems." We also employed Kania and Kramer's (2011) "collective impact" model, manifesting in the context of ISS working with an "engaged department" (Kecskes, 2013), as a major lens through which to examine this case. Sub-concepts supporting collective impact included are co-production (Ostrom, 1996) and reciprocity (Putnam, 1993) and looking toward student learning outcomes aligned with those advanced by the aforementioned visionary scholars.

Case data collection

Following Yin's (2003) recommended processes, multiple sources of evidence were collected during course planning, execution, and reflection each term. Further, both data triangulation (use of several sources of evidence essential in case studies) and investigator triangulation (faculty sharing experiences as participant-observers) provided rich evidence from multiple sources from which to analyze and report this case. Data triangulation included the following:

- Reviewing documentation: early documents generated during collaborative planning among ISS as convener, the public administration faculty, and GL community partners; quantitative data of activities generated in each of the three terms; faculty field notes and photographic images

- Reviewing archival records: Lents community data from websites and documents, GL data from websites and documents

- Conducting a semi-structured interview of GL community partners during spring term, which was recorded and transcribed, and collecting written responses to the same interview questions submitted by one additional partner not present for the interview

- Collecting physical artifacts—samples of informational material generated term by term at GL for communicating to local residents about planned and ongoing opportunities for shared dialogue on moving the orchard project forward

- Reviewing and coding student final, common writing assignments as authentic performance-based assessment

Faculty triangulation (Yin, 2003) provided an opportunity for the faculty as participant observers to collectively share experiences, inform each other of lessons learned as the sequence of terms progressed, and collect, interpret, and analyze data over three terms. For this case, the process was undertaken in the spirit of collaboration and co-inquiry with institutional and community partners, students, Fellows, and among the three primary public administration faculty to advance the most thorough critique of data (Shani and Pasmore, 2010).

Discussion of findings

As previously stated, our overarching research questions were simple and focused on the "what, why, and how" of the engagement. The simple answers are that people and communities changed, perceptions shifted, communities grew stronger, relationships were strengthened, and social capital was produced, dispersed, and reinvested for social sustainability. In the following sections we explore the impacts of the project on our five key actors: students, community partners, community members, ISS, and faculty in an effort to highlight the benefits, costs, and lessons learned throughout the year.

Student outcomes

Student outcomes varied but aligned with current scholarship on service-learning. Students contributed to thoughtful citizenship by engaging in authentic service with the community. The project increased students' capacity for developing a sense of personal efficacy and commitment, gaining a deeper understanding of social issues, lifelong learning and problem-solving skills for community action and involvement, and acquiring post-formal reasoning abilities necessary to address complex, "ill-structured" social problems (Eyler, 2002, p. 519), all of which were exemplified in review of students' experiences. Further, students adopted soft and hard skills related to community engagement, were able to assess and affirm their own civic values when confronted with real-world praxis, and experienced significant paradigmatic shifts when confronted with issues of privilege, diversity, equity, and social sustainability.

On an instrumental level, students augmented a hard skill set by developing critical and effective written and oral communication skills, learning and practicing best practices for canvassing, data collection, and analysis, and computer skills through the input of data into online survey instruments. However, more notable were the more qualitative outcomes experienced by students, such as empathetic communication techniques, dialogue facilitation, team organizing practices, project planning, giving and receiving feedback, conflict resolution, and real-world problem-solving. We specifically focus here on what we would note as transformational learning moments. Themes for student learning were analytically isolated by qualitatively coding their common writing assignments over the year. The themes that emerged included: 1) exercising praxis, or deep learning in action; 2) shifts in self-conceptions and personal capacity for community leadership; and 3) critical thinking where students were empowered to address their own significant challenges and repeatedly provide their own critiques.

Praxis: connecting theory to practice

Students continually demonstrated how they let theory inform their practice and vice versa within community-based settings and in the classroom. One such example was deep learning around communicating with the public during door-to-door canvassing and in community meetings. In class, students read an excerpt from Stephen Covey's *Seven Habits of Highly Effective People* (Covey, 2011) in which empathetic listening and cultivating a habit of "seeking first to understand" was emphasized. This reading extended students' theoretical understanding of "listening" to incorporate the adoption of intentions in order to understand from "the other's" paradigm, or from another person's frame of reference. In practice, time after time, students noted how they channeled Covey's lessons when listening to both positive and negative feedback from the community. One student recalled:

> When approaching peoples' doorsteps, I had to be in a mindset of, "How do these people really feel about the orchard? What do they want, what do they like, and dislike?" [A]nd made sure that I never made it about my opinions. This exercise of approaching people in a community and asking what they thought, with the goal to really understand, really enlightened me. Peoples' responses were incredibly insightful and productive. Everyone wants to be heard.

Further, students were able to recognize how empathetic listening was implemented in participatory community processes. One student noted:

> I encountered empathetic listening quite often during the design unveiling. People would ask questions and the presenters would try to rephrase the question in a way to make sure the person who asked knew they

understood where the question or concern was coming from...we were able to use this skill to show the res idents that we actually cared what they were saying.

Students displayed a keen understanding in their shift from selective and judgmental listening to empathetic and deep listening, and became aware of how important this skill was for engaging the residents in the Lents neighborhood, especially as they relayed community concerns around issues of homelessness and illegal drug use around the orchard site.

A second example of deep learning was student reflection on democratic processes including deliberation, framing for problem-solving, and collaboration. Students came to see how democracy is both a means and an end to creating healthy communities, and thus, healthier democracies. They articulated a direct understanding of how and why these pro-democratic processes were being carried out in the community:

> My experience with GL and democracy might seem limited, but there was a lot to be seen. Each step that was taken [by GL] was thought out and evaluated by everyone who was willing to participate...showing that [GL is] more interested in how it can affect others (vs. themselves) shows that they are attempting to get as many people as possible to participate in a democracy within their community.

Further, this experience had a significant impact on international students as they explored notions of American democracy and representation. One student stated:

> When we had the design meeting, I was surprised by the number of neighbors who attended the meeting. [In the meetings] neighbors changed their weekend schedule and came to discuss options about the orchard. The meeting was really organized and neighbors came to mutual agreements without arguing. What I saw in the design meeting were strangers representing their own ideas... In my country, Yemen, usually only elders represent small communities in decision making.

Students also demonstrated increased knowledge around the role and practices of civic associations as promoters of pluralist desires, a concept integral to healthy democracies (Putnam, 1993; McKnight and Block, 2012):

> McKnight and Block mention to an extent the power associations and organizations can wield, GL being an example of this. When an organization can harness the cooperation of its members and the involved community, great achievements can be performed... GL was able to harness this ideal power and brought the Lents community together when, alone, they were divided. By creating this community orchard, GL was able to unite the neighbors to create a positive and productive project for all those interested.
>
> Associational life binds people together and shapes a community to be dependent upon one another versus depending on consumer based organizations that only care for profiting off of us. Democracy plays a big

role in this concept because groups that share something in common always have to make a decision that is best for the group and must make decisions together.

Students seemed to conceptually understand that volunteerism and association are important, but until they became involved on the street level, the nature of associational life was not fully clear. This CBL project allowed them to witness first-hand how collective problems can be resolved at the community level by a dedicated group of engaged citizens.

A third area of deep learning and praxis occurred around issues of privilege and diversity. One of our key programmatic objectives in the Civic Leadership minor is to provide students with regular and repeated interactions with people with whom they may not normally interact, with the expectation that these experiences will allow students to confront and deconstruct their stereotypes, unpack their own and others' sense of privilege, and harness these new understandings toward positive social change. Topics of power, privilege, and diversity were deliberately integrated into the course content and students had profound shifts in their understanding of equity, diversity, privilege, and food access.

One student noted that they had never considered that access to food was a privilege until they were able to see how this impacted the quality of life in the Lents neighborhood. Students also shared concerns about how the community perceived issues of class and homelessness, as well as how they could incorporate more diverse leadership into the project team. One self-identified student of color noted that the community had a leadership diversity issue but also struggled with how this might be resolved. This was informed by both the student's experiences in the community as well as by the course materials:

> In "Frankly not about food forests" they express how the majority of the leaders seen in their eyes "consist of white folks with resources, privilege, and above all else, influence and access" (Toi, 2013). I can see how putting Toi's opinion in the context of the community orchard can be a problem to many, because our community partners all happen to be white, and many might have the same opinion as Toi…I do believe that having more diverse leaders [as] part of the community orchard project will be helpful, but that is a tough situation because we do not want to tokenize anyone.

Or, another student became more familiar with her own sense of privilege in relation to course texts and to the context of the engagement activities themselves:

> The first element [essential for civic engagement] is giving yourself room to learn from others and most importantly from yourself… I personally agree with Jeremy Dowsett's [2014] article because even though I am a person of color I also had to learn that I had privilege, and that not only white people have it. I strongly think that as a person of color we also have to learn that part of us in order to let allies in.

This points to deep learning on the part of these students; this also reminds faculty about the need to ensure sufficient class time for discussing these issues. Important to note is that the GL partners also identified that diversifying leadership was of significant importance to them as well. Other examples of praxis around equity included a nursing student noting how it was helpful for him to see those he served in his job in the emergency room within their own neighborhood contexts thus giving him greater empathy for neighborhood access to healthy lifestyles.

Another "aha" moment occurred when a student was empowered to use her bilingual skills to help other students convey information to community members and noting how she felt useful in those scenarios yet sad that without her presence these members would not have access to the same information as English-speaking community members. These points mark just a few of the transformational learning moments that occurred as a result of conducting a CBL project in a diverse neighborhood.

Shifts in self-conception

Service-learning has proven impacts on students' own "self-concept" in relation to the cultivation of civic values and skills (Morgan and Streb, 2001). While we as educators attempt to nurture self-concept, "a much more effective approach is to allow students to learn that they can have a positive impact on their community by actually making a difference" (Morgan and Streb, 2001, p. 155). Working on this project made students feel as though they could cause change; this increased students' level of belief in their own civic competence. Students were able to clearly see the connection of local problems to more macro solutions, felt as though they had made a significant difference in the lives of others, saw themselves as being able to engage in similar work in the future, and realized their own capacity for community-level leadership. One student noted a transformational moment in his own conception of leadership:

> I was sort of worried because I didn't understand what civic engagement was and how it pertained to the leadership aspect—that was what I was interested in learning about to add to what I've already picked up during my military service... I came to realize that in order for one to become an effective leader one must first know how to engage those who one plans on leading and this started at the micro level, which was me... But not only did I need to relearn what it means to be a part of the community, I also needed to re-evaluate who I am as a person and how I can contribute my skills to help make a difference.

Students also expressed a sense of empowerment for future leadership:

> Overall, this class has given me a wonderful knowledge base and template to move forward with my career in civic leadership. The many tools and people I have met will guide me into a greater understanding of how to become a better leader... I look forward to seeing the continued community building and projects...that will be the start of the resurgence in

> Lents. As citizens of our neighborhoods, cities, nations, world, and universe it is our responsibility to create a sustainable world for all. We must continue to look at people for the skill sets they bring to the table. We must continue to hear them and not just listen. As a community, we must remember to collaborate. Nothing can be done if we decide to go at it on our own.

As faculty, we also observed that many international students voiced their positive opinions about this project in relation to similar but often more challenged change efforts in their home countries. Further, several students modified their formal course of study based on their increased interest in the active application of their community experience. These examples, among many others, exemplify significant changes in students' self-conception.

Critical thinking and problem-solving

Students need to be regularly confronted with "unscripted problems," provided with significant opportunities to address them, and afforded occasions to demonstrate their responses in significant and public ways that count (Geary-Schnieder, 2015). A final student learning outcome was that students became empowered to address the challenges associated with democratic community change. There is evidence that this occurred due to students' repeated self-critiques, solution generation activities, and discussion of the impact of community engagement work going forward in their lives:

> I feel I have made a small difference in the lives of the Lents community by my actions and interactions during the canvassing sessions, I know that I want to stay informed about the Lents project along with finding or creating projects of my own in my neighborhood that will make a change for the better for my neighbors and the neighborhood. This was an enlightening and sometimes intense class but a real eye opener... All my life I have been searching for my purpose, for that one thing that I was meant to do. This course has opened up new avenues by increasing my knowledge and perception of life, community, and self... I feel I want my role in the community to be a pro-active, meaningful, partnership in decision making ability for my community and with other "have nots" like me.

Students critically reflected on what would happen once their volunteer work was complete and made suggestions for improvement of the project in areas such as better accessing community members' talents, tools for making the project "stickier" (Gladwell, 2000, p. 89) with the creative use of social media and technology, and how longer time frames for canvassing might improve student ability to engage in more empathetic listening. Two examples of critical thinking employed to improve the project's future were noted:

> Technology, I believe, was a flaw in the GL playbook. There was not enough outreach via technology. To me this meant that more connectors

were needed to find people in the community who had the special skill of using technology and social media to the project's advantage.

Moving forward, this project could be greatly added to if the project members sought out to learn the gifts of their neighbors... I'm sure the members of the committee are great at some of these things [carpentry, painting, gardening], but how much better would this project be if everyone in the community was involved and got to share their gifts?

Community partner outcomes

Through semi-structured interviews with community partners we attempted to garner the most important impacts for GL. Along with providing greater volunteer capacity to cover more ground in the community as well as an external source of data collection, some more qualitative, substantive outcomes emerged such as increased accountability, leadership development, data-driven impacts for increasing capacity, creation of community feedback loops, clarifying mission, values, and goals, as well as a shift in GL's own perception about partnering with institutions outside of the community of interest. First, Green Lents was better able to be accountable for translating intentions into structured actions on a reasonable timeline. Partners specifically articulated the university's role in helping them achieve better accountability:

> One of the things that was really obvious from the beginning was that having a partnership with PSU students really pushed us to put events on the calendar. So things we wanted to do, if we wanted you to help us do them, we had to plan ahead, we had to get dates on the calendar, and then it also gave us deadlines. We had to have our materials ready, our brochures ready... It helped us translate good intentions into actions.

Here, PSU faculty, students, and ISS acted as accountability mechanisms to enforce the creation of schedules that had to be maintained. Partners noted that while this was challenging, it created the positive results of keeping them on task and able to quickly respond to community needs.

A second partner outcome was that GL developed leadership capacity for its own projects. At the time of the project, GL was in the process of entering a capacity building program in order to be able to hire a full time AmeriCorps paid staff. Because this paid staff was able to more directly communicate with our undergraduate Fellows on the project, the partners witnessed a direct increase in connection among collaborators. Further, this partnership provided the opportunity for GL members to evolve into adaptive leaders and increase their own leadership skills including public presentation, organizing, canvassing, volunteer management, planning, communication, grant writing, as well as improving flexibility and creativity. One issue that emerged in the first term was that during the community meetings, GL felt "inundated by PSU students." Thus, in the second and third iterations of the course, the partners set a limit on student attendance at public meetings and provided other opportunities for students to engage such as assisting with soil testing meetings and other public events.

Third, a substantial set of data evolved from this project that will continue to bear fruit as GL continues in its capacity building phase. The partners articulated this as one of the most important benefits associated with the project:

> This is one of my favorite things about our partnership with PSU. I'm holding a packet of information that put the data that was collected at public meetings and door-to-door into a visual form. I can hold this up now and I can say to people "This is why we're building a community orchard. Because what our neighbors have said they would value about that space is, number one, growing food and harvesting, but close behind that is building community, which is why we're going to do it in this way…"

Not only has the student data generated informed service delivery, but also it has helped GL attain grants and move forward very quickly with other aspects of the project. During this project year, the nonprofit received two large grants to continue the orchard project—demonstrating that active citizen engagement was critical to success in receiving the grants. GL was also able to use student-generated data to secure funding for blackberry removal and soil testing on the orchard site, as well as provide resources for new paid leadership positions. GL staff further mentioned that the "information [collected and organized by students] provides a foundation for how we're working with community and how we're building opportunities for leaders in the project and the neighborhood."

A fourth partner outcome was that the project helped to create a continuous feedback loop between community members and GL organizers that would not have existed without the nearly 100 volunteers collecting input on the street level. In particular, the partners described previous antagonism in the community when other organizations attempted to do similar work. Community members have stated to GL that in the past they have shared their opinions and nothing happened:

> We've done canvassing in the past and the feedback I've gotten was "why didn't you come back? Why didn't you call me? I gave you my number"… so having those students there to help us do call downs was a huge benefit and some of the feedback we were hearing is "Oh yeah, I heard about that… Oh yeah, we know about that project" [which is] really unheard of in a lot of situations.

This project, as the canvassing questions built upon previous data, demonstrated to community members not only that they had been heard, but that they were being asked again and again to help refine the process and outcomes.

Fifth, the partners expressed how the project helped them to better clarify their own mission, values, and goals and get better organized for implementation of the different phases of the project. They stated, "We're trying to narrow our mission and provide a service for our community and for potential leaders in the community, and this helped us really define some of those ways we can do that." Further having to articulate their mission to PSU students, forced them to "sit down and work a little bit deeper, and articulate a little better, and be a little more clear." They recognized that the small group organizers on their team all had an idea of what the aim of the project was, but that this needed to be better articulated to others in the community. PSU students acted as a sounding board for GL to refine that process.

Finally, GL expressed a deep satisfaction with the success of the collective impact model noting how each actor was integral to the success of the project. They came to see PSU students not only as passive data collectors and information conveyors from outside the community but as collaborators and co-producers. One of the organizers explicitly expressed her weariness with having outsiders come in on a locally based project but noted her "aha" moment facilitated by one of the faculty in the project.

> [The faculty member] helped me reframe when I was struggling at one of the public meetings to introduce everyone who was in the room, and I was thinking I would introduce him and "his" PSU students, and he said, "How about 'our' PSU students?" And I thought, "Oh, they're 'our' PSU students." And it just turned for me a little bit. They're project partners. They're not strangers coming from an institution downtown. They're partners to help this project. They're very much our students, and they're learning from us, and I think that kind of collaboration could eventually, if that keeps happening successfully, diminish a lot of the antagonism that our neighbors have.

Community partners were also able to directly see impacts that not only their *collaboration* but also their *co-education* had on PSU students when students from previous terms began to become more involved. Some inspired students searched for (and found) orchard-related internships, others even changed their majors to better align with this type of community engagement and community change work.

Community member outcomes

As a result of this project, community members saw their input translated into action, were more positive in successive canvassing interactions, and articulated a sense of shared community vision. This is evidenced not only by the increase in participation in the second round of canvassing but in changed community perceptions and overall greater investment in the second and third rounds. While the unit of analysis of our study was not the individual community member (neighbor), our interview and interactions with our community partner (GL staff) surfaced interesting and unanticipated observations that may point toward positive individual neighbor-level impact regarding the project, and perhaps even regarding the changing ethos of the neighborhood itself:

> The students were the ones going around to hundreds of households [which] allowed team members on the orchard project [GL staff] to go directly to the immediate residents. So, for example, instead of knocking

on 100 doors, I was able to go to the people who live immediately adjacent to the lot—who were a little more sensitive—and stand on their doorstep for 45 minutes and talk and develop relationships. Especially for those who never go to a public meeting, [I was able to] hear their concerns, directly face to face, one on one, and that was really hugely beneficial for the project. Their [neighbors'] relationship to the project transformed over the year. They still have concerns about the neighborhood and what's happening on the street, but they're no longer turning those concerns into resistance against the orchard. One of the guys, who was at the beginning against the project, but also saying, "Well if you're going to do it, you need security lights," and "I have security cameras, so I can help you monitor the site," and he was all about sort of this defensive, fortress mentality…but then he said "Let me know if you need anything, because I can connect you with mulch, and contractors who would probably do the work for free if they just got their logo in your newsletter." So he's offering me resources now, he's not standing back criticizing, he's involved, he has a stake in it. I've definitely seen his demeanor change over time. I wouldn't be able to do that again if it weren't for the capacity that was built by ISS and PSU and the student interns [Fellows].

Institutional/faculty outcomes

Institutionally, a robust community–university partnership (CUP) was built. Within that context, ISS utilized the year-long, three-course connected CBL approach to test the development of a new "Fellows" program, described above. The presence of the Fellows in the classroom and community (one was dedicated to each) significantly increased the capacity of the faculty member and the main community partners. Fellows' involvement had a multiplier effect on the project. In essence, they were able to capture, interpret, and share data and assist in ways that simply would not have occurred without them. Their presence: 1) allowed faculty more time to concentrate on creating and enhancing an engaging learning environment; and 2) helped GL capture outcomes that they were almost immediately able to utilize in (now successful!) grant applications to the City of Portland and other funding agencies.

As faculty, we regularly provided significant classroom and community-based leadership experiences for the Fellows. This helped break down power hierarchies in the classroom, thus providing students another view of democracy in action.

More broadly, this collaboration with ISS helped faculty establish a multidisciplinary lens for the course that intentionally included social sustainability. Further, the many impulses in the classroom increased all actors' need for planning and expectations of accountability. While challenging at times, these connective pieces of the project significantly increased the capacity of all involved: faculty could teach and learn more and better with students, ISS could facilitate a CUP much better than without the Fellows, and GL capacity was increased well beyond expectations.

Finally, aligning with the engaged department model, key actors in the Division of Public Administration have decided to utilize this model again in the coming year. To extend familiarity with the model in the academic unit a combination of new and "veteran" faculty are scheduled to participate in a similar, three-term connected CBL project in the next academic year.

Analysis and areas for further investigation

Based on our firsthand experience, cataloging, and analysis of this extended community engagement effort, we cautiously posit these few claims:

- Students are more aware of the complexities associated with community change and of their biases; they are more informed community change actors. Most of these claims could be made for participating faculty and community partners as well.

- The building of community capacity in the neighborhood targeted by GL was significantly accelerated, broadened, and deepened due to student engagement. ISS Fellows further enhanced community and classroom capacity.

- Participants on all sides feel the partnership was reciprocal and respectful; this builds confidence and enthusiasm for future CUP initiatives for all involved.

- The targeted neighborhood community is now more socially sustainable; faculty, students, institutional actors, community partners, and neighbors have all demonstrated a commitment to increasing social sustainability through partnership.

- Theoretical propositions discussed earlier—principally engaging departments, co-production, social sustainability, and collective impact—have all informed and are now informed by our collective action.

While we are pleased with our collective effort to gather and analyze data from multiple sources to begin to determine what difference this effort has made, we are left with many more questions than answers. To highlight a few areas of inquiry for further investigation, we wonder:

- What would happen if PSU's Civic Leadership program remained committed with GL for several more years? And, how might that engagement change if new faculty are involved? If new courses were involved, including Master's in Public Administration level and/or doctoral level courses? What inhibits or inspires us to pursue these options?

- What could happen (what might we observe in students, community, etc.) if other core courses in PSU Civic Leadership minor were to join in the mix?

- What medium- and long-term impacts is a course like this having on students' civic sensibilities, career choices, etc.? How might we track these students to determine impact five years from now? What measures would we use to document change?

- Similarly, what medium- and long-term impacts is a course like this having on Lents community members? On the community partner, GL? How might we track and measure these changes and over what time period?

- What effect might expanding this focused CBL collective and engaged department initiative have on faculty teaching, research, and service? How would we capture and measure those changes?

- What specific pedagogical strategies, CBL and otherwise, could be explored and tested to augment specific educational outcomes that we desire? To augment specific community member and community partner (i.e., GL) desired outcomes?

- If we were to attempt to enhance those outcomes how would we determine which of those outcomes (educational, community capacity-oriented, instrumental and constitutive outcomes, etc.) are most worth augmenting?

- Is there opportunity for enabling learners in the fully online academic environment to participate in this type of CBL project? If not this type of engagement, which type of CBL engagements work best in the online environment?

Conclusion

While the subject matter of this course and focus of our community partners did not directly address the 21st century's truly "wicked" problems such as global warming, fanaticism of all stripes, and global conflict, among others, it did directly confront many entrenched issues of poverty, racism, marginalization, homelessness, and hunger, among others. Our strategy was informed by the last 30 years of increasing understanding about community–higher education partnerships and specifically about community-based learning as pedagogy in the context of social sustainability. We entered into an unscripted partnership that provided ourselves, the students, and community partners with unscripted challenges. As Dewey (1938) suggested nearly a century ago, we learned by doing and reflecting on our actions along the way. We have utilized the collective impact model to inform how best to interact with a university-level organization (ISS) to support this work and have tested an engaged department model while placing a priority on co-producing strategies, processes, and analyzing outcomes. This was a collective effort; our past experiences have led us to believe that students pay attention to and learn more by what they see and do than by what they hear. We invite them (and all) to look at how we have carried out our craft of teaching and learning about social sustainability in the context of civic engagement and democratic partnership in hopes that we will all find ways to enhance and extend our nascent efforts to strengthen communities and build civic leaders for years to come.

References

Battistoni, R.M., Gelmon, S.B., Saltmarsh, J.A., Wergin, J.F., & Zlotkowski, E. (2003). *The Engaged Department Toolkit.* Providence, RI: Campus Compact.

Block, P. (2009). *Community: The Structure of Belonging.* San Francisco, CA: Berrett-Koehler.

Boyte, H.C. (2004). *Everyday Politics: Reconnecting Citizens and Public Life.* Philadelphia, PA: University of Pennsylvania Press.

Coleman, J.S. (1988). Social capital in the creation of human capital. *American Journal of Sociology,* 94, S95-S120.

Conklin, J. (2005). *Dialogue Mapping: Building Shared Understanding of Wicked Problems.* Chichester, UK: Wiley.

Covey, S. (2011, December 26). Using empathetic listening to collaborate. *Fast Company Magazine.* Retrieved from http://www.fastcompany.com/1727872/using-empathic-listening-collaborate

Dewey, J. (1938). *Experience and Education.* New York, NY: Kappa Delta Pi.

Dowsett, J. (2014, August 29). What riding my bike has taught me about white privilege. *Quartz.* Retrieved from http://qz.com/257474/what-riding-my-bike-has-taught-me-about-white-privilege/

Eyler, J. (2002). Reflection: Linking service and learning—linking students and communities. *Journal of Social Issues,* 58(3), 517-534.

Fung, A. (2015). Putting the public back into governance: The challenges of citizen participation and its future. *Public Administration Review,* 75(4). doi: 10.1111/puar.12361

Geary-Schneider, C. (2015). The LEAP challenge: Transforming for students, essential for liberal education. *Liberal Education,* 101(1). Retrieved from http://www.aacu.org/liberaleducation/2015/winter-spring/schneider

Gibson, C. (2006). *Citizens at the Center: A New Approach to Civic Engagement.* Washington, DC: The Case Foundation.

Gladwell, M. (2000). *The Tipping Point: How Little Things Can Make a Big Difference.* New York, NY: Little Brown and Company.

Green Lents (2015a). About us. Retrieved from www.greenlents.org/about-us-2/

Green Lents (2015b). Home. Retrieved from http://www.greenlents.org/

Green Lents (2015c). Malden Court Community Orchard. Retrieved from www.greenlents.org/programs/community-orchard/

Harkavy, I. (2015). Creating the connected institution: Toward realizing Benjamin Franklin and Ernest Boyer's revolutionary vision for American higher education. *Liberal Education,* 101(1). Retrieved from http://www.aacu.org

Heifetz, R.A., Linsky, M. & Grashow, A. (2009). *The Practice of Adaptive Leadership: Tools and Tactics for Changing your Organization and the World.* Boston, MA: Harvard Business Press.

Kania, J. & Kramer, M. (2011, Winter). Collective impact. *Stanford Social Innovation Review,* 9(1). Retrieved from http://ssir.org/articles/entry/collective_impact

Kecskes, K. (2013). The engaged department and higher education reform: Research, theory, and transformation of the academic unit. In P. Clayton, R. Bringle & J. Hatcher (Eds.), *Research on Service Learning: Conceptual Frameworks and Assessment* (pp. 471-504). Sterling, VA: Stylus Publishing.

Kecskes, K., Nishishiba, M. & Morgan, D.F. (2014). Educating for new public governance: Civic engagement and the liberal arts. In D.F. Morgan & B.J. Cook (Eds.), *New Public Governance: A Regime-centered Perspective* (pp. 299-314). New York, NY: M.E. Sharp Inc.

McKenzie, S. (2004). *Social Sustainability: Toward some Definitions*, Working paper 27. Magill, South Australia: Hawke Research Institute.

McKnight, J. & Block, P. (2012). *The Abundant Community: Awakening the Power of Families and Neighborhoods*. San Francisco, CA: Berrett-Koehler.

Messer, W.B. & Kecskes, K. (2008). Social capital and community–university partnerships: Constructing the "soft infrastructure" of social sustainability. In J. Dillard, V. Dujon & M.C. King (Eds.), *Understanding the Social Dimension of Social Sustainability* (pp. 248-263). New York, NY: Routledge.

Morgan, D., & Cook, B. (Eds.). (2014). *New Public Governance: A Regime-centered Perspective*. New York, NY: Routledge.

Morgan, W., & Streb, M. (2001). Building citizenship: How student voice in service-learning develops civic values. *Social Science Quarterly*, 82(1), 154-169.

Nabatchi, T., & Leighninger, M. (2015). *Public Participation for 21st Century Democracy*. San Francisco, CA: Jossey-Bass.

Nishishiba, M., & Kecskes, K. (2012, February). Capacity building for the common good: PSU's interdisciplinary minor in civic leadership. *Journal of College and Character*, 13(1), 1-13.

Ostrom, E. (1996). Crossing the great divide: Co-production, synergy, and development. *World Development*, 24(6), 1073-1087.

Pestoff, V., Brandsen, T., & Verschuere, B. (Eds.) (2012). *New Public Governance, the Third Sector and Co-production*. New York, NY: Routledge.

Pond, A., & Ackerman, A. (2015, April 28). Let's build a community orchard [Portland State University Sustainability Blog]. Retrieved from https://www.pdx.edu/sustainability/solutions-blog/let-s-help-build-a-community-orchard

Putnam, R. (1993). *Making Democracy Work: Civic Traditions in Modern Italy*. Princeton, NJ: Princeton University Press.

Reason, P., & Bradbury, H. (Eds.) (2008). *The SAGE Handbook of Action Research*. London: Sage Publications.

Rittel, H.W.J., & Webber, M.M. (1973). Dilemmas in a general theory of planning. *Policy Sciences*, 4, 155-169.

Senge, P., Hamilton, H., & Kania, J. (2015, Winter). The dawn of system leadership. *Stanford Social Innovation*, 13(1). Retrieved from www.ssireview.org

Shani, A.B., & Pasmore, W.A. (2010). Organization inquiry: Towards a new model of the action research process. In D. Coghlan & A.B. Shani (Eds.), *Fundamentals of Organization Development* (pp. 249-260). London: Sage Publications. (Original work published 1982)

SNI (Sustainable Neighborhoods Initiative) (2015). Retrieved from http://www.pdx.edu/sustainability/sustainable-neighborhoods

Toi (2013, September 26). Frankly not about food forests. [Black girl dangerous blog]. Retrieved from http://www.blackgirldangerous.org/2013/09/frankly-not-about-food-forests/

Yin, R.K. (2003). *Case Study Research: Design and Methods* (3rd ed.). Thousand Oaks, CA: Sage Publications.

2

Engaged in waste

Two case studies from Portland State linking operational sustainability and student–community engagement

Brad Melaugh and Thea Kindschuh

A university is a complex social system. The internal dynamic components of an educational institution are not separate from the place in which it is situated, especially in an urban context, as exists at Portland State University (PSU). As such, perceived problems at PSU are inherently internally and externally interconnected. However, the university's hierarchical nature creates structural silos throughout the system that make collaboration problematic. Of particular importance, the functional capacity of the university (i.e., facilities, landscaping, finances, planning) is by default quite separate from the academic pursuits of students and faculty.

Due to the embedded commitment to sustainability initiatives at Portland State University, there are multiple entities that explore place-based solutions focused on student engagement, including the Campus Sustainability Office (CSO). One scope of CSO's work is solid materials management. It is the leading department that seeks to affect collective and individual waste behavior, reduce dependency on landfills as a means of disposal, and create opportunities for alternative waste management. Other priorities of the office include managing numerous sustainability programs, certifications, partnerships, data benchmarking, and enacting the Climate Action Plan.[1] This work is underwritten by their mission: fostering "partnerships across departments and disciplines that nourish institutional stewardship

---

1 https://www.pdx.edu/sustainability/climate-action

of our environment and support a growing culture of sustainability within PSU."[2] By engaging with multiple stakeholders on and off campus, CSO and other sustainability partners strive to create that culture by increasing access to sustainability programming through education, outreach, and infrastructural improvements.

Two programs highlighted in this chapter exemplify CSO's commitment to diverse and multifaceted approaches to sustainability at PSU. The Reuse Room and the Waste Audit Living Lab Experience (WALLE) both approach sustainable waste management with an emphasis on student and community engagement to foster behavior change. However, the two programs differ widely in their implementation. The Reuse Room is an infrastructural resource that relies on community participation, accountability, and maintenance to leverage a functional sharing economy for effective waste management. WALLE directly interacts with the academic face of the institution to coalesce operational sustainability and academic goals by offering an audit of a dumpster on campus as a scholarly pursuit. These two cases offer a glimpse into the variety of programming needed to effectively reach an entire urban campus community. In this chapter, we will simultaneously examine these two programs with the intention of isolating the features that make them successful examples of student engagement for sustainability initiatives.

Theoretical framework

Educational theory

A primary focus of WALLE is the student learning experience. As such, multiple learning theories have informed the development of the program. The following theories are not exhaustive of the informing framework of WALLE, but are examples of the major theories involved. Additionally, all of these theories are relative to the context of cooperative learning, described by Johnson and Johnson (2009, p. 365) as "the application of social interdependence theory to education." Social interdependence theory, they continue, "exists when outcomes of individuals are affected by their own and others' actions" (Johnson and Johnson, 2009, p. 366).

Experiential education

Identified extensively as an essential component to a holistic approach to education, experiential learning offers the chance for learners and educators to interact with content and place in a way that allows participants to form their own understandings based on their personal and collective experiences. Several models by Dewey, Lewin, and Piaget suggest a certain pattern in experiential learning processes (Kolb, 1984). While they may differ slightly, there are certain themes that

---

2 https://www.pdx.edu/sustainability/campus-sustainability-office

are consistent throughout the various models. In each model, reflection on and a revisitation of the experience are present and necessary.

Effectively implemented, experiential learning opportunities have the potential to deeply affect the behavior of learners. Students form their own understandings of the world around them, therefore taking with them a deeper connection to their learnings (Kolb, 1984). Embodied learning through tangible experience can be an accessible route to behavior change.

Transformative learning

Transformative learning is inherently experiential in nature. As Mezirow (1997, p. 5) describes, transformative learning "is the process of effecting change in a *frame of reference.*" Learners and educators typically undergo a noticeable shift in understanding and consciousness when a previously unexamined way of knowing or being comes into question. In sustainability education, this is especially relevant; the learning community is expected to conjure solutions to problems that are interconnected and ill-defined.

It requires an "aha" moment or a period of cognitive dissonance to coax a learner into a new state of educational alertness. These moments are not prescribed, they are conditionally arranged. Educators create the conditions for transformational learning, and learners must bring their own openness and willingness to engage in a transformative process. It is worth noting that transformative learning experiences are rarely effective on 100% of the individuals in a learning community. Each person brings their own biases and life experiences that make them more prone to or less available for a transformative learning experience (Baumgartener, 2001).

Service-learning

Let Knowledge Serve the City is a commonly touted catchphrase of Portland State University. Merging academics and civic engagement has readily accessible benefits for the university, the partner community, and the students. By engaging in service-learning, students have the opportunity to engage with the community in ways that make their academic pursuits relevant to the world around them, which implies deeper learning. However, service-learning requires due diligence to ensure both the community and learners are benefiting from the interaction. If relationships are ill-formed and communication is inconsistent, service-learning could provide a disservice to both the community and the learner.

Waste data analysis

The longevity of PSU's reuse programs and WALLE rely heavily on tangible operational results, including waste cost savings, waste volume reduction, and embodied emissions reduction.

Cost analysis

There are costs associated with a disposal waste stream at all levels. It costs money to produce, transport, use, dispose of, transport again, and bury/recycle any product. Therefore, with each product that is used or reused, a potential cost savings exists.

Embodied emissions

Greenhouse gas (GHG) emissions are typically seen as direct effects of an action, for example: the carbon emitted from driving a car to work, or the methane produced from a confined animal feeding operation. At PSU, CSO calculates embodied carbon emissions taking into account the GHG produced in the fabrication of products used by the campus. The tool developed by Carnegie Mellon University called Economic Input–Output Life Cycle Assessment[3] is essential in calculating embodied emissions based on material category and price.

University studies

The development and success of the WALLE program has been supported by the University Studies (UNST) program at Portland State. UNST is a general education program in which many undergraduate students are enrolled. The courses are organized thematically, and provide an interdisciplinary framework to supplement students' chosen majors of study. While the four-year program is intended to guide the students through their whole undergraduate degree, the first-year Freshman Inquiry structure is designed as a three-term-long course exploring a variety of topics through a specific thematic lens.

Underpinning the entire program are four core goals: 1) critical thinking, 2) communication, 3) diversity of human experience, and 4) social responsibility (White, 1992). The openness of the program's goals, the structure of the Freshman Inquiry experience, and the program's emphasis on innovation make it an ideal access point to insert new co-curricular programming.

Case study

Program overviews

WALLE

The Waste Audit Living Lab Experience (WALLE) is a program sponsored by the Institute for Sustainable Solutions (ISS) and designed and executed by the Campus

---

3 For further information see: www.eiolca.net

Sustainability Office (CSO). Coalescing the expertise and interests of CSO with the support and connections of ISS proves to be a partnership with lasting benefits.

WALLE is an academic experience that can exist in numerous iterations, depending on the needs of the people involved. It is a framework for an independent waste audit curriculum intended to be integrated organically into already existing three-term long Freshman Inquiry (FRINQ) courses. WALLE is available to *enhance* the class work already being done and *deepen* the understandings that students walk away with, not to co-opt the course goals. In its first year of implementation (academic year 2015–2016), WALLE is being integrated into two sections reflecting each of the following FRINQ themes: "Sustainability" and "Portland". These two themes are readily accessible to accept the content of WALLE.

Structurally, WALLE consists of three stages: 1) a waste audit, 2) an interruption, and 3) an efficacy study (follow-up waste audit); each stage coincides with one academic term in a FRINQ course. The goals of a WALLE experience are co-created by members of CSO, ISS, and the UNST instructor before the beginning of the academic year. During the goal setting process, the WALLE curriculum is dissected and instructors have the opportunity to both select activities and supporting resources as well as suggest their own. As such, WALLE is alive and constantly growing.

WALLE utilizes the potentials of experiential, transformative, and cooperative learning theory to facilitate the exploration of waste-related questions that have deeper implications for general sustainable practices. For many students, though not all, waste behaviors are automatic and they may engage in unconscious disposal; these learned behaviors can become engrained in an individual's daily life, and require more than just factual knowledge to reverse or unlearn.

A priority of the program is to allow students space to take action based on their observations and analyze the effects of their intervention. Experiential and transformative learning opportunities (stage 1) catalyze the students to implement a targeted campaign for waste reduction (stage 2). They then have a chance to revisit the same dumpster as a team to assess the efficacy of their campaign (stage 3). This cooperative learning process facilitates group accountability for individual and collective behavior change among the participants of WALLE.

Reuse Room

The PSU Reuse Room is the central hub of the campus's reuse program—an open-to-all collection of office, school, and home supplies that optimizes universality and accessibility as effective tools of community sharing and waste reduction. Overseen by the CSO, the Reuse Room engages campus and community members in a "give, take, share" model while addressing the university goals of reducing the embodied emissions from purchased goods. By offering an alternative to new materials consumption on campus, the program presents an engaging and localized system of social, environmental, and economic sustainability. Sharing economies are popping up all over vibrant communities, from tool libraries to mini book libraries on street corners; all that is needed is a space and a sharing of values. Reuse at PSU addresses these needs, providing a framework for the program to become a model for other community-based programs.

The Reuse Room runs entirely on donations from the campus community. Donations are left in the room at the convenience of the donor, and users may take whatever items they choose by signing out the items on a clipboard on the door. A part-time student CSO employee attends to the collection and analysis of this data, as well as the organization and promotion of the space.

Data collected from the Reuse Room's voluntary sign-out sheets includes an item amount and description. This data is then extrapolated by staff to imply a wider set of data, such as cost savings and emissions prevention (see below). By engaging users of the space in this process and thus in the continued success of the Reuse Room, the reuse program seeks to increase stakeholdership while educating users about the combined large-scale impact of their seemingly small actions.

The organization of the room fluctuates with community needs. For example, as university departments and students move, the room sees a considerable influx of household or office goods. Additionally, holidays and special events all contribute to a constantly changing supply. Promotion consists of student-designed logos and signage as well as events targeted toward specific campus departments, demographics, and themes. These range from university library clean-outs to Earth Day clothing exchanges, the flexibility of which offers an ever-changing and engaging approach to reuse.

Conditions of implementation

The goals of the Campus Sustainability Office, as described above, underpin much of the work of the case studies explored in this chapter. As these programs exist both in direct partnership with other departments and in service of the university as a whole, the programs are additionally informed by the needs of the PSU community. In this section, the specific conditions that exist to make these programs valuable and functional are outlined.

Need for data

Both WALLE and the Reuse Room exist in part to satisfy the CSO's need for a robust set of data on PSU's waste behavior. As outlined in the Climate Action Plan, PSU has set the goal of reducing the landfill-bound waste to 10% by weight of the total waste produced as a community. At the time of writing, PSU currently sends 70.1% of its waste to the landfill. Numerous waste audits to date have shown this material to be largely composed of compostable, recyclable, and reusable material.

A primary goal of these two programs is to provide CSO with detailed data sets that can inform and influence the direction of future waste reduction programs on campus. Reuse data provides numbers of items collected, as well as descriptions of item type, weight, cost and embodied greenhouse gas emissions. All of these data help illustrate the social, economic, and environmental impact savings of the reused items. While significant declines in waste haul totals have not yet been noted since reuse program implementation, higher item totals in the Reuse Room's data collection show increased usage and diversion, suggesting that visibility of and accessibility to reuse opportunities is a growing campus priority.

Waste audits through WALLE provide a detailed analysis of the contents of a dumpster, which is categorized by material and recyclability. Additionally, a full WALLE experience will provide data around the efficacy of certain waste reduction campaigns, and qualitative data that examines the behavior change potential of these experiential learning opportunities.

Partnerships and outreach

The internal and external partnerships necessary for effective implementation of these two programs are of considerable note. WALLE is a collaborative program by nature, and would not exist were it not for the support of ISS and partnership of UNST. These partnerships were pre-existing features of the university that were leveraged for successful implementation of the program. In particular, the ISS Living Lab program, described below, is paramount in providing an institutional foundation to WALLE. Prior to the Living Lab partnership, individual waste audits were conducted with varying amounts of consistency through outreach efforts, including pursuing existing connections to reach undergraduate instructors. Additional necessary partners include PSU's waste hauler, and janitorial service providers. As WALLE's focus is waste, it is important to provide students with the full perspective of how waste is handled at their university. University Studies is an integral partner in the development and institutionalization of a program like WALLE. To root a co-curricular program in one academic department (UNST) that values interdisciplinary and experiential learning provides stability.

PSU reuse programs harness a wide variety of partners to cultivate a culture of reuse on campus as well as effective and efficient materials management methods. Funding and staffing are provided by the CSO and ISS, and continued collaboration with campus Facilities and Property Management, Surplus program, Office of Information and Technology, and academic departments ensures efficacy and engagement. Year-round events engage community partners such as Free Geek (a community technology resource) and Ole Latte (a local coffee cart), and the annual campus move-out program utilizes charities such as the Cascadia Gaia Movement (clothing donations) and Community Warehouse (household reuse programs).

Two programs: a story of waste

WALLE

Before WALLE existed in its current form, CSO was available to perform waste audits with university groups. After a 2013 campus-wide waste audit facilitated by

Community Environmental Services, it became apparent that a profile of PSU's waste is a necessary dataset in CSO's portfolio. A consistent glimpse over time into the make-up of PSU's waste became a priority for the waste management team. Continued waste audit experiences with undergraduate students frequently sparked thought-provoking conversations among participants, and the potential for transformation became apparent.

One waste audit in February of 2014 served as a catalyst for the eventual development of WALLE. CSO performed an audit of the dumpster at the art building with a studio art class. From this experience, students noticed the excessive number of coffee cups (14.1 pounds) in the dumpster from a 72-hour period. The students felt inspired to use their studio class to take action in response to the coffee cups. Some created a short video clip called *Trash Talks*, and others designed posters that directly targeted the problem of disposable coffee cups in the art building. A waste audit quickly became more than a waste audit.

Since then CSO staff have been giving short informative and safety presentations to classes prior to an audit, and following a week later with findings based on weights and observations. Up to this point, this was the extent to which students were involved in any other capacity than sorters during the audit, unless facilitated by the instructor.

CSO's data need was being met, but it was still unclear whether there was any lasting behavior change. While assessment of behavior change is difficult to quantify, there was simply no data or direct outreach to optimize the perspective-shifting potential of the experience. Fortunately, the Institute for Sustainable Solutions (ISS) was launching a Living Lab initiative that seeks to programmatically and financially support the PSU community in sustainability projects. It is in this partnership that a need for a formalized waste audit experience emerged. While the CSO worked to develop a curricular package to deepen the experiences of the waste auditors, ISS connected to instructors of FRINQ courses within the UNST program.

The 2014–2015 academic year saw ten individual waste audits performed by undergraduate classes in conjunction with CSO's developing WALLE program. Throughout the process, WALLE's structure was increasingly informed by the experiences and feedback of the students, instructors, and CSO staff. ISS sponsored the Waste Audit Living Lab Experience to allow a lead waste auditor to be hired to devote more intentional time to this program. While it was too late in the academic year for a FRINQ class to adopt the full three-phase structure of WALLE, relationships were being built that would serve as the foundation for the 2015–2016 academic year of implementation.

Continued financial support from ISS strengthened the UNST partnership. WALLE became incentivized and four instructors have signed up to integrate the program into their courses for the first year of implementation. Instructors met with CSO and ISS representatives for four meetings to ensure thoughtful and coordinated implementation. While this level of financial and programmatic investment may not be feasible in all university settings, a certain level of commitment and planning is necessary to fully commit to an interdepartmental and co-curricular program.

Reuse Room

As Portland State is made up of buildings situated in Portland's downtown urban core, years of internal moves and transitions inevitably resulted in high accumulations of office supplies and materials that needed an outlet other than the dumpster. PSU's Surplus program through Facilities and Property Management was able to coordinate collection and redistribution of larger furniture items. The Office of Information and Technology did the same for computer equipment; however, neither of these programs catered to small office supplies or to the residential and student campus community. The need for an open space to address this issue was realized in 2005, when a former mailroom in a mixed-use building was allotted to reuse by the campus Space Allocation Committee. The years following saw fluctuations in efficacy as the volunteer-run room experimented with opening hours, staffing and data collection. Today, this program runs the gamut of materials sharing, from small-scale, peer-to-peer exchanges to campus- and community-wide clean-ups and donations.

Spring 2013 saw a programmatic overhaul including an overall expansion of the Reuse Room, diversification of reuse projects throughout campus, and re-branding. A new logo, increased online presence, and a series of student-designed posters helped to expand the reuse aesthetic so prevalent already in Portland. Growing the student move-out program led to including a wider variety of materials in the room, from office and school supplies to household goods and art materials. A greater variety of items increased traffic to the space, while the reliable stock of files, folders, and binders provide a foundation of dependable items to come back for. Surprisingly few items stay in the room long-term, and turnover is remarkably fast.

Similar models exist at a growing number of universities nationwide, illustrating the limitless place-based iterations of reuse models. On an urban campus, the Reuse Room is located inside a classroom and departmental office building, ensuring secure access as well as diverse traffic. The room is located on student orientation tour routes, near freshman and sophomore inquiry computer labs, establishing itself as an important university resource to new students. Other campus reuse programs vary in scope and accessibility, from being staffed and available certain days of the week in a location that is open to the outdoors, as at the University of Ottawa,[4] to a full-fledged warehouse of goods assembled during move-out like the Post-Landfill Action Network.[5] Despite space constraints on an urban campus, PSU's reuse program has had high success rates through pop-up events such as building-by-building office cleanouts, clothing exchanges, and systematic

4 https://sustainable.uottawa.ca/free-store
5 www.postlandfill.org

reuse collection programs such as Mug Runners, which collects, washes, and redistributes durable coffee mugs left behind in computer labs. This suite of initiatives maximizes reuse potential while minimizing space needs. However, this also makes visibility a challenge as many of our reuse efforts are conducted behind the scenes.

At this point, PSU reuse programs are experiencing a need for spatial expansion, and are calling on specific departments to host reuse rooms of their own. After the 2014 waste audit with the art department, a need for an art-specific reuse room was identified. By partnering with professors and increasing interest in peer and student circles, a space in the art building was secured and allotted to a reuse program. An additional partnership with a student visual media course created and designed a brand aesthetic for what is now known as the Supply Studio. Place-based stakeholder engagement like this is an example of the micro-communities within the larger culture of reuse on campus we hope to see emerge. Secondary benefits of the space include a space for idea sharing and community cultivation.

The Portland State University Reuse Room is a dynamic example of developing a culture around sustainability on a university campus. PSU's reuse program has reached this point by addressing concerns of students, staff, faculty, and community members and pairing these concerns with university offices to ensure implementation and program sustainability, creating a place-specific, community-oriented materials sharing model in the process.

Barriers

Data consistency

Due to the open-access model and voluntary sign-out method of the Reuse Room, data accuracy is being sacrificed for simplicity and maximum participation in the reuse program. While an employee within the CSO tends to the data entry and analysis, the raw data, reliant on community participation, is representative of just a snapshot of the total usage of the room. This issue also arises in reuse events, as continual flow of patrons can muddy data sets. Almost every reuse event partners with a third party community organization, and this provides data inconsistencies as well; different organizations may provide weights versus itemization, some utilize estimates rather than measured totals, and the value of individual items inevitably varies. At this time, one part-time student employee is responsible for the maintenance and translation of this host of information, and this leads to a preference for simplicity over accuracy.

Communication and resource sharing

As with any stakeholder-based program, continual outreach and communication of results, needs, and updates are continually developing. While the reuse program utilizes social media, student-designed posters and videos, and community news organizations, the Reuse Room is still often called a "best-kept secret." Increasing engagement by sharing ideas and stories as well as material goods and expanding to include a wider variety of materials in larger, more accessible spaces may increase visibility and awareness long term.

Outreach to other universities requires continual effort as well; as each university develops its own reuse program (from surplus to move-out to a free store), model and data sharing become increasingly valuable to maximize efficacy and minimize pitfalls. Presenting at local and national conferences, creating toolkits, and sharing open-source data models in accessible platforms all require continued efforts.

Outliers and special waste

Invariably, dumpsters may be filled with outlying material that does not provide a representative sample of the university's waste. Over time, these inconsistencies will be averaged out, but for a single waste audit experience, they can provide an anomalous cross-section of campus waste behavior. For example, during a waste audit conducted in April 2015 with a FRINQ class, the students found an excessive amount of construction waste. While this is invaluable information, it throws off the data set when trying to ascertain a standard breakdown of typical dumpster material. This experience helped CSO to ensure other departments were following protocol for special waste (construction waste). It also gave students an idea of issues surrounding responsible waste disposal. Perhaps students weren't aware that construction waste is better disposed of separately to optimize potential for reuse and repurposing.

From a data management perspective, it's easy to adjust for a large outlier such as construction waste. However, it begs the question of how often this happens. Waste audits through WALLE occur very infrequently when compared with the amount of waste that leaves the campus monthly, which amounts to approximately 30 truckloads. Examples like this show that the data collected from periodic snapshots often leave extenuating circumstances undiscovered.

Student interest

It is extremely important to note that the WALLE experience is not a transformative or positive experience for all students involved. It is rare that an entire group of first year students has a positive reaction to putting on Tyvek suits and gloves, opening bags of waste, and individually sorting out pieces of trash. In fact, there are typically a few students who eagerly take to it, while the majority of participants are apprehensive at best. Some students feel more comfortable taking photos or engaging with passers-by, while others are avid dumpster divers.

However, it is neither easily observable nor immediately noticeable how an experience may interact with an individual's learning process. Students come to PSU with a diversity of life experiences, creating an extremely valuable dynamic in a learning community. Additionally, each student has their own personality and interests. Therefore, some are more reticent than others to face their waste. This does not mean that an experience isn't as meaningful for those who do not participate. The mere fact that a class is sorting a dumpster may be catalyst enough to create a transformative perspective shift.

This also makes assessment of transformation an amorphous thing to conduct. Baumgartener (2001) and others have performed assessment on transformative learning experiences, which tends to be an intense longitudinal study process. The scope of WALLE at this point in time precludes intentional formal assessment on the learning experiences of students. To date, cursory surveys have been distributed that assess the relevance to coursework and provide a space for feedback.

Waste impact

Ten waste audits were performed from January 2014 and April 2015 at various locations around campus. Students sorted 3,643 pounds of landfill-bound waste and found that only 30% of that was true landfill waste. Other material could have been composted (33%) or recycled (11%). The remaining 26% is considered "special recycling," meaning material that can be reused, repurposed, or recycled at specialty recycling locations. This data is representative of most sorts performed by CSO, and the 2013 waste profile compiled by CES.

Categorization of materials taken from the Reuse Room has been collected since February 2013. Since then, total monthly monetary value of items taken has ranged from $573 (March 2013) to a high of $8,655 (June 2014), while weights of items have ranged from 164 pounds (March 2013) to 1,852 pounds (June 2014). Calculating greenhouse gas emissions avoided by utilizing reuse began in May 2014, and monthly totals of carbon and carbon equivalent emissions avoided have ranged from 1.31 pounds of CO_2 (May 2014) to 6.01 pounds (September 2014). Since February 2013, $88,938.30 worth of goods has been reused by the PSU community, keeping 21,970.83 pounds out of landfill. Since May 2014 the emission of 24.78 pounds of CO_2 to the atmosphere due to new material production has been avoided. These are conservative estimations as of December 2014.

Conclusion

Co-curricular and infrastructural programs maximizing student and community involvement are necessarily dependent on the multiple needs and assets of a university. Within the realm of waste, WALLE and Reuse Room demonstrate the need for sustainability programming to identify strategic partners, a use for data collection, space for programs to emerge, and time for experiential and transformative learning through active student and community engagement. While Portland State University offers many of these structural features readily, the success of these programs is anchored in the students' and other community members' authentic engagement in the process, rather than being a passive receptor of sustainability programs.

As a symptom of overly consumptive societal norms, excessive waste is often overlooked as a resource for academic and social engagement. It is a problem that is also a solution; it is a way for students, faculty, staff, and community members to take action, reduce collective environmental impacts, build community, and slowly work towards a university culture less dependent on blind disposal.

References

Baumgartener, L.M. (2001). An update on transformative learning. *New Directions for Adult and Continuing Education, 89*, 15-24.

Johnson, D.W., & Johnson, R.T. (2009). An educational psychology success story: Social interdependence theory and cooperative learning. *Educational Researcher, 38*(5), 365-379.

Kolb, D.A. (1984). *Experiential Learning: Experience as the Source of Learning and Development.* Englewood Cliffs, NJ: Prentice Hall.

Mezirow, J. (1997). Transformative learning: Theory to practice. *New Directions for Adult and Continuing Education, 74*, 5-12.

White, C. (1992). A model for comprehensive reform in general education: Portland State University. *The Journal of General Education, 43*(3), 168-237.

3

What happens when high school students publish books?

Cultural sustainability in a university–community partnership

Per Henningsgaard

In 2009, U.S. Secretary of Education Arne Duncan announced that the federal government would devote $3.5 billion in funding to an initiative targeting the nation's lowest-achieving public schools (U.S. Department of Education, 2009). The following year, $34 million from this initiative was distributed among ten Oregon schools (Hammond, 2010b). The single largest payout—$7.7 million, which was $2 million more than any other school—went to Portland's Roosevelt High School (Hammond, 2010b). Approximately three-quarters of Roosevelt High School students qualify for free or reduced-price lunches, and roughly the same percentage belong to an ethnic minority; these figures are among the highest in the state (Roosevelt High School, 2014). Furthermore, in 2009, Roosevelt High School "established itself as Oregon's lowest performing high school: Only 39 percent of students in the class of 2009 graduated on time, and sophomores' … passing rate of 40 percent on the state reading test was dead last" (Hammond, 2010a). The injection of $7.7 million over a three-year period would fund a variety of plans that were meant to send both test scores and graduation rates soaring.

Among the proposed changes that helped the Portland School District and Roosevelt High School secure this competitive funding from the federal government was its commitment that, "for the next three years, it will have extra counselors to put students on a college track, and daily after-school tutoring"

(Hammond, 2010b). And so it was that the Roosevelt High School Writing and Publishing Center came into existence in 2011. The purpose of this new entity was clear in the minds of its creators:

> We have designed the Roosevelt High School Writing and Publishing Center to serve three distinct functions:
>
> - Enhancing academic writing skills for graduation, college and career;
>
> - Raising the visibility of youth voice and writing in the community; and
>
> - Sustaining our near-peer mentoring opportunities and the Writing and Publishing Center itself (Roosevelt Rough Writers, 2012).

The latter two functions ultimately led to a university–community partnership that would include an example of community-engaged teaching at Portland State University.

One of the most innovative efforts of the Roosevelt High School Writing and Publishing Center involved its decision to establish the Freedom Fighters Project. As part of this initiative,

> students sought out and interviewed important Portland-area adults who've made a difference... The students call their subjects "Freedom Fighters," and they have gone far beyond what high school students normally do to share their stories—through writing, public speaking, a book and now a museum-quality exhibit (Hammond, 2012).

This initiative is most obviously connected to the leadership's desire that the Roosevelt High School Writing and Publishing Center "rais[e] the visibility of youth voice and writing in the community" (Roosevelt Rough Writers, 2012). The students wrote every profile that went into the first Freedom Fighters Project pamphlet they produced back in 2012, and they also wrote all of the content for the exhibit. The pamphlet and the exhibit, which appeared in at least five different locations around Portland, have the ability to then connect that "youth voice" to the broader community (Roosevelt Rough Writers, 2012).

An article about the Freedom Fighters Project in the pages of the state newspaper, *The Oregonian*, caught the attention of Dennis Stovall, Director of Publishing at Portland State University (Hammond, 2012). Stovall subsequently attended an exhibit of the Freedom Fighters Project, where he struck up a conversation with some Roosevelt High School students who were involved in the initiative. The students, upon hearing that Stovall had worked for many years as a freelance writer and later as the owner and operator of his own publishing house, immediately expressed an interest in Stovall's expertise. They were well aware that there was room for improvement in the Freedom Fighters Project pamphlet and exhibit; specifically, they recognized that the pamphlet and exhibit would have been improved by the participation of someone with Stovall's background and abilities, especially in the areas of print design and production. Stovall's role as the director of a master's degree program at an urban university renowned for its commitment to community engagement gave him a stake in the conversation, as well.

The Department of English at Portland State University offers graduate work leading to a master's degree in writing with a specialization in book publishing. Stovall served as director of this program from its inception in 2001 until his retirement in 2011. The master's degree program in book publishing at Portland State University is at the forefront of publishing education nationally and has been recognized for its excellence by publications such as *Publishers Weekly*, which described the program as a place where "publishing education gets innovative" (Habash, 2013). Students gain a comprehensive view of the industry through the program's required foundational courses. Seminars conducted by expert faculty are augmented by a variety of experiential learning opportunities, the most notable of which is Ooligan Press, a publishing house staffed by students in the master's degree program.

Publishing three books a year and selling them in bookstores across the nation as well as online, Ooligan Press provides a hands-on experience that is not replicated in any other master's degree program. Students participate in every step of the publishing process—from manuscript acquisition to editing, from design and production to marketing and sales—with guidance and supervision provided by expert faculty. Students take lessons from the classroom and apply them to real-world publishing challenges, resulting in numerous award-winning and bestselling books that span every genre. Participation in Ooligan Press is required of all students in the master's degree program.

The model of Ooligan Press, along with Stovall's involvement with the Roosevelt High School Writing and Publishing Center, inspired another particularly innovative effort. Indeed, arguably *the* most innovative effort of the Roosevelt High School Writing and Publishing Center involved its decision to establish a student-led publishing house that goes by the name Unique Ink Publishing. This initiative, like the Freedom Fighters Project, is related to the leadership's professed desire to "rais[e] the visibility of youth voice and writing in the community" (Roosevelt Rough Writers, 2012). Indeed, "Unique Ink's mission is to publish regionally themed books featuring student work along with that of professional and aspiring writers in the area" (Schmidt, 2013), which would certainly have the intended effect of "raising the visibility of youth voice" (Roosevelt Rough Writers, 2012).

The original vision for Unique Ink Publishing, however, extended beyond satisfying this single key function of the Roosevelt High School Writing and Publishing Center. Unique Ink Publishing was also meant to help meet a second key function: "sustaining our near-peer mentoring opportunities" (Roosevelt Rough Writers, 2012). The leaders of the Roosevelt High School (RHS) Writing and Publishing Center elaborate on the purpose of this function in the center's foundational documents: "RHS will institutionalize a culturally responsive near-peer mentoring model of service delivery that improves college access and retention for current and former students" (Roosevelt Rough Writers, 2012). Near-peer mentoring at the high school level is meant to increase college retention by teaching students "how to effectively utilize a Writing Center to receive feedback and refine their writing" so that "graduates of RHS will utilize the Writing Centers on the college campus they attend" (Roosevelt Rough Writers, 2012). To this end, the Roosevelt High School Writing and Publishing Center set out to establish "formal partnerships with at least four colleges to provide a mechanism for college students to serve as near-peer mentors" (Roosevelt Rough Writers, 2012). It was in this context that Stovall and students enrolled in the master's degree program in book publishing at Portland State University came to support the activities of the Roosevelt High School Writing and Publishing Center and, more specifically, Unique Ink Publishing.

To initiate this collaboration, Stovall taught a graduate-level class titled "Practicum in Classroom Publishing" in the summer of 2012. Only a few students from the master's degree program in book publishing enrolled in the class, but English Department and Portland State University administration allowed the class to continue because of their commitment to community-engaged teaching. The administration also recognized that this was a new initiative, and if they wanted it to succeed they had to support it in these early stages, even if that meant running a class that did not recoup its instructional costs.

A group of approximately one dozen Roosevelt High School students traveled to the Portland State University campus several times weekly during the summer of 2012, giving Stovall and this first class of graduate students plenty to do. Over the course of these visits, the graduate students "mentored [the] high school students in the process of publishing by helping them to create a publishing company and plan the creation of a book about Portland" (Ooligan Press, 2012). This process both satisfied a desire for "near-peer mentoring opportunities" in connection with the Roosevelt High School Writing and Publishing Center and allowed the Portland State University graduate students to reflect critically on their own education (Roosevelt Rough Writers, 2012). More specifically, the graduate students were testing a pedagogical model in which they had already been unknowing participants via Ooligan Press; that pedagogical model goes by the name "classroom publishing."

The concept of classroom publishing was developed by Stovall over many years, resulting from his desire to "help teachers understand publishing and how it might be best used by them or their students" (PSU, 2014). Stovall eventually partnered with an experienced educator and textbook writer, Laurie King, to write a textbook titled *Classroom Publishing: A Practical Guide to Enhancing Student Literacy* (King and Stovall, 1992). The book was published in 1992—nearly a decade prior to Stovall's employment at Portland State University—by Stovall's own publishing house, Blue Heron Publishing. *Classroom Publishing*

> put forward new ideas on how the publishing process can be used to advantage in almost any classroom, either as an adjunct to an existing curriculum or as the foundation for an entire curriculum in any subject, with any budget, and with any level of technology... It was recommended and sold for use "elementary through high school" by the National Council of Teachers of English (PSU, 2014).

A revised, second edition titled *Classroom Publishing: A Practical Guide for Teachers* was published by Ooligan Press in 2010. This edition was authored by students in the master's degree program in book publishing at Portland State University. Consequently, the second edition was not only a book about classroom publishing but also a product of that process.

During that first summer in which Stovall taught the "Practicum in Classroom Publishing" class utilizing a pedagogical model expounded in *Classroom Publishing*, "State Farm ... awarded the Roosevelt High School Writing and Publishing Center a $94,000 grant to set up its publishing operation and publish its first book" (Portland Public Schools, 2012). This grant from State Farm was awarded by its Youth Advisory Board, which "awards $5 million each year in grants to student-led service-learning projects. Service-learning integrates community service with classroom learning to increase student engagement and raise achievement" (Portland Public Schools, 2012). On top of the $7.7 million in competitive funding from the federal government, this State Farm grant was obviously a major boon to Roosevelt High School and, in particular, its Writing and Publishing Center. The funding greatly accelerated plans for Unique Ink Publishing and its first book.

Unique Ink Publishing's first book, released one year later in July 2013, was an anthology titled *Where the Roses Smell the Best: A Literary Companion to Portland* (Unique Ink, 2013). The book was "written by Roosevelt High School students as well as established authors and poets" (Schmidt, 2013). Among the better-known writers who contributed to the book are novelist Brian Doyle, poet and memoirist Kim Stafford, *Oregonian* columnist Steve Duin, Pulitzer Prize–nominated journalist Renee Mitchell, and Oregon Poet Laureate Paulann Petersen; the mayor of Portland, Charlie Hales, wrote an introduction. Contributors, including several of the aforementioned high-profile writers alongside Roosevelt High School students, participated in five book launch events at various locations around Portland in the month of July. *Where the Roses Smell the Best* was stocked in three Portland-area bookstores; it was also made available in every room of the Heathman Hotel, a luxury boutique hotel in downtown Portland, as part of its "Book by Your Bedside" program (Portland Public Schools, 2013).

A Roosevelt High School student involved in the publication of *Where the Roses Smell the Best*, Zachary Learned, observed that he had "learned important career survival skills in the process, including how to send business emails and use Excel" (Ooligan Press, 2013). Learned's observation fits a claim made in the second edition of *Classroom Publishing*: "Some part of the publishing process is accessible to virtually everyone; those students who might not write confidently may excel in designing the book, creating its website, or handling the announcement of its publication" (King and Stovall, 2010, p. xv). Indeed, the Roosevelt High School students who worked toward the publication of *Where the Roses Smell the Best* performed all of these tasks and more. For example, they arranged for their book to be stocked in local bookstores and at the Heathman Hotel. They also organized the book launch events and wrote the press releases that ensured local media would attend and report on the occasion. Empowering the students—that is, giving them control of all aspects of Unique Ink Publishing—was a conscious decision made by the leadership of both Portland State University and Roosevelt High School in an effort to ensure that this particular university–community partnership would be a sustainable cultural project.

The concept of sustainability manifests itself in two very different ways in this example of community-engaged teaching. First, there is the interest in creating a sustainable cultural project. On this issue, there is an obvious consonance between *Classroom Publishing* and the Roosevelt High School Writing and Publishing Center. As was previously mentioned, one of the "three distinct functions" that is meant to be served by the Roosevelt High School Writing and Publishing Center is the function of "sustaining our near-peer mentoring opportunities and the Writing and Publishing Center itself" (Roosevelt Rough Writers, 2012). The back cover copy for the second edition of *Classroom Publishing* also mentions sustainability: "This book discusses new projects, as well as tips from educators about how to sustain more traditional long-term publishing projects like school newspapers and literary magazines" (Ooligan Press, 2010). Clearly, there is a shared interest in sustainability, arguably born of an awareness of the difficulties inherent in institutionalizing an initiative that began as something much more personal. It is not at all uncommon for an initiative that has developed and been successful because of a personal investment of time and expertise to stumble when attempts are made to institutionalize that initiative so that it can continue in spite of any personnel changes.

Some of these difficulties are evident in the particular university–community partnership documented in this chapter. For example, Stovall taught the "Practicum in Classroom Publishing" class in both the summer of 2012 and the summer of 2013, even though he retired from Portland State University in 2011. I was hired and assumed the title of Director of Publishing at Portland State University in 2012. After two summers of offering the "Practicum in Classroom Publishing" class to a small number of graduate students who acted as mentors and instructors to Roosevelt High School students, beginning in the summer of 2014 the master's degree program in book publishing took a different approach. Now, the master's degree program encourages its students to enroll in an independent study for which they receive credit. I supervise these independent studies, but the graduate students who sign up for them spend the majority of their time working directly with the cohort of Roosevelt High School students who are involved with Unique Ink Publishing at the time. Clearly, I am committed to the collaboration between the master's degree program in book publishing and the Roosevelt High School Writing and Publishing Center, but Stovall's involvement is still crucial to the success of this endeavor; since the summer of 2013, he has continued to volunteer with the Roosevelt High School Writing and Publishing Center. Perhaps even more indispensable is the involvement of Kate McPherson, Community Engagement Specialist at Roosevelt High School. Drawing on the $7.7 million it was awarded in federal government funding, Roosevelt High School hired McPherson in 2011 to lead the Roosevelt High School Writing and Publishing Center. To this day, her involvement remains critical to the success of the organization and, in particular, of the singular and time-intensive undertaking that is Unique Ink Publishing.

By first training Roosevelt High School students in skills such as writing, editing, design, production, marketing, and business management, and then empowering these same students by giving them control of Unique Ink Publishing, this university–community partnership is attempting to build a sustainable cultural project. Hopefully, this is not the sort of project that will simply disappear when its charismatic leader finally burns out, because the students themselves are its engine and its greatest advocates.

In addition to providing vocational skill training for high school students, Unique Ink Publishing was conceived as a vehicle for the production of books that possess unique cultural value; this is the second way in which the concept of sustainability manifests itself in this example of community-engaged teaching. Throughout the centuries, the book has proven to be an unparalleled format for the preservation of ideas. The student staff of Unique Ink Publishing take advantage of this capability by publishing books that preserve ideas they perceive to be underrepresented but, nonetheless, culturally valuable—something they are uniquely qualified to judge as students at one of Oregon's poorest and most ethnically diverse high schools. For example, *Where the Roses Smell the Best* contains work by writers from underrepresented populations such as high school–age writers, writers of color, working class writers, LGBTQ writers, and more. By publishing these writers' words and ideas in a book, and ensuring that book is properly marketed and distributed so that it gets into the hands of as many readers as possible, Unique Ink Publishing and the Roosevelt High School Writing and Publishing Center are helping preserve and sustain these ideas for consideration by future generations.

Used in this context, the term "sustainability" clearly refers to the fourth pillar of sustainability—cultural sustainability. Of course, as has been asserted by researchers with much more impressive credentials on the subject of cultural sustainability, "Culture is capable of being integrated within sustainable development in three more-or-less separate … ways, or 'roles.' These are derived from a literature review of scientific articles using the concept of 'cultural sustainability'" (Dessein *et al.*, 2015, p. 28). In this case, the third role—"culture as sustainable development"— seems most applicable (Dessein *et al.*, 2015, p. 29). This role

> sees culture as the necessary overall foundation and structure for achieving the aims of sustainable development. By recognising that culture is at the root of all human decisions and actions and an overarching concern (even a new paradigm) in sustainable development thinking, culture and sustainability become mutually intertwined, and the distinctions between the economic, social and environmental dimensions of sustainability begin to fade (Dessein *et al.*, 2015, p. 29).

The assertion, in this excerpt, that "culture is at the root of all human decisions and actions" is perhaps why this third role seems most applicable to the case of Unique Ink Publishing and the Roosevelt High School Writing and Publishing

Center (Dessein *et al.*, 2015, p. 29). To be sure, the terms "decisions" and "actions" are clearly significant to the researchers who use them here, because they use them elsewhere, as well, in their discussion of this third role, "culture as sustainable development" (Dessein *et al.*, 2015, p. 29). For example, they write, "Culture in this approach refers to a worldview, a cultural system guided by intentions, motivations, ethical and moral choices, rooted in values that drive our individual and collective actions" (Dessein *et al.*, 2015, p. 32). The gist of their argument seems to be that a decision must be made that is ultimately cultural before the economic, social, and environmental dimensions of sustainability even become a possibility.

This way of understanding cultural sustainability is particularly relevant to the business of book publishing. After all, the book publishing process always begins with the selection of a book to publish. The preeminent book on the subject of sustainability and the publishing industry, *Rethinking Paper & Ink: The Sustainable Publishing Revolution*, frames the issue in the following manner: "Truly responsible publishing starts with book acquisition. … Acquisitions editors, who decide which manuscripts to publish, do have to … [weigh] a book's potential social or cultural value against the methods used to make it" (Carver and Guidry, 2010, p. 59). The authors of *Rethinking Paper & Ink*, Jessicah Carver and Natalie Guidry (2010, p. 59), elaborate on this point:

> The acquisitions editor functions as a gatekeeper between the worlds of unpublished manuscripts and published books. A sustainably minded acquisitions editor will be conscious of the gravity of the decision to bring a manuscript to the printed page with regard to the long-term [cultural] and environmental consequences as well as short-term financial gains.

Clearly, culture in this context is an initiating force that gives birth to the possibility of making economically, socially, and environmentally sustainable decisions—but only after a decision about cultural sustainability has first been made.

As long as Unique Ink Publishing continues to fulfill its mission to publish "regionally themed books featuring student work along with that of professional and aspiring writers in the area," it is sure to serve as a vehicle for the production of books that possess unique cultural value (Schmidt, 2013). Accordingly, the particular university–community partnership documented in this chapter will continue to serve as an example of community-engaged teaching with a focus on cultural sustainability.

The outcomes associated with this example of community-engaged teaching are threefold: outcomes for the high school students who are involved with Unique Ink Publishing and the Roosevelt High School Writing and Publishing Center, outcomes for Roosevelt High School itself, and outcomes for the graduate students at Portland State University who are involved with this project. For the high school students, there exists an abundance of research—not necessarily specific to this project—that testifies to the benefits of this type of endeavor. For example, one of the most frequently cited articles on the subject of classroom publishing is Dennis Rowen's (2005) "The write motivation: Using the internet to engage students in writing across the curriculum." Rowen (2005, p. 22) writes, "We know that [students] take more care in their writing when they know their writing will be on display for all to see". In "Students' awareness of audience in Web-published science writing," Nathan Bos and Joseph Krajcik (1998) refer to the internet as a mode of "publication for a local, national, or worldwide audience" (p. 3) and state that students experienced some "motivational benefits" as a result of writing for an audience (p. 30). These types of observations certainly apply to the high school students who are involved with Unique Ink Publishing; after all, everything they do that is associated with a book's publication—from writing stories and poems for inclusion in an anthology, to designing the book cover, to writing press releases, to speaking at book launch events—has a very real audience of fellow students, readers from the general public, media outlets, booksellers, and more. For example, another major release from Unique Ink Publishing is an anthology titled *No Box Can Hold: A Modern Study of Identity and Self-Discovery* that, like their first anthology, combines the voices of Roosevelt High School students and community members. *No Box Can Hold* is clearly intended for the broadest possible audience. Unique Ink Publishing has also released two small pamphlets—*Invasion of the Head-Scratchers: Survivors' Guide to Scholarship Essays* (Unique Ink, 2014) and *Youth and the Law* (Unique Ink, 2015b)—written entirely by students and meant mostly for their peers at Roosevelt High School.

For Roosevelt High School itself, the outcomes associated with this example of community-engaged teaching are more difficult to pin down. Nonetheless, it is notable that a news story on the subject of Roosevelt High School's transformation at the conclusion of its three-year federal grant uses *Where the Roses Smell the Best* to illustrate its main points. After observing that "the book launch caps a transformational three years for Roosevelt High School," the article goes on to document the most significant benchmarks of the school's improvements:

- **Graduation Rate:** Rose from 42 percent in 2009–10 to 57 percent in 2011–12.

- **Math, Reading:** The percentage of students meeting or exceeding the state math standards rose 25 percentage points in math—from 32 percent in 2009–10 to 57 percent in 2012–13—and 37 percentage points in reading—from 39 percent in 2009–10 to 76 percent in 2012–13 (Portland Public Schools, 2013).

These gains are remarkable in such a short period of time, and while it would be irresponsible to lay all of the credit at the feet of Unique Ink Publishing and the Roosevelt High School Writing and Publishing Center, they have surely played a role. As was observed in the aforementioned article,

> Three years ago Roosevelt High School struggled with low achievement, flagging enrollment and a dispirited community even as the school and partners worked hard to bring change. Today the Heathman Hotel hosted Roosevelt students who helped write and publish the school's first book and placed a signed copy in the storied Heathman Library—helping cap

the high school's three years of growth and transformation (Portland Public Schools, 2013).

The collaboration between Portland State University and the Roosevelt High School Writing and Publishing Center was instrumental in delivering these positive outcomes for Roosevelt High School.

The outcomes for the graduate students from the master's degree program in book publishing at Portland State University are also significant. For those involved with this project, there is the benefit of teaching high school students some of the publishing-related skills that they have been honing as graduate students. Research on the subject of learning by teaching presents unambiguous conclusions: "Teachers learn while they teach … and while they prepare to teach… Expecting to teach appears to encourage effective learning strategies such as seeking out key points and organizing information into a coherent structure" (Nestojko *et al.*, 2014, p. 1047). In other words, the graduate students who taught high school students how to, for example, write back cover copy for a book, likely enhanced their own abilities as compared to their uninvolved graduate student peers. Furthermore, reflective practice is a well-acknowledged factor in the improvement of teaching and learning, with pioneering work on this subject done by Donald A. Schön as early as 1983. The first step in reflective practice is

> *setting the problem* [which] involves two stages, *naming* (an understanding of the situation is developed and the "things" to which the practitioner will attend are named) and *framing the problem* (boundaries are established, and a "logic" or discipline is created for the problem, defining the context in which the named things will be attended) (Pereira, 1999, p. 342).

By practicing classroom publishing but not identifying these practices to their students, faculty in the master's degree program in book publishing were flouting this very first step of reflective practice. Naming and framing these practices—in other words, making these practices explicit—is the first step toward a more comprehensive reflective practice, thereby potentially opening up a unique realm of practical and pedagogical advantages for the graduate students from the master's degree program in book publishing at Portland State University.

Perhaps, then, it is worth adding a fourth outcome associated with this example of community-engaged teaching. This final outcome is for Portland State University itself: adding yet another approach to its already impressive roster of examples of sustainability-focused community engagement in higher education. Clearly, what happens when high school students publish books is that everyone connected to this enterprise comes out a winner.

References

Bos, N., & Krajcik, J. (1998, April 13–17). *Students' awareness of audience in Web-published science writing*. Paper presented at the meeting of the American Educational Research Association, San Diego, CA.

Carver, J., & Guidry, N. (2010). *Rethinking Paper & Ink: The Sustainable Publishing Revolution*. Portland, OR: Ooligan Press.

Dessein, J., Soini, K., Fairclough, G., & Horlings, L. (Eds.) (2015). *Culture in, for and as Sustainable Development: Conclusions from the COST Action IS1007 Investigating Cultural Sustainability*. Jyväskylä, Finland: University of Jyväskylä.

Habash, G. (2013, February 7). Publishing education gets innovative at Ooligan Press. *Publishers Weekly*. Retrieved from http://www.publishersweekly.com

Hammond, B. (2010a, December 18). Can Portland's Roosevelt High School turn itself around? New focus on great teaching raises hopes. *The Oregonian*. Retrieved from http://www.oregonlive.com

Hammond, B. (2010b, July 7). Portland's Roosevelt High gets $7.7 million to propel a turnaround. *The Oregonian*. Retrieved from http://www.oregonlive.com

Hammond, B. (2012, January 15). Civil rights stories, in black and white. *The Oregonian*. Retrieved from http://www.oregonlive.com

King, L., & Stovall, D. (1992). *Classroom Publishing: A Practical Guide to Enhancing Student Literacy*. Portland, OR: Blue Heron Publishing.

King, L., & Stovall, D. (2010). A letter from the authors of the first edition. In Ooligan Press, *Classroom Publishing: A Practical Guide for Teachers* (pp. xv-xvi). Portland, OR: Ooligan Press.

Nestojko, J.F., Bui, D.C., Kornell, N., & Bjork, E.L. (2014, May 21). Expecting to teach enhances learning and organization of knowledge in free recall of text passages. *Memory & Cognition*, 42, 1038-1048. doi: 10.3758/s13421-014-0416-z

Ooligan Press (2010). *Classroom Publishing: A Practical Guide for Teachers*. Portland, OR: Ooligan Press.

Ooligan Press (2012, October 8). The partnership between Ooligan Press and Roosevelt High School [Web log post]. Retrieved from http://ooligan.pdx.edu

Ooligan Press (2013, July 28). Roosevelt High School students present anthology at Powell's [Web log post]. Retrieved from http://ooligan.pdx.edu

Pereira, M.A. (1999). My reflective practice as research. *Teaching in Higher Education*, 4(3), 339-354.

Portland Public Schools (2012, August 31). State Farm grant will expand Roosevelt writing center. Retrieved from https://web.archive.org/web/20151019164826/http://www.pps.k12.or.us/news/7866.htm

Portland Public Schools (2013, October 16). Roosevelt caps transformation with launch of first book. Retrieved from http://insurancenewsnet.com/oarticle/Roosevelt-Caps-Transformation-with-Launch-of-First-Book-a-405719

Portland State University (PSU) (2014, December 4). Dennis Stovall named Rittenhouse Award winner. Retrieved from http://www.pdx.edu/ubets/news/dennis-stovall-named-rittenhouse-award-winner

Roosevelt High School (2014). 2014 Oregon School Performance Ratings. Retrieved from http://web.archive.org/web/20150308075048/http://schools.oregonlive.com/school/Portland/Roosevelt-High-School/

Roosevelt Rough Writers (2012). Our purpose. Retrieved from http://rooseveltroughwriters.org/about-us/our-purpose/

Rowen, D. (2005, February). The write motivation: Using the internet to engage students in writing across the curriculum. *Learning and Leading with Technology*, 32(5), 22-23, 43.

Schmidt, S.M. (2013, July 24). Student publishers' book coming up roses. *Shelf Awareness: Daily Enlightenment for the Book Trade*. Retrieved from http://www.shelf-awareness.com

Schön, D.A. (1983). *The Reflective Practitioner: How Professionals Think in Action*. New York: Basic Books.

Unique Ink (2013). *Where the Roses Smell the Best: A Literary Companion to Portland*. Portland, OR: Unique Ink Publishing.

Unique Ink (2014). *Invasion of the Head-Scratchers: Survivors' Guide to Scholarship Essays*. Portland, OR: Unique Ink Publishing.

Unique Ink (2015a). *No Box Can Hold: A Modern Study of Identity and Self-Discovery*. Portland, OR: Unique Ink Publishing.

Unique Ink (2015b). *Youth and the Law*. Portland, OR: Unique Ink Publishing.

U.S. Department of Education (2009, August 26). Obama administration announces historic opportunity to turn around nation's lowest-achieving public schools. Retrieved from http://www.ed.gov/news/press-releases/obama-administration-announces-historic-opportunity-turn-around-nations-lowest-achieving-public-schools

4

Promoting international urban sustainability through innovative community–university partnership

The case of Hoi An, Vietnam

Shpresa Halimi, Julia Babcock, and Marcus Ingle

Portland State University (PSU) has a successful record of more than ten years of transformational programs, partnership, and policy work on the ground in Vietnam, playing a leading role in shaping Vietnam's sustainability agenda since 2003 (Latz *et al.*, 2009). The university's engagements have been diverse and include applied research on urban water pollution in partnership with a Vietnamese higher education institution in the south; curriculum development on the topic of "Leadership for Sustainable Development" with a national political academy and policy officials in the north; and technical collaboration on eco-city development with urban agencies in central Vietnam (CPS, 2015). This chapter focuses on PSU's story in shaping the future of the coastal city of Hoi An by approaching sustainable development processes and practices through a collaborative, solutions-seeking lens that led us on a cross-cultural journey with our Vietnamese partners.

Background

Hoi An ancient town is located in central Vietnam in Quang Nam Province, on the north bank near the mouth of the Thu Bon River. It is an exceptionally well-preserved small-scale port active from the 15th to 19th centuries, bridging cultures and products from Southeast and East Asia with the rest of the world. Its decline, due to the growth of Danang as a major port in the later 19th century, silting of its major river, and the subsequent lull in commerce, ensured that it has retained its tradi-tional urban fabric to a remarkable degree (UNESCO, 2015).

Recognized as a UNESCO World Heritage site since 1999, Hoi An has strong, unique architectural bones that have remained intact for centuries. Though no longer prominent as a port, Hoi An continues to serve as a place for cultural exchange as the crossroads between north and south Vietnam and through its fusion of Asian cultures from China, Japan, and beyond. Further international influences have emerged due to growth in tourism, with around 1.6 million tourists from around the world visiting Hoi An and surrounding sites in 2014. The cultural landscape that supports the 100,000 residents and growing tourism industry is dependent on the coastal environment with deltas, estuaries, wetlands, rivers, seashores, dunes, and islands enhancing both the vistas and vulnerabilities of the underlying land uses.

In addition to maintaining its historic heritage, Hoi An seeks to secure its future by adapting green principles to guide investments in the expansion of its infrastructure. As user demands rise, the existing systems can't keep up with growth pressures without major structural changes and retrofits. For example, several international resorts have been built along the East Sea shoreline that frequently have tour buses, taxis, and cars moving tourists from the inner city to the beach. Many of the roads were constructed for farm use to connect rural citizens to the local markets and are overwhelmed by these large vehicles traveling at high speeds. The old town has been designated as a bicycle and pedestrian zone during peak hours to avoid costly roadway expansions that could otherwise diminish the character and safety of the riverfront streets, museums, markets, and housing. In the future, Hoi An will have to leverage funding from developers and investors to ensure there is a balance between the pace of growth and the level of infrastructure to support citizens and tourists alike as the city becomes more modernized.

The city leaders in Hoi An recognize these critical changes and challenges for the sustainability of Hoi An and have made subsequent internal changes while also reaching out for external support. In 2009, a formal commitment to the eco-city concept was made at the 16th Party Committee Congress of Hoi An city where they pledged to:

> continue to build Hoi An following the criteria for a secondary eco-city, as one of the cultural centers of Quang Nam province, as the province's tourist city and one of the important tourist places of the country, with

safety, friendliness and new attractions (People's Committee of Hoi An, 2009).

The ultimate goal was "to build eco-cities while preserving distinctive traditional villages." Sustainable development has been defined as the primary goal, to create "an environment that is spacious—green—clean—beautiful and safe, turning Hoi An into the first ecological city of the country."

With this orientation of momentum, Hoi An then established the project "Building Hoi An into a living laboratory of best living quality" in Vietnam from 2010 to 2030. Initial approaches include green growth and job creation, promoting sustainable transportation, developing eco-tourism and environmental preservation, managing urban economic growth, and strengthening urban–rural linkages.

Addressing the eco-city development challenge

Traditionally, Vietnam employs a hierarchical, top-down governance approach that emphasizes control, speed, and efficiency, embracing structural planning solutions that often fail to factor in emergent environmental and social consequences (Painter, 2014). Vietnam's new legal framework for "Oriented Strategy for Sustainable Development" (Decision 153/2004/QD-TTg) envisions a more integrated, adaptive approach to the "eco-development" of livable cities linked to rural poverty alleviation. However, this eco-development strategy is not being fully implemented due to serious knowledge gaps and capacity shortages. Without urgent action, Vietnam's rapid urbanization and high rates of growth seriously threaten the country's quality of life and ecological integrity (Ingle and Halimi, 2007).

To address these implementation challenges, Vietnam is embracing the use of Provincial Development Strategies (PDS) and City Development Strategies (CDS) which incorporate sustainability dimensions into strategic planning efforts at the local and regional scale. Concurrently, "Eco-city Development" has been identified as a potential strategic driver for integrated PDS/CDS implementation. UN-Habitat Vietnam, a United Nations program working toward a better urban future, is the lead agency for strengthening provincial and city planning and management capacity to integrate issues of urban–rural economic development, eco-city development, environmental sustainability, ecosystems services, climate change, and social equity.[1]

Because of a history of relative openness politically and culturally in the central region, UN-Habitat partnered with Quang Nam Province and Hoi An City in pilot testing their development strategy approach. They articulated one core need as: generating innovative and inclusive participatory solutions for Eco-Development PDS and CDS implementation through shared-power leadership and multi-level

---

1 For further information, please see http://unhabitat.org/vietnam

governance (UN-Habitat, 2011). This need embodied two relatively recent areas of agreement among sustainability scientists. First, that the major drivers of sustainability are human in nature, so strong local leadership and management are essential to innovation and implementation. Second, that solutions need to be place-based beginning at the local level and need to encompass "simultaneous actions at multiple scales" (Allen *et al.*, 2012).

Given PSU's active involvement in Vietnam, its expertise in and commitment to addressing urban sustainability issues, and Portland's reputation as one of the most livable cities in the USA, UN-Habitat Vietnam approached PSU with a request to assist with the sustainable planning of Hoi An in 2010. Since then, PSU has collaborated with UN-Habitat and Hoi An on a number of activities as summarized in Figure 4.1 and further elaborated in this chapter.

Figure 4.1 **This heuristic places the public work—the orchard case study—at the center. Informing the work are theories and action focused on civic leadership and social sustainability in the pedagogical context of community-based learning**

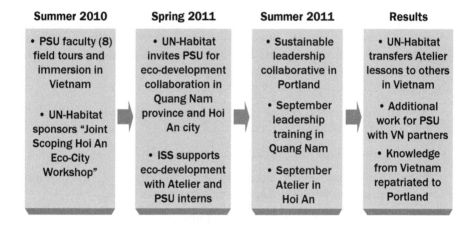

Early beginnings: scoping workshop in Hoi An

PSU as an institution strives to become a leading public urban university "known for excellence in student learning, innovative research, and community engagement that contributes to the economic vitality, environmental sustainability, and quality of life in the Portland region and beyond."[2]

2 PSU Visions, Mission, Values and Priorities, http://pdx.smartcatalogiq.com/en/2014-2015/Bulletin/Welcome-to-Portland-State-University/Vision-Mission-Values-and-Priorities?site_pref=gofull

In a June 2011 letter to PSU faculty and staff, PSU's President reaffirmed this vision, saying the university must aspire not only to provide an excellent education for students but to "serve as a model for the urban university in the 21st century; a place where campus and community are inextricably linked, and where we can find solutions to the seemingly intractable challenges that face societies locally and globally" Wiewel, 2011). In addition to urban sustainability, PSU is committed to internationalization and achievement of global excellence (PSU, 2015). In 2010, a team led by the Vice Provost for International Affairs worked on developing the Internationalization Strategy for the University, which, among others, included a set of recommendations for the expansion of international faculty development opportunities (PSU, 2010).

The first immersion international faculty development program with a focus on urban sustainability issues in Vietnam was designed in 2010 and the timing coincided with the request from UN-Habitat to assist with eco-city development in Hoi An. As the first step in the process a "Joint Hoi An Eco-City Scoping Workshop" was conducted to discuss a practical approach among local officials, relevant international organizations, experts, and interdisciplinary faculty members within a close collaboration between UN-Habitat and PSU. An interdisciplinary team of eight PSU faculty traveled to Hoi An to facilitate the scoping workshop. Participants from the People's Committee, Hoi An City Mayor's office and several departments, community groups, Da Nang University, and United Nations agencies (UN-Habitat, UNESCO, ILO, and FAO) also attended the scoping workshop.

The objectives of the Hoi-An Eco-City Scoping Workshop were:

- To learn from best practices of urban sustainability from a leader (Portland/PSU) in the field

- To share concepts of "integrated urban sustainability"

- To have a solution-oriented discussion on current challenges and seek innovative approaches for the Hoi An eco-city plan in the future

- To identify applicability and feasibility of future projects in the form of PSU–Hoi An cooperation based on local thinking and planning perspectives

At the end of the scoping workshop, a vision for Hoi An eco-city was developed along with key focus areas for a more unified approach to eco-city planning. The scoping workshop developed strong professional and personal relationships among the major partners in the process including city leaders and stakeholders (in the government, mass organizations, local academic institutions, and commercial enterprises), UN-Habitat representatives (including other UN and donor agencies), and PSU.

As a follow up step to the scoping event, PSU sent an intern to Hoi An to maintain relationships and advance solutions by conducting community surveys and collecting local field data in consultation with a broad range of local stakeholders through the local government and UN-Habitat.

The Sustainable Leadership Collaborative in Portland

After the first workshop, PSU and UN-Habitat continued their collaboration and worked together to find innovative ways to support eco-city development efforts across Vietnam.

Two PSU faculty who had attended the scoping workshop developed a proposal and submitted it for funding to the Institute for Sustainable Solutions, the hub for sustainability at PSU supporting interdisciplinary research, curriculum development, student leadership, and meaningful community partnerships. The proposal emphasized developing a space for innovative eco-development strategy implementation in Vietnam at and across multiple eco-system and biophysical scales. The primary focus of the Collaborative was to facilitate the implementation of Hoi An's eco-city development plans.

The proposal was funded, and a Sustainable Leadership Collaborative kick-off event took place in Portland in summer 2011. In designing the Collaborative, PSU recognized the impact of creating multi-dimensional partnerships between academics and practitioners across disciplines to address complex and dynamic "wicked challenges." Wicked problems are characterized by complexity, uncertainty, interdependence, and dispute, and tend to be found in highly interconnected social-ecological systems (Davies *et al.*, 2015; Brown *et al.*, 2010).

The Collaborative was a multidisciplinary learning laboratory session to discuss successful models that contribute to sustainability in Portland that may be adaptable for Hoi An. Throughout the work sessions, PSU faculty, students, and staff as well as community practitioners captured their ideas around what challenges Portland has overcome in the last few decades, from multi-model transportation to green infrastructure and waste management and what lessons hold promise for adaptation to the Hoi An and Vietnam context. The team also discussed the aspects of Hoi An, such as ecotourism and historic preservation, that could provide important lessons for the future development of Portland (Ingle, 2013).

As a result, the team designed an interactive solutions-driven "Atelier" course. An Atelier (adapted from the French word for artisan's workshop or studio) course addresses real-world problems at multiple scales by involving faculty and students from many disciplines, local decision-makers, and other stakeholders in collaboratively finding integrative solutions to such problems (Wainger *et al.*, 1996). Ateliers focus on specific problems at the interface between human and natural systems. The main elements of Ateliers include: 1) transdisciplinary, whole-system, problem-based learning; 2) community/client sponsorship; 3) stakeholder participation; 4) creating a common language; 5) blurring of the distinction between faculty and student, research and education; 6) ensuring knowledge transfer to future generations and building of local capacity; 7) adaptive management and flexible working groups; and 8) appropriate and practical communication of results (Farley and Costanza, 2010).

The organizing principles for the Atelier derived from Portland's EcoDistrict Framework. An EcoDistrict is defined as "a neighborhood committed to improving its sustainability performance over time with empowered people, green buildings, smart infrastructure" (Portland Sustainability Institute, 2011). The framework includes nine performance areas important to neighborhood sustainability: Equitable Development; Health and Well Being; Community Identity; Access and Mobility; Energy; Water; Air and Carbon; Habitat and Ecosystem Functions; and Materials Management. The performance areas cover the great challenges faced by urban systems and the opportunities neighborhoods have to meaningfully address those challenges through performance-based metrics. Portland Sustainability Institute, currently known as EcoDistricts, is the key player in the development of the EcoDistrict framework.

The team composed of PSU faculty, students, and community partners from the Portland Sustainability Institute (now EcoDistricts) and Portland Bureau of Planning and Sustainability traveled to Hoi An in September 2011 to outreach with local partners and conduct the Atelier. UN-Habitat provided the team with translated versions of city and sectoral development plans which served as background documents for the Atelier design.

Prior to the Atelier, two team members and two student interns with support from UN-Habitat and faculty from the Ho Chi Minh National Academy of Politics delivered a leadership training including several practical tools on "EMERGE: Public Leadership for Sustainable Development" in Quang Nam Province to help facilitate the adoption of the Provincial Development Strategy (PDS). PSU trainers facilitated a strategy dialogue between Quang Nam leading officials and key stakeholders on the main elements of the PDS. They shared several practical leadership tools from the EMERGE framework, a public leadership approach and curriculum co-produced by the Mark O. Hatfield School of Government at Portland State University and the Ho Chi Minh National Political Academy in Hanoi, Vietnam. The EMERGE framework is designed to empower public officials to address and embrace complexity while leading their organizations and countries toward sustainable development (Magis *et al.*, 2014).

Hoi An Eco-City Development Atelier

Following the scoping workshop the city developed proposals and started implementing sustainability projects which sought to rationally and harmoniously combine economic development, social development, and environmental protection. In order to effectively achieve this balance, the city recognized a need to review and adapt lessons learned from international models of sustainable eco-city development.

To address this need and the one identified at the scoping workshop, in September 2011 PSU, in collaboration with UN-Habitat, hosted a three-day Atelier in Hoi An. The audience of more than 40 participants was actively engaged in the eco-city "solutions-seeking" journey with the following objectives:

- To assess the progress of implementation of the eco-city development proposal from the 2010 eco-city development scoping workshop based on thorough analysis of context, key issues, and local practices of Hoi An.

- Practice strategic planning process for eco-city development through issues analysis and prioritization, evidence-based "target" development, feasibility analysis, and solutions finding, based on extensive discussion among various stakeholders, international and local experts.

- Share experiences and approaches to eco-city planning between Hoi An leadership/stakeholders and PSU/Portland sustainability professionals.

- Further strengthen relationships between Hoi An, UN-Habitat, and PSU/Portland and other local stakeholders.

Participants conducted an analysis and evaluation of Hoi An's existing eco-city proposal and other plans (e.g., transportation, tourism, Master plan) and identified interventions/existing projects using an adaptable framework: the "EcoDistrict Performance Areas." The performance areas were grouped under three overarching themes: Socio Cultural and Governance; Natural Resource Sustainability; and Green City Planning/Urban Services. Participants conducted an eco-city framework analysis by comparing Portland's EcoDistrict goals with Hoi An's goals and identifying performance areas that lacked clear goals.

After goal setting, participants had an opportunity to develop project prioritization skills and determine which projects yet to be implemented had the highest potential to contribute to the achievement of eco-city goals by addressing multiple performance areas. They also applied feasibility standards to projects and reached consensus on which projects had to be implanted first.

Reviewing and refining eco-city goals and projects helped to create ownership within the community for future action. As an exercise to establish ownership and responsibility for projects and actions, participants worked in teams to sign a sheet which established what actions they could take in the short or long-term that would contribute to eco-city development in Hoi An either as individuals or as an organization.

The Atelier provided a unique hands-on, "solutions-seeking" experience for all participants in the process. As a result Vietnamese participants learned about eco-city development tools and real place-based issues related to sustainable urbanism and how to interact openly and respectfully with a wide range of stakeholders. At the same time, the PSU team had the opportunity to apply a transdisciplinary, collaborative, service-learning approach in the Vietnamese context.

Post Atelier developments in Hoi An and Portland

A month after returning from Vietnam the PSU team convened a "post-Vietnam reflective practice" to debrief the Atelier experience with our internal, innerdisciplinary team and share lessons learned with PSU and the wider Portland community and discuss curriculum improvements for the EcoDistrict work in Portland.

Through continued partnerships, one of the commitments made by the PSU team to the Vietnamese partners was for additional students from Portland State University to travel to Hoi An for 10-week periods or longer to collaborate with Hoi An City officials and communities on the implementation of various eco-city projects in the areas of transportation, natural resources management, water, energy efficiency, climate adaptation including greenhouse gas reductions, and sustainability governance and leadership. PSU was able to send four interns in the subsequent year. One of the interns worked on the environmental aspects of the Quang Nam Provincial Development Strategy and developed a River Basin Coordination Organization proposal for Vu Gia Thu Bon River Basin to encourage regional collaboration. Another intern conducted a study to assess Quang Nam's province tourism assets and projected demands. One of the Atelier participants returned to Hoi An in 2012 to assesses the progress made towards eco-city goals and reported on upgrades to waste management facilities and composting including empowering work for the women's union to manage recycling programs. One of the student interns worked with Hoi An City and Cham Islands to develop a study tour for the Executive Master of Public Administration students who visited Hoi An for several years.

In October 2012, a delegation from Vietnam including UN-Habitat staff as well as the Mayor of Hoi An and the General Secretary of the Quang Nam Communist Party and Vice-Chairman of the Quang Nam People's Committee came to Portland to present their experience at the EcoDistrict Summit. The Summit is an annual event which gathers city professionals from across the globe for information-rich education sessions, keynotes, and workshops designed to share best practices from the USA and beyond.

The presentation was well-received and the delegation further had successful field tours with local government officials around watershed management, land use, and climate adaptability.

In 2013, Portland State University was invited to present and participate in poster sessions for a Green Growth Investment Forum in Hoi An. The key objectives of the Forum were to promote green growth-related strategies and initiatives in Quang Nam province and the region as well as linking key investment opportunities toward green growth with donors, development agencies, and potential investors. A PSU professor who led the design of the eco-city Atelier attended the Forum and co-presented with a Vietnamese fellow about the models to implement green growth with high return on investment through public–private partnerships. A representative from the state of Oregon co-presented with a sustainability expert from Portland State University about Oregon state policy that has led to broad, long-term outcomes such as the 2001 Sustainability Act.

As a result of the Atelier and the PSU, UN-Habitat, and Quang Nam partnership, a process of transformation was initiated and furthered in Vietnam and Portland.

Quang Nam Province (QNP) made a commitment to further professional development of public officials. In 2013, the province signed a memorandum of understanding with the Center for Public Service (CPS) at PSU. QNP and PSU agreed to four primary areas of focus for this collaboration: 1) cooperation on human resource development for Quang Nam province, through the CHRD (Center for Human Resource Development) in Tam Ky; 2) implementation of the Hoi An eco-city strategy; 3) working with PSU's emergency management team and other international scientific organizations on emergency response in Quang Nam including earthquake monitoring and integrated water management; and 4) pursuance of research collaboration and potential funding mechanisms for climate adaptation and governance.

One of the Atelier participants from Hoi An (Cua Lo Cham Bioreserve) was selected to participate in the Professional Fellows Program—a program funded by the Department of State and implemented by the Center for Public Service. He spent five weeks in Portland learning about ecosystem services, sustainable fisheries management and collaborative governance. Upon return to Vietnam he initiated several changes in his organization including the development of the Marine Protected Area plan. He also led the successful campaign to abolish the use of plastic bags on the island for locals and tourists.

At PSU, transformation occurred at different levels. The Atelier approach was validated in the international context and the lessons learned from that experience informed the subsequent work of the Atelier team members. For example, the team member from the Portland Bureau of Planning and Sustainability was able to incorporate some of the lessons learned around incorporating cultural values into project prioritization in Vietnam into his daily work with neighborhood-scale planning. He also gave a presentation to the EcoDistrict Summit where he shared with an international audience some examples of the adjustments he had made to develop a "climate resilient" EcoDistrict in Portland, after he returned from Viet-nam. He was also featured in *Portland Monthly* (Dundas *et al.*, 2013) for his work in Hoi An.

The Center for Public Service crafted an International Sustainability Investment Strategy (ISIS) for Vietnam (CPS, 2012). The vision of the ISIS for Vietnam was: "By 2015, PSU's regional, national and international profile as an 'urban sustainability university of choice' related to faculty, community and student engagement with Vietnam is significantly raised." The strategic intent of the ISIS was to significantly raise PSU's international sustainability profile by communicating the high visibility benefits of the Vietnam portfolio for faculty research, community engagement, and student education.

As a result several programs were initiated:

- In 2012, CPS received a grant from the State Department to implement a Vietnam–USA Professional Fellows Program with a focus on sustainable economic empowerment. This was a two-way exchange program for mid-level professionals from Vietnam and USA.

- Portland State University has established and sponsored the Vietnam Oregon Initiative (VOI). The initiative was launched in May 2014 at PSU (CPS, 2015). The goal of the VOI is to create new synergies that can leverage the existing diverse relationships across government, business, and academic sectors between the State of Oregon and Vietnam for mutual trust and deepened partnerships. In September 2014, Portland State University was awarded a grant from the US Mission to Vietnam to support the acceleration of the VOI. In 2015, VOI assisted the US Mission to Vietnam with a year-long series of national and provincial events commemorating the 20th anniversary of the normalization of diplomatic relations between the US and Vietnam. On July 6, 2015, Hoi An City and Quang Nam Province hosted a VOI launching event in Vietnam in collaboration with Portland State University and the U.S. Mission to Vietnam.

- In early 2015, PSU replicated the Atelier approach in another World Heritage site in Vietnam, Ha Long Bay. Ha Long Bay is one of Vietnam's major international tourist attractions and a natural UNESCO World Heritage site. It also sustains a range of other economically important activities such as aquaculture, fisheries, harbor, mining, and transportation (USAID, 2015). These economic development activities have increasingly placed pressure on the Bay, degraded the environment, and made the livelihoods of communities who are dependent on the Bay more vulnerable. Two PSU Hoi-An Atelier program directors traveled to Ha Long City to conduct an Atelier organized by a consortium of local environmental NGOs and funded by USAID, which focused on local engagement for sustainable development.

Successes and challenges

PSU has undoubtedly influenced the nature of discussions about sustainability in Hoi An. By encouraging public–private partnerships and bridging the gap between academia and local government PSU has shown that good planning comes from empowering the community to build a vision together in order to create ownership in implementation. From the initial widening of the net of practitioners involved in the Atelier to the range of social entrepreneurs and foreign investors present at the Green Growth Investment Forum, it is clear that PSU has been part of transforming the collaborative approach to problem solving in Hoi An. As an example, following the Atelier, Vietnam National University of Hanoi together with UN-Habitat and PSU faculty applied a climate change analysis to the area to help fill gaps in environmental analysis around increases in flooding and storm hazards.

The Hoi An initiative presented a unique opportunity to craft locally relevant, collaborative, community-based solutions to the challenges faced by Vietnamese stakeholders during the design and implementation of eco-city development strategies. Some of the major successes of this initiative include:

- A roadmap for eco-city development which created, inclusive of social, economic, environmental, and governance goals.

- Mutual learning took place during the Atelier. The PSU team introduced and applied in the Vietnamese context a framework that was developed in Portland. The feedback the PSU team received from the Vietnamese stakeholders initiated a series of revisions that were made to the EcoDistrict framework.

- The Atelier was the first of its kind offered by PSU in an international context. An interdisciplinary team of PSU faculty, students, and community partners working collaboratively with the Vietnamese stakeholders co-produced the eco-city development framework. Most Vietnamese stakeholders understood and embraced the collaborative approach. The collaborative process offered a viable alternative to the Vietnamese top-down, hierarchical approach to addressing local challenges.

- Activities conducted by PSU enhanced branding of Hoi An as a World Heritage site committed to sustainable development. PSU faculty and students appreciated the opportunity to contribute in a meaningful way to addressing a real-world problem and benefited from the learning that occurred during the Atelier through the interaction with the Vietnamese stakeholders.

While the delegation from Vietnam was visiting Portland for the EcoDistrict Summit, an unusual earthquake hit Quang Nam Province in an area that had not historically experienced such events. It was suspected that recent dam construction in the area was the catalyst for the destruction. The Quang Nam Provincial leaders were coincidentally meeting with United States Army Corps of Engineers (USACE) officials in Portland about dam and reservoir infrastructure along the Columbia River at the time and were able to share their concern about the disaster and how to respond. There was an empathic exchange between the sides; the USACE staff recognized the power of the moment when the Army was able to share its sympathy as well as its technical expertise when just 40 years earlier our countries were at war. Unfortunately, when the delegation returned home national politics were in play that precluded USACE from providing additional support on the ground through local analysis. Nonetheless the power of these exchanges in the spirit of collaboration and information sharing was exemplified by this timely meeting.

Despite successes the partnership experienced a number of challenges:

- The scoping workshop, the Atelier and subsequent activities were sponsored by UN-Habitat and PSU. Even though Vietnamese stakeholders were committed to eco-city development, local resources were not made available for the implementation of different programs and activities, which affected the ability to successfully implement some of the high impact projects. In the years to follow, there were changes to Hoi An City leadership. The Mayor who had participated in the scoping workshop and Atelier and also visited Portland retired and the new leadership was not as committed to eco-city development.

- Working in a different culture requires skillful use of language, otherwise concepts can be lost in translation. When PSU brought the EcoDistrict Framework to Hoi An we found that certain American nomenclature didn't work, such as investing where you can get the most "bang for your buck." One way to overcome this obstacle was to create a matrix that was left relatively open for stakeholders to rank their own priorities based on their own metrics as agreed upon in small groups. This empowered stakeholders to speak relationally about what was important to them in the moment in their own language.

Transferable insights

Over the last ten years of successful engagement with Vietnamese stakeholders at different levels and sectors, PSU has learned that the development of mutually beneficial, long-lasting collaborations takes time. To be successful, such collaborations need to be carefully tailored to the Vietnamese context and they require substantial financial resources. The analysis and evaluation of the Hoi An case suggests the following key recommendations when designing international Ateliers and building collaborations in the future:

- **Articulate the need for eco-city development**. For the Atelier process to be started off correctly and sustained over time, city leaders need to understand and embrace the urgent need for an eco-city development process. This includes a recognition that eco-city development requires a long-term strategic perspective, and that the pathway to success is neither clearly identifiable at the outset nor easy to achieve and sustain over time.

- **Co-production**. The development of the Atelier content has to be done through an iterative process using a "co-production" and "co-delivery" approach. Don't underestimate the need to share power and build trust. Listen carefully to all key stakeholders (Halimi *et al.*, 2014).

- **Put relationships first**. Partnerships must be built on a shared understanding of local and organizational assets. PSU has been successful in Hoi An and Vietnam generally because it has put a strong emphasis on relationship building to ensure that trust is built person to person. Authentic desire for exchange is important for long-term implementation to show that each side sees mutual benefits in the partnership for years to come.

- **Local context**. Successful introduction of the Atelier approach in a different context must ensure that its features are closely aligned with the political, economic, environmental, cultural, social, and governance characteristics of the local context. The joint scoping workshop organized in Hoi An a year prior to the Atelier afforded the PSU team the opportunity to understand the Hoi An context and analyze major stakeholders. When the PSU team designed the Atelier, the team met in Portland to review background documents and better understand the local context. Team members who were Vietnam experts and had attended the scoping workshop shared information about Hoi An's history as World Heritage site, its governance characteristics as well as current sustainability status. The team also benefited from the data collected by the PSU intern who spent several months on the ground and was fully immersed into the Hoi An culture.

- **Local political context**. Involve local political leaders early on in the process by inviting them to attend planning meetings, scoping workshops, and Ateliers, and create opportunities for them to demonstrate commitment and leadership and take actions on the Atelier commitments.

- **Information sharing**. Attract the attention of the media, tell stories and disseminate results early, often, and broadly among all key stakeholders. Atelier dialogue and documents should be summarized in a proceedings report and shared with the leaders so as to develop further commitment to action.

- **Continuous funding**. Initial seed funding is key to ensuring the success of the early stages in the process. The seed funding (secured through grants or other external sources of funding) should be used strategically to leverage additional resources that allow the continuation of project activities beyond the grant cycle. Funding will only be sustained if partners see mutual gains and returns on their investment over the long term.

References

Allen, J., DuVander, J., Kubiszeski, I., & Ostrom, E. (2012). Institutions for managing ecosystem cervices. *Solution*, 2(6), 44-49.

Brown, V., Harris, J., & Russell, J. (2010). *Tackling Wicked Problems through the Transdisciplinary Imagination*. London: Earthscan.

CPS (Center for Public Service) (2012). International sustainability investment strategy for Vietnam. Retrieved from https://www.pdx.edu/cps/vietnam-partnerships-leadership-trainings

CPS (2015). Vietnam partnerships and leadership trainings. Retrieved from https://www.pdx.edu/cps/vietnam-partnerships-leadership-trainings

Davies, K., Fisher, K., Dickson, M., Thrush, S., & Heron, R. (2015). Improving ecosystem service frameworks to address wicked problems. *Ecology and Society*, 20(2), 37-42.

Dundas, Z., Perry, G., Denies, R., Lundberg, L., Frochtzwajg, J., & Feingold, T. (2013, January 25). Twenty five Portlanders who are changing the world. *Portland Monthly.* Retrieved from http://www.pdxmonthly.com/articles/2013/1/25/25-portlanders-who-are-changing-the-world-february-2013

Farley, J., & Costanza, R. (2010). Payments for ecosystem services: From local to global. *Ecological Economics*, 69, 2060-2068.

Halimi, Sh., Kecskes, K., Ingle, M., & Phuong, P.T. (2014). Strategic international service-learning partnership: Mitigating the impact of rapid urban development in Vietnam. In P. Green and M. Johnson (Eds.), *Crossing Boundaries: Tension and Transformation in International Service-learning*. Sterling, VA: Stylus.

Ingle, M. (2013). EMERGE Public Leadership for sustainable development: A reflective case application from the Portland region of Oregon, U.S.A. In Ngo Duc and Tran Thi Thanh Thuy (Eds.), *Strategic Political Leadership in Vietnam*. Hanoi, Vietnam: Ho Chi Minh National Academy of Politics.

Ingle, M., & Halimi, Sh. (2007). Community based environmental management in Vietnam. *Public Administration and Management*, 27, 95-109.

Latz, G., Ingle, M., & Ficher, M. (2009). *Cross-border capacity building: selected examples of Portland State University's involvement in tertiary level educational reform in Vietnam.* Paper presented in the PICMET Conference, Portland, Oregon.

Magis, K., Ingle, M., & Duc, H. (2014). EMERGE: Public leadership for sustainable development. In D. Morgan & B. Cook (Eds.), *New Public Governance*. New York: M.E. Sharpe.

Painter, M. (2014). Governance reforms in China and Vietnam: Marketisation. Leapfrogging and retro-fitting. *Journal of Contemporary Asia*, 42(2), 204-220.

People's Committee of Hoi An (2009). Proposal to build Hoi An into an eco-city. No. 1970/DA-UBND, Hoi An, Vietnam.

Portland Sustainability Institute (2011). *The EcoDistricts Toolkit: Assessment*. Retrieved from https://ecodistricts.org/wp-content/uploads/2013/03/4_Toolkit_EcoDistrict_Assessment_v_1.12.pdf

PSU (Portland State University) (2010). Strategy for comprehensive internationalization. Retrieved from www.pdx.edu

PSU (2015). Strategic plan. Retrieved from www.pdx.edu

UNESCO (2015). Hoi An ancient town. Retrieved from http://whc.unesco.org/en/list/948

UN-Habitat (2011). *UN-Habitat Vietnam Annual Work Plan*. Hanoi, Vietnam: UN-Habitat.

USAID (2015). *Ha Long Bay—Cat Ba Alliance*. Retrieved from http://www.usaid.gov/sites/default/files/documents/1861/FS_HaLongBayAlliance_Eng.pdf

Wainger, L., Ryan, P., Cowling, R., & Costanza, R. (1996). Ecological economics in South Africa: Valuation and management of fynbos ecosystems. *Ecological Economics Bulletin*, 2(1), 12-13.

Wiewel, W. (2011, June 15). *End of year message from President Wiewel*, Portland State University. Retrieved from http://www.pdx.edu/ces/news/end-year-message-president-wiewel

5

Bridges to a brighter future

University–corrections partnerships
as a sustainability issue*

Deborah Smith Arthur

Sustainability is an important concept, framework, and goal, and a large part of the lexicon of higher education campuses nationwide. According to the Institute for Sustainable Communities, "A sustainable community is one that is economically, environmentally, and socially healthy and resilient… [It] manages its human, natural, and financial resources to meet current needs while ensuring that adequate resources are equitably available for future generations."[1] Portland State University, a green campus and a nationwide leader among institutions of higher education in sustainability efforts, defines sustainability much the same way, including "addressing the world's toughest challenges—from poverty and globalization to climate change and urban development."[2]

Generally, sustainability projects and efforts are aimed at supporting healthy communities through means such as: waste reduction, anti-gentrification efforts, affordable housing initiatives, effective energy conservation, protection of natural areas, food systems analysis and support, development of and support of active

---

* Special thanks for their assistance with and contributions to this chapter: Stephanie Bolson, Volunteer Manager, Multnomah County Department of Community Justice; Kathleen Fullerton, Director, Hope Partnership; Molly Gentzsch; Courtney Gibb, Wesley K., Seanna Kerrigan, Capstone Program Director; Scott M.; Frank Martin, Education Director, Oregon Youth Authority; Brian P.; Deborah Rutt, PSU Faculty and Instructor of the Women's Prison Gardens Capstone; Amy Spring, PSU, who offered the first Inside Out course in Oregon in 2006; Griffin T.

1 Definition of sustainable community. Retrieved from http://www.iscvt.org/impact/definition-sustainable-community
2 https://www.pdx.edu/sustainability/graduate-certificate-in-sustainability

transportation networks, and environmental justice advocacy. However, often notably missing from the conversation is an examination of the impact of mass incarceration on communities. Vast numbers of people have been removed and isolated from their communities through our country's system of mass incarceration, thereby devastating the social capital of these communities. Substantial community and social supports are necessary for successful reintegration upon release. In order to adequately address the complete idea of a sustainable community, then, efforts to support successful reintegration of those who have been incarcerated back into their communities must be considered and included in the sustainability discussion and framework. Through numerous university–corrections partnerships, Portland State University includes the issues of mass incarceration and reintegration into its sustainability portfolio.

Roughly 2.3 million people are incarcerated in this country. In Oregon, we admit over 5,000 people per year into adult correctional facilities (Oregon Department of Corrections, 2015) and roughly 1,200 juveniles are incarcerated in any given year (Sickmund et al., 2015). It is expected that 95% of those released from prisons and jails will return to the community, and recidivism rates remain stubbornly high (Petersilia, 2005). Incarceration disproportionally impacts low-income communities, and in particular communities of color. In these communities experiencing high incarceration rates, the informal and formal social ties that strengthen and sustain communities are constantly disrupted, and the social and economic fabric of the community is decimated. With the mass depletion of human capital, an economically, environmentally, and socially healthy and resilient community is impossible to achieve and sustain (Bernstein, 2014).

A resilient community is one that is able to recover, and even grow, from catastrophe—in this case, the depletion of human capital due to mass incarceration. People experiencing incarceration are removed, separated, and isolated from their communities, and often times are unable to maintain social ties. Thus, upon release, many need to begin anew the process of connecting. This is a difficult task when they have experienced years of isolation, have been living devoid of pro-social connections, and have learned to survive in a closed system with much different values, rewards, and incentives than are experienced outside of prison walls (Schenwar, 2014).

Another difficulty includes attempting to reintegrate into a community whose members may operate only upon assumptions about incarcerated people based on media exposure, and therefore often perceive formerly incarcerated people as dangerous and to be avoided. Community resistance to policies and initiatives that provide the community and social supports necessary in assisting with successful reintegration is a significant barrier (D'Auria, 2011).

By partnering with correctional facilities, institutions of higher education have a unique opportunity to contribute to healthy and resilient communities by supporting successful community reintegration for formerly incarcerated people. University–corrections partnerships address this issue from two distinct and equally important postures. First, formerly incarcerated people who have been educationally prepared, who have developed community connections and pro-social relationships, who have experienced cognitive transformation, and have increased their perceptions of themselves as having expanded opportunities, are more likely to be successful in reintegration (Bucklen and Zajac, 2009). University partnerships with correctional facilities can help develop educational preparation and pro-social relationships and supports for people experiencing incarceration. Second, university students are positioned well for examining their assumptions and gaining new perspectives. By partnering with correctional facilities and moving beyond the classroom to personally engaging with the "other"—in this case, the person experiencing incarceration—in a real and meaningful way, students are given full opportunity to examine and potentially shift the way in which they think about people experiencing incarceration and the reentry programs that would support them. Community-based learning courses are the perfect soil for unlearning cultural judgments and for developing relationships with the "other" (Eyeler *et al.*, 1997). These relationships, built within a context of shared intellectual inquiry, have the effect of dismantling assumptions, familiarizing the "other," creating empathy and understanding, and oftentimes shifting perspectives on larger policy issues. The civic engagement model of reentry highlights pro-social relationship building as being integral to successful community reintegration (Bazemore and Stinchcomb, 2004). University–corrections partnerships can assist with the development of pro-social self-identities of people experiencing incarceration and simultaneously foster community willingness to accept and support the reintegration of the formerly incarcerated person, a factor that is crucial to successful reintegration (Bazemore and Stinchcomb, 2004).

This chapter will examine three Capstone courses at Portland State University that partner with correctional facilities and allow university students to engage directly with people experiencing incarceration, thereby contributing to successful community reintegration and overall community sustainability.

Juvenile Justice Capstone

The final step of the general education program at PSU, Capstone courses are small, interdisciplinary, community-based learning seminars. Each course has a community partner—a wide variety of civic, public, and nonprofit agencies and organizations—and senior level students from across disciplines work together to contribute to the community in a meaningful way. Capstone courses build interdisciplinary cooperative learning communities and take students out of the classroom and into the field to understand and find solutions to important issues.[3]

---

3 University Studies Capstone website: capstone.unst.pdx.edu

The Juvenile Justice Capstone course examines both the history of the juvenile justice system as well as current issues, most notably the treatment of youth offenders as adults. Academic work involves readings, discussion, and reflection. This course partners with the Multnomah County Department of Community Justice (DCJ), specifically the Juvenile Services Division. Portland State University and the Multnomah County DCJ have a long-term partnership, of over 12 years. The Juvenile Services Division of Multnomah County DCJ operates the Donald E. Long Juvenile Detention Home (JDH). This facility houses youth, typically ages 12–18, from Multnomah, Clackamas, and Washington counties. The majority of youth are being held in detention pre-adjudication, and the average length of stay is 14 days, but youth can spend anywhere from 1 to 241 days in the facility. Roughly 60% of youth are incarcerated under Oregon's Ballot Measure 11, codified under ORS 137.700. This law requires automatic waiver to adult criminal court for youth aged 15 and older charged with certain crimes, as well as mandatory minimum sentences upon conviction.[4]

In partnership with DCJ, the Juvenile Justice Capstone brings "The Beat Within, A Publication of Writing and Art From the Inside" into juvenile detention in Multnomah County. Founded in San Francisco in 1996, the mission of The Beat Within is:

> to provide incarcerated youth with consistent opportunity to share their ideas and life experiences in a safe space that encourages literacy, self-expression, some critical thinking skills, and healthy, supportive relationships with adults and their community... [The Beat is] committed to being an effective bridge between youth who are locked up and the community that aims to support their progress towards a healthy, non-violent, and productive life.[5]

The Beat Within operates within numerous juvenile detention facilities across the country.

In order to participate in this Capstone, PSU students must first pass a background screening through the Multnomah County DCJ. This requires substantial time and resources on behalf of DCJ staff, especially considering that PSU's 10-week terms means that roughly 15 Capstone students are undergoing the clearance process at DCJ approximately every 12 weeks. The strength of the partnership is dependent upon the willingness of DCJ to facilitate this process. However, DCJ also recognizes and appreciates the benefits to their clients and the support of their mission that the partnership with PSU provides.

In preparation for facilitating Beat Within workshops, the class tours the detention facility and begins the process of being oriented to the culture of detention. Additionally the class reviews The Beat Within Volunteer and Training Manual as well as Editing Guidelines. By the third week of the term, students are visiting units in detention in small groups once a week and facilitating workshops.

---

4 Multnomah County DCJ Juvenile Services Division website: https://multco.us/dcj-juvenile
5 http://www.thebeatwithin.org/about-us

The emphasis of the partnership is not on developing youth into polished writers, but instead on positive pro-social engagement between university students and incarcerated youth. The Beat Within is the vehicle for that engagement. On days when youth may not want to participate in the writing or art, a discussion about college or a game of dominoes ensues. The key is the pro-social engagement between the detained youth and the PSU student.

Capstone students type and lightly edit each piece of writing, and submit it to The Beat Within. The editorial board at The Beat Within reviews the submissions and pieces are chosen for publication. Each young person who submits work receives a personalized response from The Beat Within.

While extensive nationwide research of The Beat Within is lacking, research of youth and volunteers who participate in The Beat Within in California detention facilities demonstrates that The Beat Within is indeed a conduit for positive community engagement. Many youth report an increase in consistent reading patterns, and a sense of feeling validated when their work is published. They report that participation in The Beat Within helps them make good choices, and that the personalized response they receive from editors at The Beat Within helps them to feel connected to multi-generational communities. Further, participation with The Beat Within develops a habit of reflection that supports positive familial and community engagement upon release (Catching, 2013).

At the end of each term, all participants in the Capstone class, the PSU students, instructor, incarcerated youth, and DCJ staff, reflect upon the experience of working together in a closing circle held within juvenile detention. This is a time to reflect on how the experience has impacted the participants personally and collectively. Generally all participants echo the sentiments highlighted in the research. Youth overwhelmingly express that they are grateful for the engagement with the Capstone students, and that they feel no judgment from the students, which helps them feel more like "normal human beings."[6] They appreciate having the opportunity to be listened to, and the chance to share their stories and their feelings. The engagement with Capstone students helps them to feel connected to people and to the world outside the walls of detention. Capstone students very commonly express that the experience of working with the youth has changed them profoundly. They have learned that the youth are "brilliant, unique, smart, talented, thoughtful, kind and reflective" which is not how they perceived incarcerated youth prior to the course.[7]

From the perspective of the Department of Community Justice, the Capstone class and Beat Within workshops enhance their mission by "assisting youth in developing creative problem solving skills, empathy, and tools to express emotions appropriately."[8] In fact, the course was recognized with a "Volunteer of the Year" award from Multnomah County in 2011. In the words of one staff person, Capstone

6 Comment by anonymous incarcerated youth, December 2014
7 Comments from course surveys
8 Personal communication with S. Bolson, Multnomah County DCJ, 14 May 2015.

has "become a part of the culture of detention,"[9] and provides pro-social engagement and community connections that DCJ staff necessarily cannot provide.

According to a Positive Youth Justice model of youth rehabilitation, positive, pro-social relationships are imperative to a youth's success. When, through a strengths-based approach, disadvantaged young people are connected to pro-social relationships, skills, and opportunities, they have the opportunity to transform in positive ways (Butts *et al.*, 2010). In the words of Michael Meade, "Treat them as if they are carriers of meaning, and then all of a sudden, they will begin to act in a meaningful way…" (Neale, 2004). By bringing The Beat Within into juvenile detention and working with detained youth, The Juvenile Justice Capstone provides an opportunity for that meaningful identity transformation for youth. Simultaneously, university students are given the opportunity to examine and transform how they perceive those labeled as juvenile delinquents and how they understand criminal and juvenile justice policy.

Women's Prison Gardens Capstone

Students in this Capstone review, research, and reflect on the impact of incarceration on women, their families, and communities. Students study the circumstances of women in prisons and the diversity of individuals in correctional facilities through readings, video, dialogue, and reflective writing. For the community-based learning element, students work in the prison garden at Coffee Creek Correctional Facility (CCCF) in Wilsonville, about 20 minutes south of PSU. They are directly engaged with incarcerated women, contributing to the development of a prison garden program that addresses the unique needs of women inmates. As with the Juvenile Justice Capstone, students must undergo a background clearance process prior to being allowed to participate at the prison. However, this course does allow for student participation in alternative, but related, community-based learning projects for students who might not achieve background clearance.

The garden at CCCF began as a horticulture project through Portland Community College in 2001, but quickly lost funding. In 2009, a group of volunteers revived the garden program (Piper, 2012). Now fully thriving, the garden at CCCF encompasses roughly 23,000 square feet of vegetables and flowers, producing 5,000–6,000 pounds of food each year. Fresh produce from the garden is provided to the prison kitchen and donated to a local food bank. The main purpose of the garden is to teach gardening skills and to encourage women to lead healthier lives upon their return to the community (Daley, 2012).

---

9 Personal communication with I. Lefebvre, Multnomah County DCJ, 22 April 2015.

An instructor who already had an established connection with the correctional facility developed this course.[10] Prior to the development of the course, she was working with the facility manager to revive the garden and develop the gardening program at the prison. That established relationship helped a great deal with developing the partnership between the Department of Corrections and PSU. The instructor also had previously prepared with the Inside Out Prison Exchange Program at Temple University, which was instrumental in shaping how the course developed. Founded in 1997 through a partnership between Temple University and a Pennsylvania prison, Inside Out "increases opportunities for men and women, inside and outside of prison, to have transformative learning experiences that emphasize collaboration and dialogue, inviting participants to take leadership in addressing crime, justice, and other issues of social concern" (Inside Out, 2014). Starting with one course partnership, Inside Out has now trained hundreds of instructors who have taught hundreds of Inside Out classes in 40 states and internationally (Inside Out, 2014).

The initial intent for developing this course was to engage more volunteers in the gardening program at Coffee Creek Correctional Facility. The Capstone Program at PSU, with its heavy emphasis on community-based learning pedagogy, seemed a logical place to turn for increased involvement. It quickly became clear that students were already thinking a great deal about the larger criminal justice system, many feeling that mass incarceration was problematic. They were eager to examine these issues more deeply. This Capstone offers students that opportunity through direct engagement with incarcerated women and the gardening program. Through this partnership, students not only develop their own gardening skills and knowledge, but also explore the impact of incarceration on people and communities. The partnership humanizes incarcerated women and to allows their voices to be heard. Students are also introduced to organizations and individuals advocating for and serving incarcerated people and their families.

While the Juvenile Justice Capstone, through The Beat Within, utilizes writing and art as a tool for pro-social engagement, the Women's Prison Garden Capstone utilizes gardening as the tool for that engagement. Research of gardening programs in prisons indicates that gardening behind bars can soften the effects of the harsh prison environment while at the same time preparing inmates for reintegration into society. Learning to garden offers pro-social tools for self-support and coping with stress (Lindemuth, 2014). Beyond the organic gardening skills, however, the gardening program at CCCF and the partnership with PSU Capstone offers both incarcerated women and students an opportunity to engage with one another as peers. They also push beyond the stereotypes of one another they may have held previously.

---

10 Deborah Rutt teaches the Women's Prison Gardens Capstone at Portland State University. She is also the Garden Coordinator at Coffee Creek Correctional Facility, Oregon's state prison for women.

When asked to discuss their experience at the close of the term, Capstone students commonly report that they were very nervous before entering the prison, but that once they met the women and began the process of learning to garden together, they were surprised to find that the women were "just people" and were kind and helpful. Many indicate the process of engaging with the women as peers, as equals, was powerful and "life changing" and that the experience made them understand the criminal justice system in a new way. Many reported a deepened political awareness and compassion.[11]

The women incarcerated at CCCF have expressed that the gardening program and the engagement with Capstone have helped them to grow in ways they would not have expected. The women are often nervous to meet Capstone students, as they may feel shame about being in prison. Once they show off their garden to the students, however, and teach gardening skills that they have developed, the women exhibit increased confidence in their ability to make meaningful contributions in this setting, and they do seem to relate to the university students more as peers, sharing information and learning together. Increased visits to the prison garden would only strengthen this peer-to-peer relationship. Many women indicate that the gardening program and the engagement with Capstone helped them to "feel more connected," and to imagine different possibilities for themselves after release.[12]

By using organic gardening as a tool for pro-social engagement, which has obvious additional links to sustainability efforts, both university students and incarcerated women gain a sense of taking action together toward a healthier environment at the prison and beyond, strengthening their identities as agents of change.

Metamorphosis: Creating Positive Futures Capstone

This Capstone provides an opportunity for a small group of students from PSU and a small group of students incarcerated at MacLaren Youth Correctional Facility (MYCF) to work together in a structured peer and collaborative learning environment. Together, students examine a variety of social justice issues facing today's world, and explore their role as agents of change. Each week, the class meets at MYCF in Woodburn, about 45 minutes south of PSU. Students study historical and contemporary examples of social change that help them understand various tools for effecting positive social change, and for maintaining personal well-being while in the midst of struggle. Participants have the opportunity to gain a deeper understanding of a variety of social justice issues through readings, film, and discussion. Additionally, as a whole group, students decide upon and complete a

11 Comments from course survey.
12 Comment from course survey

community-based learning project, addressing a social justice issue agreed upon by all. All students have equal ownership of and participation in the project, and thus contribute to the positive transformation of themselves, their community, and the world.

This course is based upon the model of the Inside Out Prison Exchange Program. In this model, "inside" incarcerated students study alongside "outside" college and university students, with class meetings taking place inside the correctional facility. Living up to the program's goal of social change through transformative education,

> Inside Out begins with the assumption that all human beings—whether they reside behind bars or on the outside—have innate worth, a story to tell, experiences to learn from, perspectives that provide insight, and leadership to contribute to the community... (Davis and Roswell, 2013).

This course developed as a partnership between PSU, The Oregon Youth Authority, and Hope Partnership. The goal of the Oregon Youth Authority (OYA) is to "help youth offenders lead crime-free lives and become productive members of their communities".[13] OYA has physical custody of many youth offenders who have been convicted under Oregon's Measure 11, the mandatory minimum sentencing law that also requires automatic waiver to adult court for certain crimes, and committed to the Oregon Department of Corrections. OYA can hold youth up to age 25, and a substantial portion of the population at MYCF are youth who were convicted under Measure 11 but are now in their early 20s. Most of them have graduated from high school while in custody, and some of them were already engaged in college courses online. Due to its collaborative nature, Inside Out would need to be modified in order to work well in a true "juvenile" facility, with outside students being first or second year university students (Nurse, 2013). At MYCF, however, with a population largely in their early 20s, the model works well with the senior level—same age—Capstone students.

Hope Partnership (Hope) is a program of Janus Youth Programs, Inc. Hope Partnership "creates community connections through special workshops, groups and classes focused on arts, life skills, vocational training and transition services for incarcerated young men..."[14] Hope understands that helping incarcerated young men to feel valued and valuable is an important way to reduce recidivism, and that to collaborate as peers with community partners develops that feeling of value within the young men at MYCF. Thus, Hope Partnership is a conduit through which OYA can introduce positive programming to the young men at MYCF.

In partnership with OYA, Hope Partnership, and PSU, and based on the Inside Out model, this Capstone was developed. As with the Women's Prison Gardens, the instructor was already a volunteer with the Oregon Youth Authority, and had previously established relationships with administration of both OYA and Hope Partnership, as well as staff and incarcerated young men at the institution, thus

13 http://www.oregon.gov/oya/Pages/index.aspx
14 http://www.janusyouth.org/programs/residential

paving the way for the development of the course.[15] Additionally, the instructor had completed the Inside Out Prison Exchange Program Instructor Training.

OYA's Education Director was very supportive of the partnership, as was leadership at MYCF. Initially there was concern about the distance away from campus for PSU students, but despite the distance the class fills quickly. Again, outside students must complete and pass background clearances in order to participate. Inside students are selected in a variety of ways. Some who are already enrolled in various online college courses choose to be a part of the course; others who might not previously have perceived themselves as college students are also encouraged to participate.

Different collaborative projects develop each term, based on the interests and skills of the students. An inside student describes the first project well:

> MacLaren is the largest facility operated by the Oregon Youth Authority, housing over 130 youth offenders, ages 16–24 on a 90-acre campus. In recent years there has been a lack of critical attention paid to the trees on the campus. Many trees have been damaged by storms or have been removed for other reasons. We seek not only to plant more trees to replace those that have been lost, but also to raise awareness to the need for establishing a management plan for the trees on the MacLaren campus for now and the future.
>
> The trees in MacLaren not only help the environment, but they also have many social benefits that directly affect the incarcerated youth in MacLaren. Trees have the inherent benefits of improving people's moods by reducing stress and promoting a sense of well-being. There is also research that neighborhoods with lots of trees have lower incidence of crime. Many prisons across the nation have found that inmates with murals of trees and nature painted on their cell walls respond better to rehabilitation leading to a reduction in recidivism and a safer community (Scott M.).

Students completed their research and petitioned administrators at MYCF, secured donations of fruit trees to plant on campus, and created a book about the process of working together on this project, with an emphasis on protecting the trees as a metaphor for their own personal development as human beings. In a subsequent term, students capitalized on a strange occurrence: MYCF borders several farms, and a hen somehow made its way into the correctional facility. Students quickly named her "Henrietta" and "The Henrietta Project" was born, leading to the development of a hen house and addressing the need for healthier, local food choices on the MacLaren campus.

All students—inside and outside—reflect upon their experiences at the close of the term. Reflections from inside students indicate that participation in the

---

15 It should be noted, however, that while prior relationship is certainly helpful, it is not necessary to a university–corrections partnership. Amy Spring, a PSU academic professional who had no previous experience with corrections, established the first Inside Out course in Oregon, developed in fall 2006.

Capstone course helped them to feel "more human and less like a convict."[16] They appreciated the opportunity to learn alongside and collaborate with PSU students, and felt a shared sense of efficacy and empowerment. In a *Yes! Magazine* interview the youth expressed the observation that in the Metamorphosis class the inside and outside students were "the same"; they shared equal ability to generate ideas, to collaborate and discuss issues, and they were respected equally when ideas were shared (Lalji, 2015). They also appreciated the opportunity to share with outside students what it is like on the inside.

Outside students similarly had positive experiences. They report that for them the experience humanized those who had been dehumanized, or "written off" as "bad" or "unreachable." They expressed gratitude for the opportunity to learn alongside the inside students, together creating opportunities to build valuable skills. Many report that the experience of studying and working with the young men at MYCF changed everything they thought about men and women who are incarcerated. They came to see the inside students not as "crazy," or "animals," but instead as "strong, inspiring, intelligent young men."[17]

Oregon Youth Authority and Hope Partnership administrators also feel positive about the partnership. They expressed that PSU Capstones open up a world of activism and meaningful participation in community for their youth. They indicate that youth who have participated now see a way to create a better world for themselves and others, and are better suited to take advantage of opportunities to overcome their history and become the best person they can be. According to Hope Partnership Director Kathleen Fullerton, "The partnership with PSU Inside/Out Capstone creates a normalizing environment, builds trust in community, and improves self-efficacy and confidence… because of the Capstone our youth have become excited about higher education and prospects for their future through education…"[18] And in the words of the Education Director of the Oregon Youth Authority, Frank Martin:

> The PSU Metamorphosis/Inside Out Capstone brings a greater scope of learning and purpose for all participants; the partnership brings out the best of the human spirit. Faculty and students create an academic environment that is based on socialization and education. At first there are two groups at the starting gate but later they merge as one. The finish line is a healthier community where we acknowledge care, understanding and learning of all its members…[19]

16 Comment from course surveys
17 Comments from course surveys
18 Personal communication with Kathleen Fullerton, spring 2015.
19 Personal communication with Frank Martin, spring 2015.

Limitations and challenges

There are many complicated aspects to managing a learning community that includes both non-incarcerated and incarcerated students. Due to facility rules and expectations, interactions between incarcerated students or participants and university students must be closely regulated and monitored, leaving little or no room for communication and collaborative work outside of the classroom. Additionally, courses and content must be oriented so as to never allow those incarcerated to feel that they are being studied or examined by university students. Courses with a criminal justice content are difficult to present without placing participants on the inside in an awkward position. For academic faculty without a close experience in and around the juvenile and criminal justice system, all of this can be difficult and take time to learn, understand, and manage.

Additionally, a truly equitable university–corrections partnership using the Inside Out model would include an option for course credit for *all* participants. Now that Pell Grants will become an option again for some incarcerated people, this aspect may, over time, be addressed (Anderson, 2015). [20] Adding education debt to the burdens of a person facing community reintegration is less than optimal. To truly work toward sustainability, universities should offer expanded learning opportunities to incarcerated populations at reduced tuition.

Conclusion

In all three of the examples highlighted here, university–corrections partnerships support community sustainability by providing opportunities for pro-social engagement between people experiencing incarceration and university students. There's no doubt that receiving education while incarcerated increases the chances of successful reintegration (Davis *et al.*, 2013). However, the additional component of direct engagement and collaboration with university students can serve to make those outcomes even more positive. University–corrections partnerships allow for finding common humanity, sharing stories, and enjoying and learning from pro-social relationships, thereby humanizing those experiencing incarceration, and assisting with transforming identities and perspectives… After all,

> [t]he more practice one has, the greater likelihood that one perfect the desired changes…prisoners desiring to learn more social productive behaviors do so not by sitting through endless hours of therapeutic group

---

20 "The Federal Pell Grant Program provides need-based grants to low-income undergraduate and certain postbaccalaureate students to promote access to postsecondary education." http://www2.ed.gov/programs/fpg/index.html

sessions but…by practicing socially productive behaviors which they seek to make a part of their lives (Lifers Public Safety Committee, 2004).

University–corrections partnerships serve the dual role of bolstering opportunities for those inside prison walls, and encouraging those on the outside to better understand the complex realities of who incarcerated people are, thus increasing likelihood of support for community programs and policies that help with successful reintegration. By expanding how we think and talk about sustainability efforts to include university–corrections partnerships, PSU contributes to integrated solutions and long-term perspectives of neighborhood and community sustainability.

An outside student of the Metamorphosis Capstone created a six-word essay about her experience, which nicely illustrates why university–corrections partnerships belong in the sustainability framework: "Connection bridges division and restores community."[21]

References

Anderson, N. (2015, July 31). Feds announce new experiment: Pell grants for prisoners. *The Washington Post*. Retrieved from www.washingtonpost.com

Bazemore, G. & Stinchcomb, J. (2004). A civic engagement model of reentry: Involving community through service and restorative justice. *Federal Probation*, 00149128, 68(2).

Bernstein, N. (2014). *Burning Down the House: The End of Juvenile Prison*. New York, NY: The New Press.

Bucklen, K.B. & Zajac, G. (2009). But some of them don't come back (to prison!): Resource deprivation and thinking errors as determinants of parole success and failure. *The Prison Journal*, 89(3), 239-264.

Butts, J.A., Bazemore, G., & Meroe, A.S. (2010). *Positive Youth Justice: Framing Justice Interventions Using the Concepts of Positive Youth Development*. Washington, DC: Coalition for Juvenile Justice.

Catching, L. (2013). *The Beat Within: Perceptions and attitudes among youth and volunteers— A conversational survey of Santa Clara, Solano and San Francisco Facilities*. Unpublished research. UC Irvine.

Daley, J. (2012, November 15). Portland State University helps Coffee Creek prison garden thrive. *OregonLive*. Retrieved from www.oregonlive.com

D'Auria, S.C. (2011). *The Bars that Bind Me: A Study of Female Parolees* (Ph.D. thesis). University of California, Riverside, CA.

Davis, L.M., Bozick, R., Steele, J.L., Saunders, J., & Miles, J.N.V. (2013, July 24). *Evaluating the Effectiveness of Correctional Education: A Meta-analysis of Programs that Provide Education to Incarcerated Adults*. Retrieved from http://www.rand.org/pubs/research_reports/RR266.html

Davis, S.W. & Roswell, B.S. (2013). *Turning Teaching Inside Out: A Pedagogy of Transformation for Community-based Education*. New York, NY: Palgrave Macmillan.

Eyeler, J., Giles, D.E. Jr., & Braxton, J. (1997). The impact of service learning on college students. *Michigan Journal of Community Service Learning*, 4, 5-15.

---

21 Personal communication with Courtney Gibb, spring 2015.

Inside Out (2014). Inside Out Prison Exchange Program; Annual Report, 2014. Retrieved from insideoutcenter.org

Lalji, N. (2015, August 12). School behind bars: How college kids and incarcerated youth benefit from learning together. *Yes! Magazine*. Retrieved from www.yesmagazine.org

Lifers Public Safety Committee of the State Correctional Institution at Graterford, Pennsylvania (2004). Ending the culture of street crime. *The Prison Journal*, 84(4) 485-685.

Lindemuth, A.L. (2014). Beyond the bars: Landscapes for health and healing in corrections. In K. Tidball & M. Krasney (Eds.), *Greening in the Red Zone: Disaster, Resilience, and Community Greening*. Netherlands: Springer.

Neale, L. (2004). *Juvies* [DVD]. Santa Monica, CA: Chance Films.

Nurse, A. (2013). Juveniles and college: Inside Out as a way forward. *The Prison Journal*, 93(2) 234-247.

Oregon Department of Corrections (2015). Prison admissions by county 2012/07/01 to 2013/06/30. Retrieved from https://www.oregon.gov/doc/RESRCH/docs/admissions_county_20130630.pdf

Petersilia, J. (2005). What works in prisoner reentry: Reviewing and questioning the evidence. *Federal Probation*, 68(2), 4-8.

Piper, E. (2012, July 11). *Portland State students join inmates to build prison garden*. Portland State University: Inside PSU. Retrieved from http://www.pdx.edu/insidepsu/news/portland-state-students-join-inmates-build-prison-garden

Schenwar, M. (2014). *Locked Down, Locked Out: Why Prison Doesn't Work and How We Can Do Better*. Oakland, CA: Berrett-Koehler.

Sickmund, M., Sladky, T.J., Kang, Wei, & Puzzanchera, C. (2015). *Easy Access to the Census of Juveniles in Residential Placement*. Retrieved from http://www.ojjdp.gov/ojstatbb/ezacjrp/

6

Rooted in history
Portland's Heritage Trees

Catherine McNeur

On May 20, 2015, I attended a funeral for a madrone tree that unexpectedly fell on a windless day a few months earlier in North Portland. Upset by the loss, some community members saw fit to organize a celebration of its life. There were many reasons why I might choose to attend a tree funeral. First, I was still somewhat new to Portland and this sounded exactly like the kind of quirky Portlandia event that I could tell my friends and colleagues back east about. Second, the funeral took place right in the middle of the spring quarter at Portland State when I was teaching a public history course on Portland's Heritage Trees and this fallen madrone was a Heritage Tree. How could I not go?

Portland has roughly 300 designated Heritage Trees. The program is not completely unique, but having begun in 1993, it is one of the earliest American programs, and it seems to have one of the more robust lists of landmarked trees in the country. The city designates trees for reasons ranging from the tree being large or botanically unique to it having historical significance. Urban foresters at Portland Parks and Recreation administer the program, alongside a volunteer Heritage Tree Committee that judges applications and puts a list of proposed Heritage Trees before the Portland City Council. After designation, the trees receive extra protection from being cut down, a plaque indicating their status and species, and some fame among local tree enthusiasts.

I developed the idea for this course after inviting Portland Parks and Recreation's head forester, Jenn Cairo, to come and speak in a different public history course I taught on historic preservation. While historic preservation typically deals exclusively with architecture, I was intrigued by Portland's tree landmarking program and wanted to open students' eyes to the range of ways we can preserve physical history in a city. Cairo and I spoke about the program and the fact that historians are rarely a part of the process of designating a tree. The city lacked the staff and resources to do any serious historical research. When I suggested I might be able to design a course where students could research the histories of these trees in local archives, Cairo and her colleagues were incredibly enthusiastic.

As a course on public history, this had a lot of potential. Students would have their pick of trees and projects. Public history, within the larger discipline of history, is meant to reach a broader audience than academic writing might otherwise. Every Portlander encounters street trees once they go outdoors. If we could get them to think about those trees in a new way, it might not only give them a better appreciation of the tree they bike past regularly but it also might open their eyes to some aspect of their city's history. They might consider the history that tree had witnessed, the reasons why someone might have planted that tree there, or even why certain neighborhoods might have more trees than others. Ideally, the students' work would also draw more attention to the foresters' underfunded programs so that they, in turn, could do more to protect the urban canopy.

Portland's relationship with trees has been complex. The city, which has had close ties to the region's lumber industry, is nicknamed "Stumptown" for the rapid clearing of urban land in the nineteenth century that left it bereft of trees and full of stumps. And yet, as an "ecotopia" of the twentieth and twenty-first centuries, Portland embraces its image as an environmentally conscious municipality full of parks, tree-huggers, recyclers, and bicycle lanes. The Douglas fir stands at the center of the state's license plate, hearkening back to both the lumber industry and the lush landscapes where these trees thrive. It likely has multiple meanings for different Oregonians. Portland is certainly a city that takes pride in its trees and its ecological image.

Students were attracted to the course for a variety of reasons. Some exclaimed that they "love trees!" when we went around the room introducing ourselves on the first day. Some were particularly enthusiastic that the course would involve some time outdoors. Others were lamentably honest that they chose the class simply because it fulfilled a program requirement.

I had my own goals for the students, of course. Not only did I want them to produce something that would be useful for Portland Parks & Recreation, but I also hoped that they would obtain some useful skills performing historical research. I wanted them to collaborate with the foresters and their classmates to create something unique and geared toward a specific audience of their choosing. Whether by creating a walking tour or an app, they had the opportunity to learn new skills that they could use elsewhere in their future careers.

As I developed the course, I wanted to make sure that the students were interacting directly with the arborists at Portland Parks & Recreation to get feedback on their project choices. Angie DiSalvo, an arborist who runs the Heritage Tree program, became our point person. She presented information about the program to the students on the first day of class and came back midway through the term to vet their group project ideas. At the tail end of the quarter, she and members of the Heritage Tree Committee came to hear the students' presentations. As this was the first run of the course, Angie and her staff were very flexible about what the students might produce, giving them a lot of freedom. She made herself available to them via email and invited them to make use of materials in her files.

Figure 6.1 **Students spent significant time outdoors both independently and as a class considering the history, context, and physical setting of the Heritage Trees**

Source: author

Students had to tackle a variety of projects throughout the term. The first half of the course was reading-heavy, giving them the chance to reflect on how other historians have written about trees, the kinds of sources they used, and the range of ways city residents have embedded trees with historical memories.[1] We read multiple examples where people passed down histories of trees that were not necessarily true. The myths are significant and worthy of analysis in their own right, but I wanted students to think carefully before engaging in their own form of myth making. Students were also charged with comparing Portland's Heritage Tree program to other programs in the United States and abroad. This project helped students think about what types of public programs and projects might be useful for Portland while getting some ideas from other cities.

In order for students to truly understand the trees and the city they were researching and writing about, we needed to get out of the classroom and see them in person. Students visited three trees of their choosing during their own time and talked about the kinds of information they were able to get about those trees. While many students had no problem locating their trees, several reported having colorful experiences such as taking photos of a tree only to realize a man was urinating on it, or being chased by an angry man through a shady section of a park. Luckily everyone made back it to class unharmed. We also took a tour during class, led by a history department graduate student who had had an internship with the Parks Department and was in the process of putting together a guidebook to a set of trees downtown. He spoke to students about his experience in the archives and the range of histories he had been able to uncover, and then took the class on a brief tour of four trees close to Portland State's campus. Being able to see the trees within the context of the block and neighborhood was important for understanding the tree as a plant, an artifact, and a symbol for the city's changing history.

The celebrated "heritage" of cities can take many forms, often highlighting the history of certain groups of residents over others. Many of Portland's designated trees honor Portland's pioneers and founding fathers—typically wealthy white men. As students chose trees to research, they were enthusiastic about unearthing a broader range of Portland's history and heritage, whether their research spoke to Native American history, women's history, labor history, or the history of trees in less wealthy sections of the city. When cities rely on private initiative and investments to plant street trees, most of the trees will be planted in wealthier neighborhoods. Many municipal governments and nonprofits in cities like Portland are trying to correct these historic imbalances, but these past practices continue to have impacts ranging from unequal air pollution rates to fewer designated Heritage Trees.[2] Assuming that Heritage Trees reflect and in turn build a certain kind of pride in the neighborhood, a lack of Heritage Trees can have broader social

---

1 Examples of this reading include: Lossing (1862); Campanella (2003); Farmer (2010, 2013); Hurley (2010); and Swett (2013).
2 Glenn (2015) and Rao *et al.* (2014) describe some of this work.

implications. Early on in the term, students expressed interest in drawing attention to the heritage trees in underrepresented communities.

Students had the freedom to choose a designated tree, a tree that might deserve to be designated, or, alternatively, they could look into the history of a specific tree type—such as determining why Italian plum trees became popular in the early twentieth century. Some students even chose to research "ghost trees" or trees that have since fallen and no longer exist. They chose trees that were close to their homes, their jobs, or their favorite parks and cemeteries.

Doing archival research to hunt down very specific subjects can be tricky work. Doing archival research to hunt down the history of a specific *tree* can be even harder. Few people identify specific trees in their diaries. Few photographers purposely take pictures of street trees. In a number of cases students found very little material on a specific tree and then had to get creative and expand her or his research questions. Some who faced these issues chose to look at the transformation of a neighborhood, the lives of the people who planted the tree, or the rise and fall of botanical trends. Having to seek out this hard-to-find information not only got students comfortable with detective work at the Oregon Historical Society and the Portland City Archives, but also exposed them to the difficulties of historical research. One student spent a significant amount of time feeling around the bark of a set of Douglas firs in hopes of finding 80-year-old bullet holes. At the midway point in the term, students presented their findings to each other so that their classmates could become familiar enough with the tree histories so they could use them in their group projects.

Before the city foresters returned to vet group project ideas, students brainstormed various possibilities on the class website's discussion board. They floated a range of ideas from developing walking tours to organizing community events. After meeting with the arborists and talking about their needs and typical audiences, students decided on five projects and divided themselves into appropriate groups based on their interests, with roughly two to four students per group. The projects included recording podcasts based on their classmates' research, developing tree-based walking tours in an underserved section of the city, constructing a children's activity book, designing trading cards geared toward teenagers, and creating historical content for a pre-existing iPhone app focused on Portland's trees.

The app posed the greatest challenges for both the students and myself. In the months before the course began, I reached out to the app developer who had designed a popular Heritage Tree app as part of a city government competition in 2010. The app was already on the iPhones of approximately 5,000 Portlanders and I thought it would be a great opportunity to inject some history into an app that was primarily focused on locating the Heritage Trees and identifying their species. The developer was eager to collaborate, having long considered updating the app to incorporate more material. The problem, ultimately, came down to money. Having reached out to the developer shortly before the class began, there was no time to fundraise to pay for his work. As such, the project was understandably not a priority for him. In addition, university lawyers expressed concern about protecting the students' intellectual property. The lawyer I met with wanted to make sure that the app developer would not make money from work done for free by Portland State students. Ultimately the app developer agreed that he would not charge for the app and students who contributed agreed to have their work protected by a Creative Commons license. While the app developer was generous with his time, visiting the class to discuss the app and designing a new version of the website and app based on our suggestions, the students did not ultimately have the ability to upload material until the night before the project was due, leaving them in a tight spot. Ideally, when I teach this class again I will be able to secure funding in order to appropriately pay people for their work and, in turn, better control the timelines and contributions of those helping to build content for the course.

There will almost always be some drama in any class that involves group collaboration. Some groups worked incredibly well with all members devoted to the project; others led to complaints about classmates not pulling their weight or not listening to the suggestions of others. When issues arose, I tried to assure students that they were learning a range of skills in the class, including interpersonal skills, and that any public history project they embark on after graduation would likely involve working with a range of different people with different skills, levels of enthusiasm, and points of view. Though this likely did not completely satisfy them, I did see the group work as an integral part of any public history lab, as students need to be able to talk with future employers about their abilities to collaborate on large-scale projects. History, as an academic discipline, can often be a solo endeavor. It is rare for authors to collaborate on articles or books, for instance. Public history, however, whether it involves museum exhibits, historic preservation campaigns, or even archival projects, requires collaboration to an extent that many history students might not otherwise experience in other classes in the department.

Each of the groups relied on the research their classmates had put together for their individual papers. For instance, the group that produced a series of seven podcasts wrote scripts based on their classmates' research, occasionally using the authors as actors to bring out a range of historical voices. The students who designed the trading cards similarly mined their classmates' papers for pithy facts that could be listed on the back of a tree's card. Some groups had to head back to the archives to do additional research to fill out their projects, as was the case with the students who designed a series of walking tours in North Portland.

Balancing what would be most useful for the Parks Department and the passions of the students proved somewhat challenging. Reflecting on these group projects and the importance that the individual research projects played in shaping what the groups ultimately could do, I have been debating whether I should have been more hands-on in shaping what subjects students chose to research. As the first run of the course, there was a lot of ground that we could potentially cover so I left it up to students to choose which trees they might do research on. If a student who studies the history of Chinese Americans wanted to look into a tree that somehow related to that ethnic group or Portland's Chinatown, I wanted them to follow their passion so that the research they did might be potentially useful for their Master's thesis or other projects they were working on. However, we ended up with a number of projects that reflected trees that no longer existed or were not yet designated. Some of those projects could be incorporated into the group work, but most could not. In future iterations of the course, I might require students to research designated trees, which might make the relevance of these projects more apparent for the Parks Department and more directly useful once they begin the group projects.

In getting student feedback at the tail end of the course, though, the freedom I allowed them to choose their topics proved to be a major boon. One student who performed research on a set of undesignated trees that were a part of a labor strike from 1934 has gone on to organize an event bringing together the community, union members, and historians to the park where the event occurred. He is working with several groups to get a historical marker at that park. While this project was not completely aligned with the needs of the Parks Department, it is an incredibly successful example of public history and community building. Ultimately my role is to make sure that the students leave the course with materials and skills they can use in the future and in this case, the student came away with both.

The freedom to choose the format for their group projects also led to positive results. One student wrote afterwards in a course review:

> I really enjoyed the flexibility of the class and how it was really up to the students to come up with their own projects. This really allowed for a lot of creativity and I think it showed in the quality of final projects that were produced.

While I wanted to make sure that at least some students worked on the app after having gotten the app developer involved with the course, students had freedom to decide exactly what kind of product they were going to produce. While some students certainly got more from their group projects than others, the overall results were inspiring. The group of students who produced the podcasts learned significant skills from recording engineers at KPSU, the university radio station. Some members of that group are now working to develop a history podcast that will air next year. There was no way that I could have anticipated that outcome when planning the course. The passion that the students brought to their projects was tied to their freedom to control them, and that led, ultimately, to more investment and more vibrant projects.[3]

As I look to repeat the course in the future, I hope to extend the kind of work that the students can produce while still maintaining some of the momentum. I plan to continue to give students freedom to explore and create projects that they will enjoy being involved with, but I will encourage them to fill in the research gaps for

---

3 To see the projects put together by the students in the course, see http://www.pdx.edu/history/heritagetrees.

trees that have already been designated and perhaps build on some of the larger projects that students from the first iteration of the class began. I hope that getting a few modest grants will help students get reproduction rights for historic photos that they can use more broadly in their publications and projects. The funding will also help us pay for professionals who can perform work such as app development that students otherwise will not be able to do themselves or learn to do during the course of a quarter.

In addition, I want to expand the role that the foresters and the Heritage Tree Committee play in the course. After having participated in this initial run of the course, the foresters have a more complete idea of what students might be able to produce and will likely have more opinions about what will be useful for the promotion of their programs. When the students presented to the larger Heritage Tree Committee at the end of the term, we began to have amazing conversations about some of the committee members' experiences in historic battles to save trees and launch the Heritage Tree law. I'd like to establish connections for students earlier in the term so they might be able to interview community members who have been so integral in saving and celebrating various trees.

Finally, a problem that will likely come up any time I teach this course is maintaining some sort of quality control for projects before they go to our community partners. There are likely to be projects that flop. I need to find a way to catch those issues earlier in the term, perhaps by meeting with the groups a week or two before the due date to see a draft of their work. Giving a disclaimer to our community partners that not all of the material will be usable is also probably wise.

While the long-term impact of the course has yet to be determined, my hope is that the work these students do will inspire Portlanders to value trees as a connection to the past. By linking trees to stories about people, neighborhoods, or larger changes impacting the city or country, those trees will no longer just be a part of the background for the Portlander walking past. In turn, more Portlanders might consider the importance of the urban forestry programs and vote for additional funding for the Parks Department. Or they might consider submitting a request to designate a tree on their property. Hopefully the tree lovers who already have the app or are already inclined to go on a walking tour about trees will learn something more about Portland's history and the wide variety of people who have made it their home.

Some of the students who have since completed the course have continued their work after the quarter ended. One is researching trees for a neighborhood association, another took an internship working with a parks conservancy organization, others are continuing to produce podcasts, and some are preparing to present their work at academic conferences. Repeatedly in emails and course evaluations at the end of the term I was told by students that they hardly expected to get as much from a course about trees as they did or that they have "never been more excited about trees." Hopefully they have come to appreciate the range of primary sources that they can tap as historians, whether in the archives or on the street.

When I attended that funeral for the madrone tree, I was fully expecting to leave with a smirk at having attended such an oddball Portland event. Instead, it was actually much more of a community building experience than a spectacle. Neighbors met each other as well as tree lovers from across the city. Long-time residents discussed their childhoods playing in the park near the tree and trick-or-treating nearby. A Portland State history student delivered a eulogy of sorts, discussing Native American history and the wide-ranging uses and meanings of madrone trees across Portland's long history. The fallen tree, which is now a "nurse log" for kids to climb on, became a symbol for the community and the neighborhood. It represented their rooted history, the transformation of the neighborhood and the city, and the ways a community can value a plant and the history it has witnessed.

Figure 6.2 **Students, members of Portland's Heritage Tree Committee, and Professor McNeur met on the final day of class to discuss the final projects and possible collaborations in the future**
Source: author

References

Campanella, T.J. (2003). *Republic of Shade: New England and the American Elm*. New Haven, CT: Yale University Press.
Farmer, J. (2010). On emblematic megaflora. *Environmental History*, 15(3), 533–547.
Farmer, J. (2013). *Trees in Paradise: A California History*. New York, NY: Norton.
Glenn, D. (2015, February 13). Want a city to thrive? Look to its trees. *City Lab From the Atlantic*. Retrieved from: http://www.citylab.com/weather/2015/02/want-your-city-to-thrive-look-to-its-trees/385455
Hurley, A. (2010). *Beyond Preservation: Using Public History to Revitalize Inner Cities* (pp. 120–145). Philadelphia: Temple University Press.

Lossing, Benson John (1862, May). American Historical Trees. *Harper's New Monthly Magazine*, 144, 721-740.

Rao, M., George, L.A., Rosenstiel, T.N., Shandas, V., & Dinno, A. (2014). Assessing the relationship among urban trees, nitrogen dioxide, and respiratory health. *Environmental Pollution*, 194, 96-104. doi:10.1016/j.envpol.2014.07.011

Swett, B. (2013). Introduction. In *New York City of Trees* (pp. 9-15). New York: Quantuck Lane Press.

7

Food access and affordability in the Foster Green EcoDistrict

Lessons from student engagement with equity and sustainability in southeast Portland

Hunter Shobe and Gwyneth Manser

Each week from May to November farmers from across the Willamette Valley set up shop on a busy street in Portland, Oregon, where they sell free-range eggs, pesticide-free apples, and local honey. On paper, the Lents International Farmers Market (LIFM) looks a little bit like a sketch in the TV show "Portlandia"; there is homemade pasta for sale, quirky live music, and abundant "buy local!" propaganda. However, the market's surrounding neighborhood bears little resemblance to the city portrayed in the TV show. Instead of coffee shops, bikes lanes, and grocery co-ops, the streets surrounding the market are lined with fast food chains and crumbling sidewalks, and convenience stores serve as de facto neighborhood grocery stores (Photo 7.1). Many of the families that frequent the LIFM rely on a food stamp (also known as Supplemental Nutrition Assistance Program, or "SNAP") matching program to purchase their weekly produce, and Russian, Spanish, and Mandarin are spoken alongside English (Photo 7.2). In a decaying urban landscape characterized by liquor and convenience stores hawking fast, cheap calories, the Lents International Farmers Market stands as both a symbol of hope, and a poignant reminder of the deep disparities between rich and poor, white populations and people of color.

Photo 7.1 **Signs outside a corner store in southeast Portland**

Source: photo by Gwyneth Manser, July 2015

Photo 7.2 **Sign outside a McDonald's in Lents that reads, "Now hiring Mandarin speakers"**

Source: photo by Gwyneth Manser, July 2015

According to the United States Department of Agriculture, the Lents Neighborhood in southeast Portland is a food desert. This means that healthy and affordable food access within the neighborhood is limited, and that the burden of inadequate food access falls disproportionately upon low-income populations. Because Lents is also one of the most ethnically and linguistically diverse neighborhoods in the Portland Metropolitan Area, this also means that food access issues disproportionately affect minority residents. According to census data, the Lents neighborhood is rapidly becoming more diverse, while the white population has increasingly relocated to more central neighborhoods (Goodling *et al.*, 2015). People of color have been forced out of the inner city, swelling Lents' total population by 10% in ten years. Although the overall population of the neighborhood has spiked, the white population has dropped from 73.9% in 2000 to 60.2% in 2010 (significantly below Multnomah County's average of 76.5%). In this time, the Black and African American population rose by nearly 200%, the Asian population rose by over 77%, and the Hispanic and Latino population rose by nearly 69% (Office of Neighborhood Involvement, 2011).

It is within this context of demographic change, poverty, and food access disparities that a research project was born. This chapter analyzes a teaching and research methodology used to engage undergraduates with local research related to food affordability and accessibility in the Lents neighborhood and at the LIFM. In the fall of 2014, 50 students in a junior level geography class entitled "World Population and Food Supply" undertook a research project to collect data about the price, place of origin, SNAP eligibility, and marketing of fruits, vegetables, meats, seafood, and eggs in 50 supermarkets, grocery stores, small international markets, farmers markets, and convenience stores in and around Lents. This work was done with the understanding that food access is an important aspect of both physical and cultural wellbeing. The research presented here is part of an ongoing study of food issues that will engage students across the university. Because the data are linked to specific addresses, the information will also be used to construct a series of maps, thus creating a visual tool for analyzing and disseminating data.

The instructor and teaching assistant of the class (the authors of this chapter) designed this project with staff members from Zenger Farm, a local nonprofit and the community partner for this project. Zenger is an urban farm with a focus on youth and adult education. Located in the Lents neighborhood, Zenger also operates the Lents International Farmers Market, which helps bring local produce to a community with limited access to fresh, healthy, and affordable food. This project was born out of the community partner's need for data on food accessibility and affordability in and around the Lents neighborhood. However, we designed a project that could be replicated in future World Population and Food Supply classes, specifically those held in the summer and fall of 2015. Thus, over time, the project has transformed into a multi-year research effort by undergraduate and graduate students at Portland State University, allowing the community partner to benefit from student engagement beyond the fall of 2014's ten-week class term.

This project is replicable elsewhere, in that it can be used as a basic template for examining food justice issues in other discrete neighborhoods, both in the Portland Metropolitan Area and beyond. By design, this project addresses the needs of the community partner as well as the needs of undergraduates, who are able to gain field research and community engagement experience. As such, our methodology intrinsically links research and pedagogy, while pulling together the three main threads of sustainability—society, the economy, and the environment.

Literature review

To situate our project within the larger framework of research and engagement related to food access and affordability, we review literature that applies a geographic and spatial lens to the study of food and social justice. Although issues of food access, affordability, and malnutrition are often associated with low-income countries, food insecurity—a "lack of access by all people at all times to enough food for an active, healthy life"—is a global issue (Conway, 2012, p. 330; Gottlieb and Fisher, 1996). Increasingly, the issue of food access is being examined in the context of high-income countries, such as the United States and United Kingdom. Food access and affordability issues have thus served as a nexus for exploring a broad variety of equity issues, including food justice, public health, transportation access, and issues relating to low-income communities and people of color.

An analysis of food justice research shows a consensus among policy-makers and academics that equity issues and shifting retail patterns have shaped a contemporary foodscape that is characterized by a patchwork of "privilege and poverty, Whole Foods and whole food deserts" (McClintock, 2011, pp. 90-91). Within the past century there have been massive changes to the ways that food is bought, sold, and produced around the globe. Since the emergence of the full-service food market model in the 1920s and 30s, food retailers have moved towards a business model that is increasingly concentrated, globally sourced and operated, and large in size (Gottlieb and Joshi, 2013). Fueled in part by growing land needs, ever-tighter profit margins, and the expansion of the automobile, grocery stores have progressively moved into suburban neighborhoods, away from the urban core and rural centers (Blanchard and Matthews, 2007; Gottlieb and Joshi, 2013; McClintock, 2011). The resultant food deserts and grocery gaps place an undue burden on low-income populations and communities of color (Blanchard and Matthews, 2007), forcing them to either rely on convenience stores for their daily food needs, or to travel long distances to access fresh, healthy, and affordable food.

Concerns over how food is produced, where it comes from, and who has access to it are increasingly being placed under the umbrella of **food justice**. Food justice is a relatively young concept that has emerged out of a desire to "challenge and restructure the dominant food system" (Gottlieb and Joshi, 2013, p. viii), and

gives voice to vulnerable communities. Sharing goals in common with environmental justice, social justice activism, and worker justice campaigns (Gottlieb and
Joshi, 2013; Gottlieb and Fisher, 1996), food justice takes a multifaceted approach
to addressing both critiques of and solutions to problems with the dominant food
system. In the past two decades, food justice and (in)access have largely been studied by focusing on areas identified as lacking access to fresh, healthy, and affordable food. In more recent years, however, these "food deserts" have also served as
a framework for exploring a wider variety of issues, including public health, transportation justice, and gentrification.

The term "food desert" first emerged in Scotland in the early 1990s, coined by a
Nutrition Task Force working with low-income communities. In this context, the
term food desert was used to describe areas where residents "lacked access to an
affordable and healthy diet" (Cummins and Macintyre, 2002; Beaulac *et al.*, 2009).
In the United Kingdom, the term food desert was primarily used to describe the
complete *absence* of food retailers. Thus, the definition reflected concerns about
the quantity, rather than the quality, of food available to residents in particular
areas (Blanchard and Matthews, 2007). Conversely, in the United States, the academic literature and policy initiatives surrounding food deserts have primarily
centered on the quality and price of available foods. This is largely because nearly
all residents in the United States have access to *some* form of food, as a result of the
proliferation of gas stations, fast food chains, and convenience stores (Blanchard
and Matthews, 2007).

In the U.S., food justice provides a unique framework for considering interstitial
food spaces that lack easy access to some combination of fresh, healthy, culturally
appropriate, and/or affordable food. The past decade of food justice work has also
spawned a plethora of related terms, including "food mirage," "food swamp," and
"junk food jungle" (Breyer and Voss-Andreae, 2013; Everett, 2011; Short *et al.*, 2007).
While these terms allow for more nuanced engagement with food environments,
they have also been heavily critiqued for their racialized subtext (McClintock, 2011)
and their role in promoting "spatialized form(s) of neoliberal governance aimed at
producing slim consumers less burdensome to the state" (Shannon, 2014, p. 259;
Agyeman and McEntee, 2014). Furthermore, although supermarkets and super-
centers tend to offer the lowest prices, a growing number of researchers have challenged the idea that increasing the number of large, full-service grocery stores is
the only means of achieving urban food security (Breyer and Voss-Andreae, 2013;
Agyeman and McEntee, 2014). Within this context of globally shifting foodscapes
and large-scale changes to the ways that food is bought, sold, and consumed, it is
critical to understand what is happening at the local level. Thus, this research seeks
to provide a snapshot of food access in a particular place, at a particular time.

Project design

The purpose of this project was to investigate and assess fresh food access and affordability within the Foster Green EcoDistrict. The EcoDistrict Initiative, which was launched by the City of Portland in 2009, aims to address environmental, economic, and social sustainability goals and issues. This project was done in conjunction with the Portland State University Institute for Sustainable Solutions (ISS) and community partner Zenger Farm, a nonprofit urban farm that focuses on educating the community about environmental stewardship, sustainability, and urban agriculture. As such, this research fits into a broader effort to understand food systems and food access in the Portland Metropolitan Area.

The project emerged from the broader ISS Sustainable Neighborhood Initiative (SNI). SNI workshops in June 2013 and June 2014 brought together community partners looking for support from PSU researchers and PSU faculty, staff, and students who wanted to integrate sustainability-related community engagement projects into existing curriculum. The workshops provided a unique space that allowed local organizations and nonprofits to speak to the PSU community about past collaborations, and to suggest which kinds of engagement work best, and which have been less successful. Small break-out groups met during the workshop and, in many cases, the introductions made during the sessions between community organization representatives and PSU teachers/researchers served to catalyze the beginning of a lasting partnership. Our partnership and project is one such case.

Beyond the initial introduction, SNI staff helped to facilitate the partnership by organizing meetings between Portland State University instructors and community members, thus enabling more in-depth discussion of what the different community partnership projects might entail. In our case, the introductory discussion turned to a focus on how an existing course assignment could be transformed to provide Zenger with the data that they needed while preserving or enhancing the assignment's learning value for students. Given the time demands that are placed on both the staff members at community organizations and the instructors at PSU, the role of ISS was vital in keeping the collaboration on track. Although ISS played less of a role once the initial project had been set up, having an organization that was able to provide logistical support and facilitate communication with the community partner was critical in getting the project off the ground.

The research methodology used in this study was adapted from a similar assignment that was given to students in previous years. In redesigning the assignment, we focused on collecting the information that best met the needs of the community partner: the price and availability of foods at the LIFM and data on what foods were being sold at supermarkets and corner stores within the community. The research design also borrowed methodology from Breyer and Voss-Andreae (2013), who used a healthy foods market basket survey design in a previous study on food access and affordability in Portland. Market basket surveys "are simply a list of defined products in purchasable form" (Monsivais and Drewnowski, 2007), and they are a well-established means of assessing food access. In order to build a healthy foods market basket data set, the fall 2014 World Population and Food Supply class was given a field assignment that tasked students with researching food access and availability in the Lents neighborhood. This involved recording the prices and origins of food in grocery stores, convenience stores, international markets, and two farmers markets within the study area.

Although investigating food origins was of less interest to the community partners, having students collect these data was a critical component of tying the field assignment back to the major themes of the class. Thus, the assignment was designed to benefit and fit the goals of both the class and the community partner. Additionally, although the original assignment was designed to be conducted independently by individual students, we redesigned the project to include a group component in order to engage students with a broader set of community retailers. While group work has many potential drawbacks, a group format lent itself well to this research project. Because the Lents neighborhood was unfamiliar to many students, we wanted to give them the option of doing the fieldwork with other students. We also felt that group work would be more conducive to students engaging in discussion with one another about the project.

By the second week of class, we established 12 groups of 4–5 students and assigned each group 4–5 stores and a number of vendors at the farmers market to research. Overall, 50 supermarkets, grocery stores, international markets, and convenience stores (in addition to the two farmers markets) in and around Lents were selected for students to visit and conduct research. Most of the food retailer locations we selected were based on a spatial dataset previously compiled by Breyer and Voss-Andreae (2013), which identified grocery and convenience stores in the Portland Metropolitan Region. At each location, students collected data on five food categories: fresh fruits, fresh vegetables, unprepared eggs, unprepared meat products, and unprepared seafood items. Attribute data regarding the retailers and the recorded food items were also collected. This included: the location that foods were grown or raised; the price of each food item; how the foods were marketed (local/organic); and whether or not the retailer accepted SNAP benefits. Students were asked to submit their data digitally as part of a Microsoft Excel document compiled by the instructor.

While Zenger Farm expressed a need for food access and affordability data, data analysis itself was outside the time frame of the initial fall 2014 partnership. However, the community partner's initial project goals were further supported beyond the ten-week academic term through a Sustainable Neighborhoods Initiative (SNI) Graduate Fellowship offered by ISS to the graduate TA (teaching assistant), which provided funding and logistical support for further investment in the class project and the relationship with the community partner. The raw data set initially generated by students was extensive, but needed significant editing and data interpretation to be usable for the community partner. Thus, the SNI fellowship enabled the benefits for the community partner to be maximized while providing educational opportunities for both graduate and undergraduate students at Portland State.

Another positive outcome of this project was its integration into the graduate TA's Master's thesis work. While the graduate TA for the class already knew her research interests (sustainable agriculture and food justice issues in urban environments), she had not yet settled on a study area for her thesis research. This class project and community partnership thus provided her with the context and raw data for her research, which expands on the data set collected by the class by seeking input from community members in the Lents neighborhood to determine their perceptions of their food environment. Through interviews and focus groups, this research will present a deeper, more nuanced perspective of food access issues than the strictly spatial and quantitative data set collected by undergraduates can provide. The SNI Fellowship and incorporation of the data into a Master's thesis help to ensure that this project is meaningful beyond work with the community partner; while the data may or may not ultimately be used by Zenger Farm, tying the effort into community-based research allows the project to benefit the Lents community, regardless.

Project outcomes

While working with community partners provides unique opportunities for collaboration and educational experiences outside of the classroom, it is critical to keep in mind that the educational goals and needs of the students must be placed at the forefront of these efforts. As such, student feedback about the assignment was critical for not only improving the data collection process, but also ensuring that the assignment was engaging appropriately with class material. Students provided feedback in three main ways: class discussion, in their written course evaluations at the end of term, and in conversations outside of class. Overall, the collective feedback suggests that—despite the challenges that some students experienced along the way—most students found this to be a valuable learning experience.

One of the major benefits of this project is that it provides a tangible means of engaging students with the community. It introduces students to a topic, teaches them how to research it, and shows them what those data look like "on the ground." Furthermore, it helps to expose students to new places and experiences; while visiting the supermarket was not a new experience for any of the students in the class, visiting a farmers market, a Russian bakery, or a Vietnamese grocery store was for many. Some students had never been to the Lents neighborhood and, thus, the assignment also served to engage them with a new part of the city. Students also indicated that they valued the chance to contribute to a community-based project and the opportunity, through active learning, to tie concepts from class to what is happening in their city. By helping students explore the benefits and challenges of research projects, this project served a pedagogical purpose, as well. Another valuable element of this project is the integration of both graduate and undergraduate research with teaching. The undergraduate research/teaching feeds into a graduate thesis project, which in turns feeds back into the undergraduate class. All the while, a relationship between the university (in the form of the professor, the graduate TA, the ISS staff, and a rotating group of undergraduate students) and community partners (in the form of the contacts at Zenger and the Lents International Famers Markets) is catalyzed and supported over a sustained period of time.

Continued feedback also enabled us to adapt the research project as needed to fit both student and community partner goals. The community partners expressed a desire for more information about the various farmers markets in the area in order to compare prices, availability, and the buy experience with the Lents International Farmers Market. That feedback was taken into account with the redesign of the field assignment for the summer 2015 class. The students' comments and suggestions fell loosely into four categories: farmers markets, logistics, the group format, and access to the research site. Each of these topics is discussed below.

Farmers market

A lot of feedback related directly to the farmers market. Because the class was held in the fall quarter (which, at PSU, runs from late September to mid-December), less produce was in season compared to late spring and summer, and fewer vendors were present at the market. Although students found going to the farmers markets to be interesting and worthwhile, there were less data to collect due to the season. Several students suggested that the instructor specifies market visits in the first two weeks of the term when there is more produce available. Students in the summer course conducted their research at peak season, which provided a richer data set for Zenger and a larger range of foods for students to examine. Students suggested visiting the farmers market towards the beginning of the day, as produce availability drops throughout the day. Many students also suggested researching more farmers markets throughout the city.

Logistics

Many students made logistical suggestions. Some were frustrated to find that some store managers and employees (particularly at convenience stores) would not allow them to collect data. One student suggested that instructors make arrangements ahead of time with store managers to ensure data could be collected, while another suggested students should do that. In order to get a good idea of what products were being sold at various locations in the study area, we allowed students to choose which fruits, vegetables, fish, and meat to research. However, some students suggested the instructors create a predetermined list of products, so that comparisons between locations would be easier to make.

Group format

As anticipated, students also voiced concerns with the group format. If one group member did not come to class or stay in contact with their classmates, the entire group's progress slowed. This was a source of stress for some students, and undermined the goals of the project. One way of dealing with this in the future is to allow students the option of working in groups, in pairs, or as individuals. This gives students more flexibility, allowing them to choose an option that best suits their own learning styles. This may not eliminate absent-group-member syndrome, but could serve to minimize it.

Access

Finally, some students voiced concern about getting to the Lents neighborhood, which is not close to campus and, for some students, was located far from their homes. While the neighborhood is accessible by public transportation, the trip typically takes at least 40 minutes in each direction. Because the farmers markets were only held on Sundays, students were required to set aside time outside of class to visit some of the research sites. As such, it is important to consider the limitations on students who live far from the study area, work on weekends, and/or lack easy access to transportation options.

Adapting the field research assignment

Student comments spurred many changes to the field assignment for the summer 2015 World Population and Food Supply class. The summer class was distinct from the fall class in a few significant ways. It met intensively for four weeks, twice a week for 3 hours and 50 minutes each day, rather than over a ten-week term. The class met from mid-July to mid-August, a time when many staple items are in season. Thus, given the condensed time frame, we were able to take advantage of the season and narrow the scope of the assignment. The field assignment for the summer 2015 class focused exclusively on farmers markets instead of including research at grocery stores, local markets, and convenience stores. The students were required to visit three farmers markets in the region, but had some choice as to which ones. This suited the community partners, who found that they were primarily interested in the farmers market data from the fall 2014. This also addressed student suggestions that the class study farmers markets across the region.

The summer assignment had students work as individuals. This provided flexibility for students, particularly with such a short time frame to do the research. Students were also instructed to record data from a vendor of their choice at the farmers market. Additionally, the assignment required that researchers record the unit price of each item to ensure consistency of data for comparative analysis, thus making the data more useful for the community partner. Students received a set list of seasonal and readily available items for which to collect price and origin data so that students all collect data on the same items, which also allows for stronger analysis (Table 7.1). The assignment also required that students record data for any foods with which they were unfamiliar, providing some context for which ethnic groups each market might cater to.

Table 7.1 **Data collection items, summer 2015**

Fruit	Vegetables	Meat	Eggs
Apples	Carrots	Ground beef	Organic
Apricots	Zucchini	Ground pork	Conventional
Pears	Onion		
Peaches	Lettuce		
Plums	Cabbage		
Strawberries	Cucumber		
Tomatoes	Green beans		
Blackberries	Kale		
Raspberries	Potatoes		
Cherries	Broccoli		

As with the fall 2014 assignment, the summer 2015 assignment required students to conduct research on the advertising, marketing, and branding used to sell these items or promote the vendor. This information was particularly useful for class discussion and student essays about the exercise. Students noticed marked differences in the ways that food was marketed at different farmers markets and by different vendors. Students were also encouraged to ask vendors specific questions about their growing practices, and to record that information. After the course concluded, we again examined feedback from students, feedback from the community partners and made our own observations in order to adapt the assignment further, to ensure the needs of both students and the community partners continue to be met. The community partners were pleased with the data collected in fall 2014 and summer 2015 and look forward to integrating the findings into their grant and programming goals.

Conclusion

Lack of access to affordable healthy food is an increasing problem in cities across the country, and Portland is no exception. Those who live in areas of relatively high poverty, such as Lents, often find themselves living in food deserts. To address these issues locally, we formed a partnership with Zenger farm to help them assess food affordability and accessibility in Lents. Our goal was to ensure that the community partners and our students all benefited from the relationship.

One of the biggest challenges of working with community partners is the disparity between academic and "real world" scheduling. This is especially true for schools like Portland State University, where use of the quarter system results in brief ten-week terms that are often at odds with community scheduling, and do not always allow enough time for partnerships to flourish. Thus, one of the biggest lessons from this project was the importance of having support mechanisms in place that allow projects like this to continue beyond a single academic term.

When the World Population and Food Supply class ended in the fall of 2014 the work for the community partnership was far from over. The Institute for Sustainable Solutions was able to provide invaluable assistance by creating the SNI Fellowship, which allowed the course's graduate TA to devote time to completing the data analysis, editing, and reporting to Zenger Farm. Due to a lack of time and funding on the part of both the instructors and the community partners it is possible that, without ISS's continued support, the data never would have progressed far beyond the classroom. Through funding and support, ISS was able to ensure that the community partnership was more structured and sustainable, thus maximizing the benefit of the work for everyone involved.

Sustaining community partnerships over multiple terms maximizes benefits to undergraduate and graduate students in that it allows time for research to develop and thus related assignments to be improved and customized. Engagement over longer periods of time also allows us to address the changing needs of our community partners and deliver them better and more extensive data.

References

Agyeman, J. & McEntee, J. (2014). Moving the field of food justice forward through the lens of urban political ecology. *Geography Compass*, 8(3), 211-220.

Beaulac, J., Kristjansson, E., & Cummins, S. (2009). A systematic review of food deserts, 1966–2007. *Preventing Chronic Disease*, 6(3), A105. Retrieved from http://www.cdc.gov/pcd/issues/2009/jul/08_0163.htm

Blanchard, T.C. & Matthews, T.L. (2007). Retail concentration, food deserts, and food-disadvantaged communities in rural America. In C.C. Hinrichs and T.A. Lyson (Eds.), *Remaking the North American Food System: Strategies for Sustainability* (pp. 201-215). Lincoln, NE: University of Nebraska Press.

Breyer, B. & Voss-Andreae, A. (2013). Food mirages: Geographic and economic barriers to healthful food access in Portland, Oregon. *Health and Place*, 24, 131-139.

Conway, G. (2012). *One Billion Hungry: Can We Feed the World?* Ithaca, NY: Cornell University Press.

Cummins, S. & Macintyre, S. (2002). "Food deserts"—evidence and assumption in health policy making. *BMJ*, 325, 436-438.

Everett, M. (2011). Practicing anthropology on a community-based public health coalition: Lessons from HEAL. *Annals of Anthropological Practice*, 35(2), 10-26.

Goodling, E., Green, J., & McClintock, N. (2015). Uneven development of the sustainable city: Shifting capital in Portland, Oregon. *Urban Geography*. doi: 10.1080/02723638.2015.1010791

Gottlieb, R. & Fisher, A. (1996). Community food security and environmental justice: Searching for a common discourse. *Agriculture and Human Values*, 13(3), 23-32.

Gottlieb, R. & Joshi, A. (2013). *Food Justice*. Cambridge, MA: MIT Press.

McClintock, N. (2011). From industrial garden to food desert: Demarcated devaluation in the flatlands of Oakland, California. In A. Alkon & J. Agyeman (Eds.), *Cultivating Food Justice: Race, Class, and Sustainability* (pp. 89-120). Cambridge, MA: MIT Press.

Monsivais, P. & Drewnowski, A. (2007). The rising cost of low-energy-density food. *Journal of the American Dietetic Association*, 107(12), 2071-2076.

Office of Neighborhood Involvement (2011). 2000 and 2010 Census Profile: Lents. . City of Portland. Retrieved from https://www.portlandoregon.gov/oni/article/375977

Shannon, J. (2014). Food deserts: Governing obesity in the neoliberal city. *Progress in Human Geography*, 38(2), 248-266.

Short, A., Guthman, J. & Raskin, S. (2007). Food deserts, oases, or mirages? Small markets and community food security in the San Francisco Bay area. *Journal of Planning Education and Research*, 26(3), 352-364.

8

Portland made

Building partnerships to support the local artisan/maker community

Charles Heying and Stephen Marotta

The evocative ideal of a self-reliant, locally distinct economy is deeply embedded in the ethic of sustainable development. Promoting homegrown economies has a venerable history as a point for resistance to colonizing and globalizing forces that have been exploitive of communities, cultures, and ecologies. Localness has become synonymous with values of autonomy, human scale, authentic and personalized, and respectful of materiality and ecological limits. As we have developed partnerships with our community of interest, we have indeed seen these values embraced and stewarded by the community, but more, the community has been defining for itself what it means to be part of a sustainable local economy.

From our side as teachers and researchers, community partnerships reveal the contextual richness of the artisan and maker community and the working relationships that we both discover and create. Without the partnerships, we would be limited to the aggregate output of surveys and constrained view of one-time interviews. With the partnerships, we are embedded in the community of actors, both public and private, who are developing the infrastructure of support for the local artisan/maker economy. Not only does this provide access to data that may not otherwise be available, it also provides access to the backstory of failures and successes where the struggles for meaning and identity are played out.

From the side of the community partners, there are considerable benefits as well. Academic researchers offer the possibility for deeper understanding of their community and their struggles to create a locally distinct economy. Some of this is contextual, but much is actionable research that can leverage a community's agenda with local policy-makers or the public. We can provide academic legitimacy, advanced skills of data collection and analysis, as well as access to research funding streams and to trained and motivated graduate student researchers.

As scholars deeply interested in and supportive of homegrown economies and the artisans and makers who are creating them, we have embraced a research process that is more resonant with values of artisan production and localism. Just as artisans attend to the integrity of their source material, become intimate with its potential and limits, and learn by engagement and error, so too have we embraced these methods in our research. Instead of standing apart from makers and artisans, observing them at a distance, careful not to intervene, we have actively engaged them as partners. Our intent is to become part of the community, learning about it as we also shape it, honoring the voices of those we engage just as artisans honor their source material. Along the way we have crafted a collaborative creative process that we believe affords us an honest perspective of the community we seek to understand. This chapter will provide a narrative of the process by which we developed important research partnerships, and how these relationships yielded valuable lessons that informed our evolving research methodology as well as blurred the line between "successful" and "failed" research.

Genesis: Brew to Bikes

The process of engagement with the local artisan and maker community began with research and writing that led to the publication of *Brew to Bikes: Portland's Artisan Economy* (Heying, 2010). In the spring of 2009, students in the Toulan School of Urban Studies and Planning at Portland State University were invited to participate as chapter authors in a proposed book about Portland's artisan enterprises. Over 40 students responded with about half ultimately committing to the project. Over the summer, we met every two weeks for instructions on interview strategies, chapter framing, and writing technique. Fourteen students submitted chapters by summer's end with more authors and chapters added over the following months.

The willingness of the students to work on the project with little more than the possibility of claiming authorship of their chapter was somewhat surprising, but less so when it became apparent that many had personal connections or significant engagement with the sectors they wrote about. These were not disinterested researchers; they were passionate followers of local fashion, food, bikes, and beer. It was a satisfying and collaborative process that continued through the drafting and publication of the book. In addition to the students' work, much of the credit for the success of the editing and publication phase was due to the enthusiasm and professionalism of the book's publisher, Ooligan Press. Ooligan is part of a unique graduate program at Portland State University that operates its own nonprofit publishing enterprise. Ooligan was not only the book's publisher, but also one of the signature local enterprises discussed in our chapter on the independent media scene in Portland. Choosing a local, student-run press was consistent with the process that produced the text, engaging students and the community in a project of interest and moving beyond the tidy research habits that suggest that passion and advocacy are incompatible with producing an honest narrative.

Ooligan Press staged the launch party for *Brew to Bikes*. As much artisan trade show as book launch, it was held at the Art Department, an industrial gallery and event space operated by Kelley Roy. The space included an office in a converted camping trailer, a first sign of hipster food cart conversions to come. Langlitz Leather displayed its classic biker outfits including one made for Evel Knievel; Tony Pereira brought his award-winning hand-made bike and signed copies of his photo in the book; David King hung out at his table for quiet conversations about his unusual headless bass guitars; Grand Central Bakery's free samples were gone before the book reading. Perhaps unsurprisingly, the hit of the evening was the free spirits tasting next door at New Deal Distillery, the first of the artisan distillers that have now evolved into Distillery Row. Working with passionate student authors, a small student-run press, and launching the book in Portland's first makerspace with the participation and support of local artisans set the tone for the engaged research process that we have since pursued.

The publication of *Brew to Bikes* resulted in a number of invitations from community groups to discuss the implications of the research for developing a sustainable local economy. The community discussions created an opportunity to more deeply connect with Portland actors who were creating an economy based on local distinctiveness and sustainable production. Several of these conversations developed into mutually beneficial partnerships. At this point, we would like to delve into two specific sets of relationships that have evolved from the publication and community reception of *Brew to Bikes*. The rest of this chapter will tell the stories of these two (entangled) community partnerships and how they have co-evolved with the authors' academic research and teaching programs.

Partnership #1: ADX and Portland Made Collective

Our relationship with Kelley Roy at ADX was a gradual build. Author Heying first met Kelley Roy and her co-author Kelley Rogers over coffee to discuss their book *Cartopia: Portland's Food Cart Revolution* (2010), one of the first books to consider this soon-to-be phenomenon. Since Heying was also writing a book about Portland's artisan community, we met to compare notes. We connected again at the aforementioned book launch for *Brew to Bikes* at the Art Department. A year later, Roy moved to a new 14,000 sq. ft facility in the Central Eastside neighborhood of Portland. The move coincided with an overhaul of Roy's business plan, and Art Department became Art Design Portland. ADX, as it has become known, is a multifunctional makerspace, training center, and custom design and fabrication shop. Over the next several years, Heying took several class trips to the facility, one of which included Stephen Marotta, a Ph.D. student participating in Heying's seminar, "Making it Local: Strategies for an Economy of Place." Heying also attended the initial launch party for the Portland Made Collective, an initiative by ADX to create a collective identity and showcase for Portland's artisan/maker community.

At the launch, Roy discussed with Heying the possibility of shared research, a conversation that was nearly dropped as subsequent meetings to identify a project were mis-scheduled or simply missed. The idea of addressing some unanswered questions from *Brew to Bikes* was pushing Heying in an unexpected direction toward seeking funding for a more quantitative look at Portland's artisan economy. At book presentations, questions about the economic relevance of the artisan sector were consistently asked. Discussing this potential research in his class, Heying asked for volunteers to participate, with the possibility that funding might follow. Author Marotta responded enthusiastically, initiating a research collaboration that started with a single term of funding but ultimately resulted in grant-funded work for the next several years.

The collaborative research program was, at first, built around a survey that Roy had asked us to design and administer. She was concerned that politicians and business leaders, on a variety of levels, were underestimating the impact of local artisans and makers on Portland's regional economy. The problem, which we referred to as "invisibility," was in essence an artifact of certain characteristics of artisanal businesses; more specifically, they are smaller, newer, and tend to eschew traditional business channels and processes. In subsequent meetings with Roy and her marketing director we learned more about Roy's need for data and for the legitimacy a study produced in an academic setting would provide. Roy was engaged in a running battle with the forces at work in determining the future character of Portland's Central Eastside industrial sanctuary. As a tenant who entered the market while the economy was in freefall, Roy had secured a long-term lease under favorable terms. But leases like Roy's were becoming less available to the small artisanal firms that had been quietly populating the area. Meanwhile, developers had begun moving in to secure and convert the warehouses and lofts for the growing "creative industries" sector, including software, marketing, and design firms that needed only office space and not specialized production infrastructure like ample floor space, industrial ventilation, and electrical service. Roy needed hard data on the economic relevance of the artisan/maker firms to make her case. She also needed to show members of the collective that they were getting something, other than visibility and a brand, for their membership fees. We served her purposes in both ways and came with the added benefit of working pro bono. The most manageable solution was to design and administer a survey to the members of her newly minted Portland Made Collective (henceforth PMC) in order to get some aggregate economic information.

At this point, however, we were relatively uninformed as to the function and mission of PMC. To help us understand the development of PMC, Roy proposed that we observe an advisory group meeting between herself, ADX's marketing director, an angel investor known as "Starbucker," a representative from Wieden

+ Kennedy's Portland Incubator Experiment, and a representative from the Oregon Entrepreneur Network. The meeting left an impact on us. The meeting itself oscillated between speculative montage and frank business discussion, covering much of the ground between topics such as rebranding of Portland to concern over whether PMC should be private or nonprofit. We left the meeting having distilled very similar insights; jointly, we were surprised at the ambiguity of participants' understanding of certain collective values. The value of localness, in particular, stood out: the idea seemed to include branding, scale of enterprise, geography, intentionality, and authenticity all at once. During the discussion, we observed that the understanding of "local" slipped uncontested from one definition to another. It was the discussion around localism (and other assorted community values) that made us aware of the importance of these definitions; the advisory group seemed to share a common understanding, despite the lack of clarity for us.

The meeting was pivotal for us. While we were beginning to grasp the importance of understanding localism to our research, no directed interview could have taken us so immediately to how loosely the concept could be framed. Following the meeting, we began to reorient our research program toward interrogating localism. The fact that this somewhat mundane meeting would truly shape our research program was a surprise; we didn't expect to gain much from the meeting outside of a better operational knowledge of PMC's development. Instead, our research focus was shifted, and in the process, we became aware of the methodological importance of direct observations of the community in action rather than relying on "by-the-book" techniques.

In the months after the meeting, we followed through on the project to survey members of the PMC. Observing the meeting helped us frame questions related to localism and solidified our decision to conduct follow-up interviews where we could probe the concept more deeply. The development of the PMC survey also taught us much about the give and take that such a community–university relationship demands. We administered the survey and prepared a report for PMC at no cost to Roy, which at time felt like considerable work for minimal reward. However, in retrospect we see the benefits of what we gained. Parallel to the survey work, we were developing a new online search methodology necessary to populate our growing database of Portland artisans. Roy gave us direct access to her membership list and a possibly more responsive audience for a survey. The PMC work also allowed us to pilot a survey we hoped later to send to the full population of Portland artisans. Academic work often proceeds slowly, but work with an immediate purpose—such as the PMC survey—can jump-start a project. We took the opportunity and it had its benefits.

When the survey was sent our expectations that affiliation with PMC would improve receptivity were confirmed. Online surveys rarely get response rates over 10%; our response rate was 42%, acceptable even for a mail out survey. The results were collated into a white paper and presented at the first annual State of the Collective event. Roy had enlisted a county commissioner, local council member Nick Fish, and US Representative Earl Blumenauer to speak, but our report provided the substantive content for the event. As we will document below, on this night we made new community connections that once again had a major influence on our research program.

In the events leading to the evening, however, we experienced a particular danger in doing community-engaged research. We had circulated an electronic copy of our white paper to Roy, as we had done for all PMC members. We used the white paper's send out as an opportunity to promote the meeting, but also to fulfill our commitment to provide the outcome of the research to PMC members in a timely way. Roy responded with a short but pointed question regarding ownership of the study and the raw data; essentially she asked "who owned the data?" It was unexpected, puzzling, and even a bit threatening; we had never thought to have this conversation with Roy before collecting the data. Since we had received no compensation for our work, there was no contractual obligation, which meant that the boundaries of our partnership had never been set. We responded with questions and statements about our responsibility under the terms of our human subjects review to maintain the anonymity of the data for a prescribed time, also asking questions about Roy's sudden concerns regarding ownership.

The upshot of our exchanges was to point to the different perspectives of business and academics. Roy's concern was establishing her right to post the study to her website and to release the study to the press, essentially claiming co-ownership of the work with the particular legitimacy of a study produced by academics. While we were very much on board with the study reaching a wider audience, we realized that it can be tricky to negotiate the uses and intentions of collaborators. By the evening of the presentation, the issue was not fully resolved, but we proceeded to make it work. The trust between Roy and us was tested, but not broken.

Partnership #2: Portland Apparel Lab

We followed the aforementioned survey of Portland Made Collective members with a series of interviews intended to ripen our account of what exactly a sustainable and locally distinct economy meant to its users and creators. We asked questions about what "local" meant to Portland's makers and artisans, how they identified with Portland and its development into a creative center, and what specific values they held to be important. These interviews were quite revealing, but for this chapter we are interested in the branches of research that have evolved from these interviews.

We conducted several interviews with artisans and makers active in Portland's fashion and apparel sector. During the interviews, a common theme that emerged was the need to quantify the output of Portland's apparel makers. The aggregate economic output of this quickly growing sector was unknown, and interviewees suggested that this was one explanation for the minimal production and support infrastructure available to Portland's artisan apparel makers. Their argument boiled down to one question, how do we understand the needs of a locally distinct economy if we know nothing about its impact or role in the larger regional economy?

The interviews alluded to the "invisibility" problem that we had experienced at the outset of our reporting for the initial PMC survey. We realized at the time survey results started to come in that we needed to check our survey responses for validity against whatever economic information was available to us as researchers through subscription databases. Guided by our librarian, we examined a handful of comprehensive small business databases, eventually landing on Reference USA as the most complete and reliable source. Given Reference USA's breadth and comprehensiveness, we assumed this to be a database that political leaders, academics, and investors would be likely to turn to for aggregate economic statistics for small businesses.

The results of the comparison between our survey responses and Reference USA's database were revealing: only 7% of the businesses we surveyed showed up in Reference USA's database. It was clear from this result that the economic impact of Portland's artisanal economy—populated by a large number of embryonic businesses—would be severely underreported. We quickly realized that there was an important gap in economic impact data at the political level in terms of local economies, and that we had an opportunity to address that gap. Indeed, this followed Kelley Roy's initial suspicion and was a hypothetical motivation for her request of a survey of her members. The survey, though, had made it clear to us that economic statistics alone would not be enough to understand the impact of Portland's artisans on the overall local economy, in part because we were increasingly questioning "localness." It seemed that deriving a quantitative economic impact study of Portland's local artisan economy required qualitative interaction with the community.

In the course of interviewing Portland apparel designers and learning more about their networks and needs, we were directed to Crispin Argento, founder of PINO Portland, an apparel company dedicated to ties, bow ties, and other accessories. Argento had begun to think about Portland's potential for being an apparel center on the West Coast. Argento believed that he had identified the many missing elements of Portland's apparel landscape, and was in the process of finishing a new business plan for an apparel-specific incubator/makerspace hybrid that he and his business partner, Dawn Moothart, were to name the Portland Apparel Lab (PAL). The launch party was approaching, and our rapport with Argento got us invited.

Attending PAL's launch party was not necessary for our research program, but we knew it was important for us to go. The event was being held at Portland's Museum of Contemporary Craft, which at the time was hosting an exhibit on Portland's artisan apparel industry. We were taken by some of the mapping of apparel enterprises that Sarah Margolis-Pineo, curator of this exhibit, had done (we were later to produce similar maps of our own findings). PAL's launch party was packed; Argento and Moothart hadn't expected such a large turnout, and seemed anxious at times, but still seemed to know almost everyone in the

room. The pre-launch mixer had already been fruitful for us, as we met new artisans that we eventually interviewed for our localism research. The presentation
opened with Argento asking the audience questions about what the apparel community in Portland was missing. The attendees were well armed with answers,
as if their frustration had finally found a channel for release. The conversation
between Argento, Moothart, and the audience was fascinating, sometimes oscil-
lating between argument and commiseration but generally constructive. We
were watching a fledgling artisan sector struggling to its feet, figuring out among
them what their real needs were as a community and not knowing how to fulfill
these needs. We were eager to help and by this point we were unencumbered by
the notion that we might somehow interfere.

A month later, after the original interviews and analysis for the PMC survey had
been completed, we presented the findings at the State of the Collective event at
ADX. Following the presentation, we were approached by many of the artisans and
makers in attendance, most of whom showed real enthusiasm for the research
findings. Dawn Moothart of PAL went out of her way to introduce us to the owners
of Spooltown, a better established and politically plugged-in apparel producer that
was eager to see some new research on Portland's small business apparel sector.
One conversation bled into another, and finally the conversation brewed into a
lively discussion of how hungry Portland's artisan apparel sector was for the type
of research we had done for Portland Made Collective. The idea for our next project
came into a clearer focus that night.

Two weeks after the ADX presentation, we decided to participate in a tour of
Portland's makers and artisans that had taken root in the old industrial spaces of
the Central Eastside. Sarah Margolis-Pineo of the Museum of Contemporary Craft
led the tour, narrating the neighborhood's history between visits. She impressed
us with her knowledge of the history of postwar economic restructuring and the
flexible and creative labor forms that it gave rise to. Realizing that she had also
been responsible for curating the exhibit on the apparel sector in Portland that
we had admired at the PAL launch, we decided to contact her to see whether she
might want to build on research she had done for the exhibit. She was immediately
excited about the possibility of a research collaboration and we spent several hours
across several meetings thinking through the design of the upcoming research.
Margolis-Pineo helped us craft a database of Portland's apparel maker community, and helped arrange a larger meeting of interested actors, including the PAL
partners, a representative of the Portland Development Commission, and a select
group of local apparel business owners.

The conversation at the meeting was fertile, and we all left with a sense of purpose. Academically speaking, this research would be the first of its kind: the maker
movement (a variation on the artisan economy) was just getting onto academia's
radar, and we had already gathered relevant data. But what made this opportunity
potentially unique was the fact that we were starting to look at the artisan econ-
omy/maker movement in terms of sectors; the idea to look at Portland's economy
in this way was not our idea as researchers, but rather it had grown out of our

relationship with the community. This provided us a chance to develop a methodology that allowed us to break small creative firms into sectors that they define for us rather than us defining for them. In other words, we had a unique opportunity to understand the organization and connectivity of Portland's locally distinct economy through the eyes and experiences of the people that participated in this economy.

While things seem to be falling into place to launch a survey of Portland's artisan apparel sector, a key actor was having second thoughts. We heard rumors that Argento, despite the extensive work that he and Moothart had invested in PAL, was running out of patience with the speed of things in Portland. He was eager to grow his neckwear company and launch his new accelerator concept, and he did not feel that a sufficient level of support was forthcoming in Portland. And although we had offered our services and spent time planning the survey project, looking for funding, and making important community connections, Argento ended up leaving for Los Angeles, a city that he believed had the necessary infrastructure and resources that Portland lacked. Shortly thereafter, Margolis-Pineo, our collaborator at the Museum of Contemporary Craft, also decided to pursue opportunities beyond Portland. Other potential collaborators were showing only superficial interest. And we were also moving on. We had just agreed to join a larger, three-city, three-university research project on the maker movement, which quickly began gobbling up our time. Our project appeared to be falling apart, and we weren't sure if we'd be able to rescue it or whether we wanted to.

We did end up shelving this project. By typical academic measures—a completed research plan, a deliverable to the community, subsequent journal articles—it did not yield what it could have. In hindsight, however, we have chosen not to consider it a failed project. We learned a great deal about the connections we would need to make in order to get such an investigation together. This project was largely a community project, designed by community members and in many ways defined by the community itself. And while we were interested in the same quantifiable economic impact data as the apparel community, our interest was also with trying to understand *what the community wanted to know about itself.* This data was perhaps more telling about how makers and artisans work within their own contextual understanding of community. In helping organize the research we created an opportunity to bring disparate community members together—many of whom did not see things in precisely the same ways—and as a result there were periods of time in which we felt not in control of the direction of the project. But we were OK with that; it was important to us to perform a style of research that served the community in a way that advanced its interests. But alas, communities are not perfect, and things fall apart.

Once we realized the project would not go forward—for us, professionally, meaning that we would not be able to get academic publications from it, and for the community meaning there would be no economic impact study of the apparel sector—we reflected on what had happened. We realized that we had learned a significant amount about the community that we had set about to study. We were able to make lasting connections that we have continued to rely on in our current research study; we learned a great deal about the specific struggles the maker and artisan communities face; and we better understood how to bridge the gap between researcher and researched. But most importantly, we are satisfied with our success in being able to help rally excitement around a research project of their choosing.

The number of connections and the amount of trust we have been able to develop through this seemingly failed research project are not trivial. We have open channels of communication with a variety of actors that were, and hopefully still are, completely aware that we were offering our services to them not only to advance our academic interests but rather to help them take their community in the direction of their choosing. It was important to us not to appear to the community as bureaucratic representatives from the ivory tower, but rather as people that believed in the shared goals of sustainably developing Portland's local economy.

Denouement

ADX and PAL are the stories of relationships, not research subjects; they are stories of learning, not successes and failures. These relationships are certainly collaborative, but they can be slippery as well. The embedded model of research we have chosen to pursue has certainly not been perfect; we have had missteps along the way, and been called out by the community for those missteps. We have had good relationships suddenly dry up for reasons we still don't understand. There have been times when we have put our feet—perhaps even our ankles—into our mouths while conducting an interview or chiming in during a meeting. These are not uncommon occurrences in a community, and we have largely been forgiven for our mistakes because we continue to put our best effort into actually producing something useful for the community. Sometimes, though, it is difficult to explain to the community what the long-term benefits of research are, which loops us back to the issue of sustainability.

Sustainability, despite all of its nebulousness, is a common value cited by many artisans when they discuss the care they inscribe in their craft. Like the artisan, as researchers we specialize in a craft; this craft can be honed, forgotten, reformulated, remembered, revised, and even fetishized. The craft requires a process by which we make our products, a process that evolves every time a researcher enters into the field. As we repeatedly hear in the community, process makes all the difference. The care for the source material is especially valuable, as the idiosyncrasies of the source material often dictate the shape of the final product. In the case of the researcher, we might think of the community we seek to understand as our source material. Therefore, we can choose how to interact with it; we can choose to allow our process to evolve with it or we can choose to impose our needs upon it. We have attempted to fall in line with the former, sometimes by succeeding in crafting relationships and other times by refusing to act on relationships as if they were utilitarian commodities.

In the end, the question we have tried to ask is: what is our product? We have chosen to think about our product as the wellbeing of the community first and the accolades of publishing our findings second. That's not to say we don't value academic production; we just want the knowledge we produce to truly serve the community.

References

Heying, C. (2010). *Brew to Bikes: Portland's Artisan Economy.* Portland, OR: Ooligan Press.
Rodgers, K. & Roy, K. (2010). *Cartopia: Portland's Food Cart Revolution.* Portland, OR: Roy Rodgers Press.

9

Partnerships for healthy classrooms

The SAGE green modular classroom project

Margarette Leite

The SAGE green modular classroom project is an ongoing community-engaged teaching and research-based initiative that leverages industry and community partnerships to develop, promote, and disseminate a healthier modular classroom for children in Oregon and across the country (see Figures 9.1 and 9.2). It serves as a model for multidisciplinary collaboration at the university level and for sustainability-focused teaching and research in the areas of cultural and environmental sustainability. More specifically, it offers a unique look at a university–industry partnership model for effective action in the marketplace that positively impacts communities in need. The initiative, based primarily at Portland State University's (PSU) School of Architecture, exemplifies a growing body of work defined as public interest design. Public interest design is an expanding field of architecture that seeks to extend its reach to the majority of people across the globe that lack access to design services. It also expands the conventional definition of architectural services to focus on the real needs of communities. The SAGE modular classroom project has evolved over the course of several years involving dozens of student participants and generating significant media attention and awards including an international SEED Award in 2013 for "social, economic and environmental design" as well as national awards from the Modular Building Institute. These efforts have resulted in the placement of approximately 50 SAGE classrooms serving 1,400 students to date in school districts across Oregon and Washington in a relatively short amount of time. The process by which this project was carried out could be most accurately described as a path of discovery for the research team and stakeholders but one based on general precepts established in related work by figures such as John Quale at the University of Virginia and his work on affordable housing (2012). While some aspects of this initiative are unique to the field, it is hoped that the successes and lessons learned throughout this elongated and eventful process can be applicable to a wide range of disciplines and project types.

Figure 9.1 **A SAGE classroom in Edmonds School District, WA**

Source: photo courtesy Peter Simon

Figure 9.2 **SAGE interior**

Source: Pacific Mobile Structures

Project overview

For the better part of the last five years, faculty and students at Portland State University's School of Architecture and College of Engineering have been involved in the design of a healthier and more energy efficient alternative to the ubiquitous modular classrooms found in a great many schools across the country. Fully one-third of all students in the United States spend at least some part of their educational lives in a modular classroom, often referred to as a "portable." In California, more than a third of all classroom space is provided by modular classrooms (Modular Building Institute White Paper, 2010). The modular building industry claims that there are about half a million modular classrooms in use around the country, representing a $4 million a year industry (2011). Given these numbers, how is it that the environmental qualities of these classrooms are not addressed in the national debate over how best to deliver a quality education to our students? Concerns have generally focused on curricular issues but environmental conditions found in many of the spaces in which students are expected to learn can also play a role in student performance, as a growing body of evidence makes clear.

In 2012, a study conducted at the Department of Energy's Lawrence Berkeley National Laboratory found that even moderate levels of about 600 ppm (parts per million) of CO_2 can negatively affect human decision-making (Satish *et al.*, 2012). (Outdoor air averages about 380 ppm.) At 2,500 ppm the study showed that certain types of cognitive activity, like initiative, drop into the dysfunctional range. It is not uncommon for high occupancy spaces like classrooms to have upwards of 1,000 to 3,000 ppm CO_2. In fact, testing of existing modular classrooms in local schools by PSU students involved in the SAGE project found that CO_2 levels were often in the range of 700 to more than 1,000 ppm (Flattery *et al.*, 2010). High levels of CO_2 are indications of insufficient ventilation, which may be a result of either poorly designed or poorly operating building systems but can also be a result of our move to more energy-efficient buildings. Poor ventilation can also result in higher indoor air pollutants, contributing to "sick building syndrome." This can be an issue in poorly designed buildings of any kind but modular classrooms, often considered temporary structures, are typically built of lower quality materials and are, therefore, more prone to these issues. Lack of regular maintenance in financially strapped schools can also exacerbate these problems. Sick building syndrome has been studied primarily in work environments of adult populations, but consider the impact that these kinds of toxins can have on smaller, growing and more active bodies (two factors key to the higher impact of contamination on children) and it is no secret that modular classrooms are often seen as the FEMA trailers of our national education system. They are universally maligned for their poor quality of construction, insufficient natural daylight, and unsightliness. They are primarily the result of the lack of resources in many school districts across the country which must resort to temporary structures to serve a permanent need. These are the negative attributes of modular classrooms.

On a more positive note, modular classrooms can be quickly erected and cost less than brick and mortar additions. They can be moved from school to school if well-constructed and therefore have the potential to adapt to changing needs. In fact, well-designed modular structures can have significant advantages over site constructed buildings because they are built in factories where conditions are strictly controlled and processes can be streamlined to reduce waste. Their adaptability makes them the only current answer to the sudden fluctuations in school enrollments that are the result of the propensity of American families to move once every five years on average. Unfortunately, with little support for decision-making with regards to quality and design, and in the face of funding shortfalls, schools resort to choosing the most affordable option. These issues are indicative of systemic problems that undermine effective change in most school districts nationally. The market does offer a number of healthy and energy-efficient modular classrooms; however, their costs are prohibitive to most school districts and so their applications are few and limited to well-funded schools. As a result, what we see in most schools across the nation are uninspiring and unhealthy classrooms.

In light of this situation, faculty and students of Architecture and Engineering at PSU sought a better solution and understood that it would require joining forces with industry partners to create an alternative. This alternative, while still affordable, would signify a bold paradigm shift in what we as a society should expect in terms of quality for the spaces in which children spend a large percentage of their young lives.

Thus began a process for drawing together and mobilizing a broad array of partners, public and private, governmental and nongovernmental, community and industry, all committed to making a difference in this area. Lacking a clear roadmap for creating and following a process, the approach taken was haphazard at times but based on the groundwork in public interest design established by leaders in the field of architecture including Thomas Fisher, Bryan Bell, and others.

On reflection, it became clear that there were a series of significant moments and associated events that, taken together, were critical to the success of the entire project. They can be defined as criteria according to the following list and can be a useful checklist for community engagement across a variety of project types:

- Fostering public debate (gathering support and interested parties)

- Creating interdisciplinary collaboration at the university level

- Engaging industry partners early in the process

- Engaging the stakeholders and keeping them connected (Oregon Solutions process)

- Taking advantage of outreach and public education opportunities

- Leveraging pro bono work and grant opportunities for support at critical stages

- Creating mutually beneficial intellectual property structures for long-term funding
- Engaging student talent at every level

Fostering public debate

In order to generate public discussion and identify interested individuals and potential community partnerships for addressing the modular classroom issue, the PSU School of Architecture teamed with the American Institute of Architects (AIA), Portland, in 2010 to hold a national symposium. Its overarching theme was "Activism in Architecture," though its intent was to focus local and regional community action on the modular classroom problem. It drew a number of national figures in the field of public interest design with the goal of mobilizing and encouraging architects, student architects, and professionals in a number of related fields to see themselves as the agents of change in their communities. The first day of the two-day symposium was reserved for speaker presentations while the second day was organized as a public "charrette" or brainstorming event focusing on modular classrooms. The studio-based format of the architectural curriculum served as the structure for managing the event. Three courses, including two design studios and one senior capstone course within the School of Architecture, were set up to address particular issues with respect to modular classrooms. The students involved in these courses organized, led, and recorded the work of the charrette groups. Charrette participants included local professionals in architecture and related fields, school administrators, modular industry representatives, and others interested in modular classrooms. Continuing education credits were available to participating architects which helped to establish funding for the event. Following a number of presentations discussing issues pertinent to modular classrooms in Portland, charrette participants were split up into groups to generate ideas in the form of sketches and bullet points which they then presented to the larger group. The drawings and ideas generated served as starting points which the participating students then brought to design completion through their coursework. This event also served to bring to the fore and gain the involvement of all the stakeholders, community members, and industry representatives that would commit to collaborating on a solution. It also initiated the long-term partnership with modular manufacturer, Blazer Industries, which continues to the present.

Creating interdisciplinary collaboration at the university level

The Institute for Sustainable Solutions (ISS) at PSU was established in 2008 to support cross-disciplinary research and curriculum across a broad range of topics involving sustainability and to help create meaningful connections between institutions and community partners. It also administers a $25 million matching grant program established by the Miller Foundation. The presence of an institute such as this in a university environment is critical to establishing a support network throughout the institution that can benefit from the expertise and resource sharing that makes multi-partner processes like the SAGE classroom project possible. ISS has been instrumental in helping to link the project to a number of the community partners involved in SAGE including Oregon Solutions and PSU's Innovation & Intellectual Properties (IIP) group. In addition, it provided grant support at a number of critical stages that helped propel the project forward when taking the time to identify appropriate outside sources and waiting for long application and response times would have derailed it.

For the SAGE classroom project, creating connections across disciplines within the university not only served to pool expertise and broaden the scope of the project, which was important, but also served as fundamental scholarship and experience for university students in the value and means of collaborative, team-oriented working models. In particular, the collaboration that emerged on this project between the School of Architecture and the Maseeh College of Engineering and Computer Science proved indispensable. Despite the obvious connections that exist between related fields like architecture and engineering, it has been the norm in many universities across the country for colleges, schools, and departments alike to function primarily independently. However, with greater appreciation for the value that collaborative working relationships are creating in the field, these kinds of connections are increasing. In the case of the SAGE classroom project, this cross-disciplinary collaboration was necessary to creating the synergy between systems and envelope design that is one of the hallmarks of the SAGE classroom. The collaboration was begun earlier with the receipt of a federal Department of Energy grant which supported the creation of the Green Building Research Lab (GBRL) in 2009, a joint resource between the two schools. The GBRL was a valuable resource for conducting hands-on research in building performance including studies conducted in local classrooms as well as for advancing performance modeling for the new classroom design. The research and design provided by students and faculty at the College of Engineering reduced the need and cost of outside engineering services but also advanced a more innovative agenda for the mechanical systems in the SAGE classroom. These students participated along with the architecture students in a variety of ways including presenting at stakeholder meetings and outreach events.

Another important cross-disciplinary partnership was established with the PSU School of Business Administration. A capstone course designed to give MBA students the chance to engage in real-world service opportunities was established to help create a business plan and to develop long-term marketing strategies for the classroom. They worked with both students and faculty involved in SAGE to interview industry and school district partners to understand the sales mechanisms for modular classrooms and researched market opportunities for creating greater awareness of the product.

As a result of this focus on cross-disciplinary work, the SAGE modular classroom team was awarded a $2,500 "Excellence in Inter-Departmental/Inter-College Civic Engagement" Award from PSU in 2012.

Engaging industry partners early in the process

National modular manufacturer, Blazer Industries, located in Aumsville, Oregon became an early partner in the SAGE classroom project thanks to the charrette event. They served initially as a source of information regarding procurement procedures, production efficiency, and cost analysis associated with modular classrooms in general, and have become a long-term partner in all aspects of making the SAGE classroom successful. They continue to be the classroom's manufacturer in this region and our consultant to manufacturers of the SAGE classroom in other territories. The importance of their involvement early on in the project cannot be overstated. Their experience was particularly critical to making the classroom affordable but much of what serves as the basis for the new design is taken from the existing model which the modular industry has perfected in terms of construction efficiency and installation practices. With them, the team could take what worked and innovate where most critical.

One of the other benefits of establishing strong, early partnerships in all projects is the multiplication of resources and contacts that can help to propel a project forward. As a result of their participation, Pacific Mobile Structures, a company with a long history of collaborating with Blazer Industries, committed to purchasing and promoting the first SAGE classroom to be built. In addition, both companies' strong reputations nationally and their connections to the national Modular Building Institute resulted in the first prototype classroom being exhibited at the U.S. Green Building Council's 2012 Greenbuild Conference in San Francisco, the preeminent event in green building and design. These types of promotional opportunities would not have been available otherwise, and its presence at Greenbuild brought attention and exposure to SAGE, at a crucial moment. Thus, the inclusion of Pacific Mobile Structures as a participant precipitated an important partnership with Portland State University. Pacific Mobile Structures, a modular building distributor in the Northwest region of the U.S. and Canada, is now the primary promoter and seller of the classroom. Their partnership is not only a working partnership but a legal one as well as they have entered into a copyright agreement with the university in conjunction with the classroom. They, in turn, have been the link to other distributors across the country such that the SAGE classroom is now contracted with three different distributors covering every state as well as some provinces in Canada. Such are the benefits of a well-connected, multi-partner entity.

One measure of the value that this project has brought to the modular building industry is the award of two national prizes to two different SAGE schools by the Modular Building Institute in 2014.

Figure 9.3 **Oregon Solutions collaboration identified on a plaque for every SAGE classroom**

Source: author

Engaging the stakeholders and keeping them connected

While these industry partners were critical to this project's success, equally critical were the numerous other partners that stepped in to provide a wide range of expertise. Early presentations and discussions about the problems with current modular structures brought to light a particular and unique government initiative in the state of Oregon called "Oregon Solutions." This initiative identifies and seeks to support groups working to address issues of sustainability in their communities. It works on the principle of community governance whereby community leaders join forces and bring together public, private, and civic stakeholders to negotiate, pool, and leverage resources to render a solution. A limited number of initiatives are selected each year based on their potential impact on communities in Oregon, and their likelihood of success. The team is led by a neutral "convener" from the community while management support is provided by the Governor's office.

Once selected, the group of stakeholders meets regularly over the course of an agreed period of time to work out the details of the project. In the case of the Green Modular Classroom Taskforce, which was designated an "Oregon Solution" in 2011, participants met every other month for just over a year. Once the project goals and tasks are laid out, the members sign a "Declaration of Cooperation" identifying and agreeing to their contributions to the process. The advantages of the existing structure provided by this initiative include generating a sense of urgency and an air of credibility to the project in the eyes of both potential stakeholders as well as the public. With this in place, we were able to assemble a team that included, in addition to the School of Architecture and the College of Engineering at PSU, PSU's Institute for Sustainable Solutions, Gerding Edlen Developers, Blazer Industries, American Institute of Architects Portland, Portland Public Schools, Oregon Built Environment and Sustainable Technologies Center (BEST), Energy Trust of Oregon, Pacific Mobile Structures, PAE Consulting Engineers, Oregon Building Codes Division, Portland Bureau of Development Services, Northwest Renewable Resources, McKinstry Engineers, Luma Lighting, EcoREAL, and MSpace Holdings. Having all important stakeholders and decision-makers at the same table made for quicker, more effective decision-making and created support through the Declaration of Cooperation for follow-through. The Oregon Solutions process allowed SAGE to consolidate and build on the consensuses and relationships built in the earlier symposium and charrette. It also helped to build support and to clarify the goals of the SAGE project among the engineers, code officials, industry, and design professionals who would be essential to its adoption in the region. The importance of the Oregon Solutions process is highlighted on the plaques that are placed on each classroom (see Figure 9.3).

Figure 9.4 **PSU students present SAGE classroom design at Oregon Museum of Science and Industry**

Source: author

Taking advantage of outreach and public education opportunities

While the immediate goal of the project was the creation and dissemination of a healthier modular classroom, the ultimate hope is that the project creates public awareness of the potential flaws of typical modular classrooms and empowers school communities to think more critically about the choices they make with regards to these types of learning spaces. This can be accomplished by either choosing to buy SAGE classrooms specifically or by working with their own facilities personnel and distributors to select healthier materials and components for their own classrooms. To this end, the SAGE team took advantage of as many opportunities to address the public as possible. In addition to the symposium at PSU and the 2012 Greenbuild conference in San Francisco, faculty and students in Architecture and Engineering involved in the project took part in events such as "Planet Under Pressure" at the Oregon Museum of Science and Industry in 2011. Here they presented a model of the classroom to parents and children as an opportunity to talk about healthy, green buildings (see Figure 9.4). Other presentations were made at green schools conferences, modular building conferences, and other professional venues. Presentations were also made to specific school communities and other organizations, some looking to adapt the SAGE model for other kinds of uses such as welcome centers, mobile health clinics, etc. In addition to promoting the SAGE classroom and healthier classrooms in general, these events gave students invaluable experience in public speaking and practice in promoting their ideas as well as organizing and taking part in public, participatory design processes.

In addition, discussions about the classroom were aired on public radio, locally and regionally, and numerous articles were written in various news outlets and magazines.

Leveraging pro bono and grant opportunities for support at critical stages

Because of the somewhat opportunistic way that the project unfolded, resources were solicited as important stages advanced and specific needs were determined. Funding for the initiating symposium was acquired mainly through fees assessed by the AIA for continuing education credits. Early, critical support for research was received from the Institute for Sustainable Solutions. This support made it possible to access important engineering services, publication support, website development, and faculty course release and create materials for public presentations. The Oregon Solutions process itself was an all-volunteer effort and the source of much pro bono expertise ranging from engineering services and consultation in energy incentives to code interpretation and lighting design, among others. A second critical stage in need of funding support occurred during the Oregon Solutions process. The classroom team anticipated the need to fundraise in order to build the first prototype classroom which they deemed an important step in influencing school districts to consider the benefits of the new classroom. At this time, Pacific Mobile Structures stepped in to fund a portion of the construction of a unit that would be exhibited at the Greenbuild 2012 conference. Their support became crucial to gaining the support of a national entity such as the Modular Building Institute. This exhibition opportunity provided a unique situation whereby much of the components needed for the prototype classroom were supplied by vendors using the opportunity to market their products in a demonstration "showroom." This supplied the classroom with windows, shades, heating, ventilation and cooling equipment, flooring, and a variety of other products.

Creating mutually beneficial intellectual property structures for long-term funding

As a mass-produced "product" with market value, the SAGE classroom enjoys a unique situation that allows it to benefit from intellectual property structures managed by the university. In this respect, the project represents an entrepreneurial opportunity for students, faculty, and the institution. On establishment of interest from distributor Pacific Mobile Structures to license the design and sell the classroom, the university entered into a copyright relationship aimed at protecting the integrity of the design and insuring a royalty structure that will provide a long-term and reliable funding stream that supports both the university and continued research and development of the classroom. Both students and faculty involved in the work are included in the copyright and are able to enjoy the benefits of the copyright ownership in the form of dividends (however modest), the percentage shares of which are agreed jointly. The intellectual property contract between the university and the distributor ensures the distributor exclusive rights to sell the SAGE classroom in its sales territory. In addition, the contract dictates that it must sell the classroom as designed by PSU so as to maintain the integrity of the design and the health and energy benefits the classroom claims. This is beneficial to both parties. However, there are challenges to this model as there is no restriction on other competitors who can copy the design, potentially with lower quality materials and systems, and benefit financially from a community's belief that they are procuring a SAGE-quality classroom. In fact several "knockoffs" have already been created. However, despite the frustration this can generate, the ultimate goal of the classroom remains to improve the quality of modulars across the nation and if the SAGE classroom is a catalyst for change in other modular classrooms even to a small degree, that is a positive outcome.

In addition to the direct benefits to the classroom, the creation of this legal partnership has given the university experience in how to enter into and protect intellectual property in a new realm of the economy in which it is not used to operating but which plays a major role in the Northwest region and U.S. economy. Contracting intellectual property for a design with as many components as the modular classroom can be very challenging and requires PSU to be proactive in promoting the innovative aspects of the classroom through varied media as the most effective strategy for protecting copyright. This ultimately establishes new knowledge that benefits future projects at PSU.

Figure 9.5 **Student and faculty SAGE team**
Source: author

Engaging student talent at every level

As a university initiative, it is imperative that educational goals for the students involved remain at the forefront of the mission (see Figure 9.5). This project seeks to demonstrate to students of architecture and related fields how they can leverage community and industry support to make a difference in their communities and in their environments. To this end, we have sought to make sure that students have been inextricably involved in all aspects of the project. Students have been involved directly with industry partners, meeting with them, discussing systems design, working through larger scaled visioning exercises to small scaled details. Student research in energy modeling and daylighting analysis has directly impacted the final design of the classroom. Students have also been responsible for organizing a number of public presentations and, as previously mentioned, students share in the intellectual property in the form of royalties and thus have the potential to benefit from their work for years to come, assuming the classrooms continue to sell. Many of the tasks taken on by the students represent atypical roles for most architects (and engineers) and are evidence of the growing field of public interest design. Design, while significant, is seen as just one component of a more varied group of desirable skills whose impact is potentially systemic for communities in need. In this changing role, architects become community organizers, advocates for social change, and curators of community design processes. With Federal and local funding shrinking, communities cannot afford to do otherwise, and the architects and engineers we train in our universities need to be ready to engage this expanded agenda. This kind of model also expands the possibilities for their roles in society. While most architecture students find work in conventional offices, students focusing on public interest design are more likely to branch out into non-profit work, planning agencies, and other careers.

Conclusions

Looking back on the process, an objective evaluation would probably acknowledge that, of the eight criteria outlined above, two of the most critical are those not necessarily available at most universities, namely the existence of a support mechanism such as PSU's Institute for Sustainable Solutions and the state sponsored "Oregon Solutions" initiative. Each of these provided timely support in terms of both research monies and in facilitating connections with partners and stakeholders. The long lead times, funding cycles, and uncertainties inherent in traditional granting processes alone would not have served this project well. As an effort that took place over the course of many years in an adventitious manner rather than as a clearly articulated plan of action, the flexibility and efficiency with which the Institute of Sustainable Solutions could offer support, even with modest amounts of grant monies, helped to propel the project at critical moments. These critical moments included support for course releases when faculty time and input was needed most, support for engineering services when student research was insufficient, and support for specific opportunities such as the shipping of the prototype to San Francisco in order to take advantage of an important opportunity to generate public awareness and in turn solicit other kinds of support such as material and equipment donations. Many of these situations and opportunities were unforeseen or unplanned and the progress of the project as a whole would have stopped short if not for the support of the ISS.

Likewise, the existence of the Oregon Solutions process provided a means by which to engage and compel local stakeholders and other partners to take part in the project on a voluntary basis. These partnerships provided pro bono expertise, leveraged yet other important partnerships, like that with the Modular Building Institute, and through the participation of so many partners, created a momentum that could outlast the efforts of any single individual.

This particular project was fortunate to have these resources at hand and this paper hopes to recommend the creation of support structures like these at other institutions. In the absence of these, however, much can still be accomplished and the best practices outlined in this paper are possible under wide-ranging and varied circumstances.

As a study in how to facilitate community-engaged initiatives in the university setting, the SAGE green modular classroom provides a number of useful lessons. It is emblematic of a shift in education and the move to make what happens within the walls of the academy more directly impactful to the community in which it is situated. While, in many respects, the project represents a unique set of circumstances and outcomes, in highlighting each of the steps along its trajectory, and the processes, events and lessons learned, we hope to provide some best practices that have relevance for other disciplines and projects that are looking to make the most of partnerships in education, research-based initiatives, and service-learning-based curricula.

References

Flattery, R., Norman, K. & Moody, S. (2010). *Cross-generational Comparison of Portable Classroom Indoor Air Quality and Thermal Comfort in Portland Public Schools.* Portland, OR: Green Building Research Laboratory, Portland State University.

Modular Building Institute (2010). *White Paper: Improving Construction Efficiency and Productivity with Modular Construction.* Charlottesville, VA.

Quale, J. (2012). *Sustainable, Affordable, Prefab: The Ecomod Project.* Charlottesville, VA: University of Virginia Press.

Satish, U., Mendell, M., Shekhar, K., Hotchi, T., Sullivan, D., Streufert, S., & Fisk, W. (2012). Is CO_2 an indoor pollutant? Direct effects of low-to-moderate CO_2 concentrations on human decision-making performance. *Environmental Health Perspectives*, 120(12). doi:10.1289/ehp.1104789

10

Crossing boundaries

Context, culture, and practice in transnational collaborations

Jack Corbett, Nydia Dehli Mata-Sánchez, and Mandy Elder

Since the publication of *Our Common Future* (World Commission on Environment and Development, 1987) a generation ago we have come to accept, at least in theory, that the search for sustainability needs to be global in both principle and practice; otherwise progress in some arenas will be undermined by deterioration in others. But acceptance in theory does not automatically produce preferred outcomes, and at levels from the local to the international we search for ways to enhance the capacity of institutions to extend and blend their capability to address environmental, economic, and social challenges. In higher education this means new approaches to generating, transmitting, and applying knowledge; new skills and emphases in pedagogy; additional resources; and finding new ways to reach multiple constituencies on and off university campuses.

Simultaneously with, and in part stimulated by, efforts toward sustainability we see a broad array of initiatives to facilitate collaboration among universities, research centers, nonprofit organizations, training programs, and other partners to mobilize talents and insights across international borders. Again, good intentions do not automatically assure productive collaboration, and effective internationalization requires development of frameworks and resources facilitating institutional practice. As this chapter demonstrates, doing so requires an ability to move beyond agreements in principle or formal statements of mutual interest to a more nuanced appreciation of practice; that is, to addressing challenges to the viability of potentially fragile inter-institutional relationships. Accomplishing this requires development of capacity as well as strategy.

Given the foregoing our discussion proceeds at three distinct but intertwined levels. At its simplest it is a reflection on international collaboration over five years between two very different universities learning to work together in pursuit of shared and complementary interests. It is a collaboration that develops in a bottom-up fashion specifically around a mutual goal of enhancing institutional capacity to respond to an expanding array of needs and concerns. At a second level this collaboration emerges and takes form among many others at each partner, a reminder that most attempts at collaboration do not take place in a vacuum but in a context of institutional histories encompassing various degrees of success and persistence. This accumulation combines with priorities and preferences to place its stamp on subsequent international efforts.

At yet a third level we see what might be characterized as "international collaboration doctrine" (hereafter ICD), i.e., the visions, histories, strategies, belief systems, and received experience transmitted to senior administrators through informal communications, formal training, or observations by respected colleagues. Unstated, of course, is whether ICD will embrace existing university capacity or be driven by other university priorities as these are not necessarily the same. Existing capacity is generally represented by collective faculty resources and experience, secondarily by academic centers, institutes, or similar units. Yet resources and experience may be the accumulation of numerous individual decisions inconsistent with contemporary institutional thinking and priorities. While effective collaboration across boundaries and cultures may require one set of capacities, university administration addressing strategic planning may require another.

The centrality of administrative process

Commonly ICD tilts heavily in the direction of strategic thinking and the development of administrative systems to put strategies in place. The American Council on Education's Center for Internationalization and Global Engagement, the Institute of International Education's Center for International Partnerships in Higher Education, and NAFSA: Association of International Educators play major roles in orienting university presidents, senior administrators, and program managers in these directions through symposia, workshops, publications, and opportunities for dialogue with experts in the field. This is not a criticism, simply an observation that when administrators receive many reminders and assertions that administration is important they are likely to respond accordingly. *Internationalizing Higher Education Partnerships* (Helms, 2015) devotes nearly two-thirds of its text to discussing administrative and management matters such as accreditation and strategic planning before shifting to an overview of cultural and contextual considerations. The rationale for such emphasis is that its primary audience is expected to be American institutions pursuing partnerships abroad (Helms, 2015, p. 6) so they need to direct internal systems appropriately.

Given the prominent place allotted to administrative and management topics in the literature and dialogue on ICD we have chosen to take the road less traveled: an exploration of some of the contextual and cultural dimensions in creating effective collaborations. We do so not to dispute the focus on administration but because there is a real danger that limiting discussion of culture and context in the face of time and energy constraints risks glossing over elements critical in the formation of institutional capacity; Helms (2015, p. 6) notes, "… compared with management issues, these themes are generally more complex". If culture and context are always at the back of the book, the end of the day, or the last panel session ICD will be the loser.

Beyond the issue of priority and precedence there is a very practical consideration for emphasizing the contextual and cultural dimensions of capacity development. An emphasis on institutional administrative process tends to direct attention to the internal operations of the university, to policies and procedures, norms and rules, practice and priorities. The result is the creation of boundaries intended to clarify decision-making, responsibility, accountability, and communications, not to mention systems to assure compliance and facilitate academic/administrative engagement. Emphasis on coordination, efficiency, and integration dominates discourse and drives managerial logic.

This internal focus, while contributing to smooth functioning of the institution, does little to build capacity to engage partners abroad or confront administrative routines markedly different from those on campus. This has been characterized as "Acting Globally, Thinking Locally" (Corbett, 2009), or bringing expectations and frameworks bounding behavior locally to a global setting and expecting them to prevail. Sometimes there is no choice, as when legal strictures establish rules governing the use of public funds or privacy considerations. But thinking locally also becomes the expression of "this is the way we do things", i.e., practice, which makes sense internally but may generate very different outcomes abroad. Addressing contextual and cultural dimensions of collaboration draws attention outward, encouraging thinking about the perspective or circumstances of prospective partners. In turn this fosters attention to the presence or absence of institutional capacity enhancing such understanding. Thus a core dilemma of ICD is that boundary-making may facilitate internal management but does not necessarily contribute to negotiating the complexities of international collaboration.

The Portland State/Universidad Tecnologica Collaboration

Although they will be explored more thoroughly in the pages that follow, woven into our discussion of context and culture are a series of observations and reflections on the ongoing collaboration between Portland State University (PSU) and the Universidad Tecnologica de los Valles Centrales de Oaxaca (UTVCO). The interaction between the two institutions might be best described as sustained episodic academic entrepreneurship initiated by individuals from both institutions who had worked together previously. Initially it consisted of occasional one-day visits to the UTVCO's temporary campus by groups of PSU students in Oaxaca for other purposes, informal lectures by visiting PSU faculty, and wide-ranging, informal discussions regarding higher education practice when circumstances permitted. By 2012 these contacts were supplemented with PSU students doing research and teaching at the UTVCO under the auspices of McNair Scholar, Fulbright, and other funding. In 2013 and 2014 UTVCO faculty and administrators spent week-long visits in Portland observing classes, meeting with counterparts, examining university–community relations, and learning more about Portland State's campus-wide emphasis on sustainability. In 2014 a joint effort created UTVCO's University Center for Women's Leadership, an initiative culminating in a group of students accompanying faculty to Portland in 2015. The 2015 faculty/administrator group focused on strategic planning, and discussions are under way regarding possible creation of a graduate level certificate in sustainability studies to be offered in Spanish. These efforts may culminate at some point in a formal collaboration agreement or memorandum of understanding but have advanced in the absence of same. In effect this is a grassroots faculty/staff/student effort with zero budget and strong support from the UTVCO rector (president). It also created other opportunities for the UTVCO in Oregon as well as for other American universities with the UTVCO.

Applying context and culture in practice

What does it mean to give context and culture a more explicit role in shaping approaches to collaboration? One might start with an appreciation of one's own institution from the perspective of a prospective partner. In the case of Portland State University's relationship with the Universidad Tecnologica de los Valles Centrales in Oaxaca, Mexico, two significant contextual dimensions come to the fore. First, as a comprehensive public university with 28,000 students, Portland State has the usual bureaucratic support system to manage student services, finances, internal operations, legal matters, communications, and all the other elements found in such institutions. As the university has expanded its international footprint the bureaucratic system has kept pace via a Vice Provost for International Affairs, an Internationalization Council, Office of International Affairs, programs to recruit international students and send its own students abroad, an Office of International Partnerships, and a strategy document guiding university activities internationally through 2020 (Portland State University, 2015). Written rules and guidelines establish procedures for proposing partnerships and establish signature authority making them effective. Portland State may have as many as 400 memoranda of understanding (MOU) or other agreements in at least 65 countries. Beyond these formal partnerships there are innumerable others that have emerged through informal, though quite durable, collaboration between Portland State faculty and foreign counterparts. Thus a specific proposal for a partnership, as in the case with the UTVCO, enters a routinized, bureaucratized labyrinth generally consistent with ICD and the university's strategic plan for internationalization.

The second dimension, external to the university, is the socioeconomic setting shaping or constraining opportunities. Two decades of chronic underfunding have left the university with very limited resources for investment in international ventures; indeed it seeks to lure international students who pay much higher tuition than Oregon students and has reduced support for non-revenue aspects of internationalization. International business interests generate scholarship funds for Vietnamese students while government or family support for students from China or the Middle East encourage PSU to expand relationships there. But, absent revenue, priorities change; although Latinos make up 12% of Oregon's population and approximately 85% of Latino immigrants originate in Mexico, there is little revenue incentive to pursue international engagement there, relegating Mexico to a lower priority. While demographics appear to favor collaboration with Mexico, a revenue metric does not. And the academic focus on capacity-building is secondary to Portland State's concern for international activity as a source of revenue. This disconnect creates awkward ambiguities in pursuing collaboration for sustainability.

Seen from the UTVCO the context of collaboration appears quite different. Less than six years old and with approximately 1,300 students it is still in an early stage of institutional development; all international responsibilities, from translating communications to negotiating agreements to greeting international visitors fall on the shoulders of a single professional aided by one or two general assistants for routine matters. The extensive institutional infrastructure at Portland State does not exist, making international engagement a work of artisanry rather than bureaucracy. In addition the university is a hybrid, one in a system of 104 technological universities responsible to the General Coordinator of Technological Universities and the Subsecretary of Higher Education and Research in the federal Secretary of Public Education yet chartered as a decentralized unit of the Oaxaca state government. These structural arrangements require the commitment of administrative effort to managing relations with state and federal offices exercising oversight or promoting programs, i.e., boundary issues are external rather than internal. The UTVCO is one of many new universities, mostly in rural Mexico, established to bring higher education closer to an often marginalized population. Furthermore Oaxaca is one of the poorest states in Mexico, 90% of UTVCO students are first generation, and most of the faculty are young with limited teaching or professional experience.

Yet in less than six years the UTVCO has established formal partnerships in six countries as well as several still in a developmental stage, ranks first among the 70 institutions of higher education in the state of Oaxaca in terms of the percentage of its students studying abroad, and has established innovative programs for faculty and students designed to counterbalance difficult economic and social conditions. It draws on the resources of the Subdirectorate of International Cooperation of the Secretary of Education, organizational connections with embassies and international agencies, and its ongoing collaboration with Portland State to address two central goals:

- Strengthen the ability of students and faculty to move beyond the constraints of place and background to function in more complex, uncertain, and demanding environments, i.e., to develop human capital.

- Build institutional capacity for innovation and flexibility, particularly through partnerships and engagement with communities, companies, and governments.

As in the case of Portland State there is a strategic perspective but it revolves around capacity development rather than revenue generation. Indeed the university's 2010–2014 strategic development plan explicitly identifies a goal of establishing five international partnerships by the end of 2014 (Universidad Tecnologica de los Valles Centrales de Oaxaca, 2010, p. 54). While the lack of institutional infrastructure to manage internationalization and partnership development results in considerable improvisation, reinvention, and occasional loss of time, it also permits agile, rapid decision-making. The Director of Outreach can walk into the office of the rector almost at will, lay out an opportunity and alternative responses, and usually receive a rapid decision. Capacity options at the UTVCO tend to be clearer than revenue options at PSU, thereby facilitating choice. While the PSU–UTVCO partnership has evolved with an eye to institutional capacity development, this comes closer to meeting the immediate goals of the UTVCO than the revenue priority of PSU.

Negotiating culture

If addressing context directs attention to organizational environments, then developing collaborative culture moves in the direction of understanding what shapes practice. As culture consists of those values, norms, behaviors, skills, language, assumptions, and similar attributes that lead to a mutually understood worldview then it is not enough to know the context of collaboration; it is necessary to grasp how counterparts make sense of and use such knowledge in operationalizing partnerships. Without an appreciation of the dynamics of organizational culture generating and sustaining partnerships, simply maintaining them may prove so complicated and costly they crumple under their own weight. A clear grasp of what we could call the "culture of practice", i.e., understanding not only what we are doing, but why we do it in a certain way and how to make meaning of what we do, becomes central to collaboration. Some examples may help as each is critical to capacity development:

Language

It is not difficult to understand why so many discussions of partnership development move quickly to language. Beyond its place as a core element of culture it plays two significant roles in shaping the nature of the partnership: 1) as the language of negotiation; and 2) as the language of operation or practice. The *Internationalization of Higher Education Partnerships* acknowledges the place of different or multiple languages but tilts in the direction of English as an official program language (Helms, 2015, p. 22). The rationale for this is straightforward in a document addressed to American higher education administrators but it begs the question as to how one creates a partnership agreement if there is no common language. And the unstated expectation is most negotiation takes place in English because senior administrators will not have sufficient fluency in the partner's language and because documents such as memoranda of understanding, contracts, and related materials need to pass review by respective American university managers or units. As these are structured around process and principles such as efficiency, skill in foreign languages for professional use is generally unlikely. As a practical matter even the UTVCO manages its interactions with German partners in English because neither has sufficient confidence in its fluency in the counterpart's language.

In this respect the UTVCO–PSU collaboration has benefitted from pre-existing capacity, meaning everyone directly engaged in negotiations and planning has not only the necessary language skills but also considerable experience arranging collaborations in other settings. This contributes not only to a sense of certainty about what is being said but also to a recognition of when non-verbalized assumptions might be coloring interactions. Even given shared experience uncertainties occur but repeated revisiting helps to catch many, something more difficult in working through translation.

But the real challenge appears at the moment of research collaboration, students speaking different languages in the same classroom, or field visits with local professionals, community leaders, or ordinary citizens. A collaboration built around long-term student exchange is fundamentally different from faculty-led, short-term programs and these are different still from thesis research or service-learning. A 2014 study for the National Association of Schools of Public Affairs and Administration demonstrated inadequate language skills on the part of American students and faculty were a principal reason for not including international study or training in graduate programs (Rubaii *et al.*, 2015). The PSU–UTVCO partnership and some of the other programs Portland State offers in Mexico seek to address this not only by providing advanced translation for groups when necessary but also by providing on-location training in Spanish for American students. Meanwhile the UTVCO secures translation through Portland State for groups of faculty and students going to Oregon even though one reason for such travel is to help said groups strengthen their English. The UTVCO is deeply committed to such travel as a means of raising an awareness of the value of foreign language skills and promoting capacity-building through immersion.

One common dilemma for translator-dependent programs reflects the training and philosophical orientation of translators themselves (Nishishiba and Corbett, 2006). To the extent translators take seriously their responsibility to be the faithful rendition of the speaker's words into the listener's language there is the inevitable uncertainty as to whether the speaker grasps the knowledge level of the audience. The tendency of some professions to use specialized jargon, to draw on acronyms or insider terminology, or to inadvertently erect additional barriers make practitioner–generalist interaction through translators problematic. Translators familiar with the nature and preparation of the audience may choose to include sidebars, supplements, or prompts to the speaker for more effective communication. To date the shared experience embedded in the UTVCO–PSU collaboration enables Mexicans going north or Americans coming south to benefit from informed translation when necessary precisely because familiarity assures the educational component of crossing the border will be served.

In short, language skills necessary both for negotiating collaboration and for making it work in practice were part of pre-existing contacts and facilitated the gradual expansion of interaction. The presence of fluent Spanish-speakers at Portland State not only aided the university's ability to meet the UTVCO on its own grounds but also demonstrated PSU's capacity to work productively in the domain of others, i.e., that it is not dependent on the language skills of others, at least in Spanish-speaking environments. At the very least, this underscores the significance of language capacity.

Academic culture

As used here the term "academic culture" refers to the mix of assumptions, expectations, behaviors, myths, norms, and other elements that make up how the faculty do their work. Negotiating collaboration involving academic culture is one of the most complex aspects of partnerships because academics tend to assume we work in universals ... research is research, after all, and classroom management is exactly that. In fact one of the central concerns of developing institutional capacity to create viable collaborations is to have insights on how faculty are accustomed to work before surprise turns to irritation and frustration or depression. Yet so much of doing faculty work is taken for granted that we do not understand what must be raised to the level of explicit consultation.

As an example, consider time management for faculty at American universities. Many work long hours but are accustomed to managing time in accord with the flow of multiple responsibilities. Faculty meet classes, attend meetings, and hold office hours but otherwise are largely free to manage time when and how they see fit. But a faculty member at the UTVCO or many other Mexican universities is expected to punch in and punch out via a clock scanning a fingerprint. And you may well be expected to punch in by hour x and punch out by hour y. Failure to do so may result not only in a scolding by the department head but also a deduction from salary. An American faculty member entering such a system would never think to look for a time clock while Mexican colleagues would never think to mention it. Conversely a Mexican colleague spending time in the United States might grow apprehensive not being able to find the clock; how will anyone know of his or her careful compliance with scheduling expectations? American faculty teaching or doing research on visiting appointments in Mexico may see themselves as exempt from local rules while senior administrators grumble about their arrogant behavior and fume at the example they set for their Mexican counterparts.

A collaboration agreement would not be as specific as detailed here but might set out the expectation that someone on either side of the relationship would help with orientation. More valuable, perhaps, would be finding someone who has experience in such a system and can provide insight to participating faculty from both institutions. The capacity to address these aspects of academic culture becomes a way to facilitate working across unfamiliar institutional landscapes. Some UTVCO faculty spending a week at Portland State were puzzled that host faculty disappeared to teach classes or hold office hours rather than simply cancel sessions because of campus visitors. Yet visiting faculty in technological universities would be surprised to find that at least in some cases proposals for a new course or timely seminar would need to receive approval in Mexico City before they could be offered. Because the overall framework of university life looks comparable, it is easy, unless systems are in place to address the unmentioned differences, to overlook potential points of misunderstanding or friction. Ironically the more routinized bureaucratized processes are the less likely they are to receive explicit scrutiny.

Thus far our attention to the academic workplace in someone else's institution has centered on the place of the individual but there are collective dimensions as well. Portland State has a long-standing institutional emphasis on civic engagement and university–community partnerships. And as this volume demonstrates, it has an equal commitment to sustainability research and action. Across the five years the UTVCO and PSU have collaborated at the individual or small group level, the UTVCO simultaneously has in a conscious and deliberate way sought to instill across the university a similar sense of interaction with surrounding communities, groups, and enterprises. The goal is not to impose frameworks and processes copied from the Oregon experience but to weigh in a systematic fashion how the human capital and technology associated with the university can be directed to applied problem-solving, and in the process of doing so reinforce in students the value of and responsibility for collective action. Oaxacan communities have a long tradition of mutual support, or *guelaguetza*, so anything reinforcing this tradition benefits not only communities but the larger regional culture as well. Work teams join with local producers of fruits, vegetables, honey, corn, and other crops to improve quality, find new markets, boost incomes, and otherwise have a positive impact. The collaboration with Portland State permits a comparison of approaches and suggests new methodologies for effective interactions.

Interpersonal relations

It is common in American higher education to see partnership agreements or memoranda of understanding governing collaboration in an instrumental fashion. They define boundaries, i.e., what is covered and what is excluded, and outline paths for operation, modification, or termination. They specify who is authorized to sign to put them into effect and when they expire. They are merely instruments moving an institutional relationship forward. But not everyone sees such documents in this fashion. A commitment to collaborate on promoting sustainability can be understood by its nature to be a long-term agreement to allocate scarce energy and resources to a common project. In this respect it is not merely a technical statement or definition of organizational connections but a pledge of trust. In such circumstances one frequently finds Mexican negotiators asking their counterparts whether the people or organization they represent are *de confianza*: can they be counted on to follow through? Again we encounter very different ways of understanding what establishing a collaborative relationship means. Americans wish to see an institutional signature because it means there is a more substantial commitment there, not simply an individual. In contrast Mexicans may see institutions as unreliable; what counts is the willingness of an individual to make a personal commitment. Thus Portland State designates the Chief Contract Officer or Director of the Office of International Affairs as the authorizing signature because it falls within the boundary of their responsibility. But these people have never appeared in the discussions creating the agreement as they are several layers down in the organizational hierarchy. American organizations would treat this as routine but working across cultural as well as international boundaries it is easy for doubts to appear; if this is a serious document where is the signature of the university president?

Establishing oneself as reliable and to be counted on goes beyond signing documents. Face-to-face contact is still very important in managing inter-institutional relations in Latin America, and one way in which one establishes a reputation for reliability is by showing up, by displaying a willingness to invest time in maintaining a relationship. Thus part of building institutional capacity to initiate or implement projects is to demonstrate one wishes them to be sustainable, and that sustainability comes through presence. Universities that understand this will find ways to make or buy the presence that in turn signifies commitment to the relationship.

A striking example of this is the successful creation of the University Center for Women's Leadership (referred to locally as CMujer) at the UTVCO. Modeled on a program at PSU, the Center seeks to provide young women from indigenous communities or backgrounds where they occupy subordinate status with opportunities to nurture leadership skills. At first UTVCO women were skeptical and uncertain as to the motives of the co-chairs from the two universities. It took months to begin to see meaningful participation. By demonstrating commitment and reliability the co-chairs have had a far more significant impact than letters or certificates of commendation. Indeed by 2015 CMujer, along with the faculty/administrative professional development seminars in Portland referenced above, had been recognized as an emerging accomplishment of the collaboration. CMujer has moved to reinforce its sustainability and reach by creating a freestanding, nonprofit support organization in the United States, Women's International Leadership and Learning (WILL), and by reaching out to networks of professional and business women in Mexico. By extending its network of organizational and funding support CMujer not only increases its own viability but generates interest from other Mexican universities. The goal, of course, is not just to assure CMujer's survival but to provide well-grounded opportunities for women from rural communities to develop skills nurturing local development.

Beyond CMujer the UTVCO draws on other facets of the relationship with PSU to promote sustainability. Portland State's nationally recognized leadership in service-learning serves to validate the formation of student–community work teams to foster innovation in local agricultural production and marketing. Workshops first in Portland and then in Oaxaca encourage transfer and adaptation of university–community partnerships not only at the UTVCO but to other institutions across the state. Taking problem-solving into the field with demonstrable results and productive outcomes underscores the value of such partnerships while offering a potential alternative to out-migration to cities or the United States. A glass cabinet in the office of the UTVCO president displays many of the specific contributions these teams, often operating on the basis of nothing more than a handshake and *confianza*, have made to community economies. And all of these relationships spring from grassroots, interpersonal collaboration toward common goals.

Context, culture, and practice

Our overall line of argument starts with the common tendency in American higher education to align efforts to build collaborative relationships in the international arena by organizing them in accord with institutional administrative process, an approach we characterized as "international collaboration doctrine." This doctrine draws on the principles, perspectives, and approaches structuring university operations, in effect treating internationalization as one more element to be managed in sync with other units. The net effect of a proliferation of internal boundaries, while consistent with doctrine, misses two important factors in pursuing international partnerships: 1) the context bounding potential partners; and 2) critical cultural elements related to practice. No matter how committed to sustainability partners may be on paper, meaningful collaboration means a capacity to transcend multiple boundaries in practice. Creating that capacity while recognizing that it means moving beyond ICD requires a willingness to address the challenges of context and culture. A prospering five-year collaboration between Portland State University and the Universidad Tecnologica de los Valles Centrales de Oaxaca in Mexico demonstrates that a grassroots initiative even without formal status or institutional resources can be sustainable and foster sustainability when flexible boundaries are not impermeable barriers.

References

Corbett, J. (2009). *Internationalizing public administration: Acting globally, thinking locally.* Pacific Northwest Political Science Association Annual Meeting, Victoria, British Columbia.

Helms, R.M. (2015). *International Higher Education Partnerships: A Global Review of Standards and Practices.* New York: American Council on Education.

Nishishiba, M. & Corbett, J. (2006). *Interpretation, instruction, and the internationalization of public administration education.* Teaching Public Administration Annual Conference, Olympia, Washington.

Portland State University (2015). *Strategy for Comprehensive Internationalization 2012–2020.* Portland, OR: Portland State University.

Rubaii, N., Appe, S. & Stamp, K. (2015). Are we getting them out of the country? The state of study abroad opportunities within NASPAA member programs. *Journal of Public Administration Education,* 21(2), 179-198.

Universidad Tecnologica de los Valles Centrales de Oaxaca (2010). *Programa Institucional de Desarrollo 2010–2014.* San Pablo Huixtepec: Universidad Tecnologica de los Valles Centrales de Oaxaca.

World Commission on Environment and Development (1987). *Our Common Future.* New York: Oxford University Press.

11

Building cultural bridges

Inclusive environmental planning and outreach through university–community partnerships

Renée Bogin Curtis and Nelda E. Reyes García

For three decades, Community Environmental Services (CES) has conducted environmental services as a research unit within the school of Urban Studies and Planning (USP) at Portland State University (PSU). Over the past five years, CES's reputation has grown, as popular businesses partnered on waste stream analyses or greenhouse gas emissions assessments and implemented materials management practices. As a consultant for a multinational company, Nike, and celebrated grocery chains, New Seasons and Whole Foods, CES helped businesses pursue waste reduction goals. These new partnerships put CES in the limelight. Yet historically, community and public partnerships created the organization's rich institutional knowledge. Drawing inspiration from their CES work and academic studies, CES students have championed environmental action in unexpected places.

In 1989, PSU students launched a class project to pilot recycling in multifamily housing. Their successful results challenged skeptical expectations and the City of Portland decided to sponsor students to implement city-wide multifamily recycling. Shortly after, CES co-founders Gerry Blake and Barry Messer began running publicly funded projects out of USP's research unit as the Recycling Education Project which became CES in 1998. Since CES's inception, public and private-sector sponsors have invested millions of dollars in return for high quality student-led work. Students gain applied skills and have direct impact on policies and practices. The City of Portland's multifamily project remains CES's longest running project. After 15 years of overseeing multifamily environmental outreach, CES students pushed to expand outreach to be more successfully inclusive of the region's growing multicultural populations.

Inclusive environmental planning in Portland

Portland is a mecca for sustainability. While environmental values appear to permeate the local culture, not everyone has equal exposure to that culture, particularly if isolated by language or cultural enclaves. PSU students at CES have encouraged local governments to better represent underserved populations for 25 years.

As the Latino population steadily grows, so does recognition of new environmental planning needs. Yet changes at the government level happen gradually and new outreach plans develop slowly. Infrequent pro-environmental behavior may indicate unfamiliarity, not deficiency of attitudes or concern.

Ideally, outreach targets the region's new residents and industry professionals involved in waste and property management. As consultants to government sustainability departments, we observed the growth of Latino residents in multifamily communities and encountered criticism of Latino recycling behaviors from garbage and recycling collectors (haulers), property managers, and non-Latino multifamily residents. Critics suggested Latinos do not care about the environment and blamed Latino families for incorrect recycling behaviors.

Thus, we encouraged local governments to investigate perceptions about local Latino populations, rather than prioritization of resource allocation towards the dominant population or "low hanging fruit." We advised new investments in underserved communities could produce longer-term results. Moreover, as a few incorrect recycling behaviors can contaminate and convert entire recycling loads into waste, a small Latino presence at a multifamily complex warrants customized outreach efforts. While most local governments recognize the potential value of Latino-focused research and outreach, they are constrained by limited budgets. Culturally specific outreach campaigns are rarely developed and community educational materials are mostly in English, or occasionally in literal, not necessarily culturally competent, translations. Occasionally bilingual presentations to on-site communities occur and dramatically improve behaviors. Further investigation into the environmental behaviors, attitudes, and concerns among local Latino multifamily communities is needed.

The current study builds on previous research in the region. In 1991, through the successful implementation of a pilot recycling program at 26 multifamily complexes, a study challenged the widely held belief that recycling is more appropriate in single family households (Katzev *et al.*, 1993). The study challenged the region's historical perceptions held by environmental planners, haulers, and property managers about environmental concerns, attitudes, and behaviors among multifamily residents and highlighted the importance of property manager or hauler attitude on recycling participation levels.

In 2006, CES collaborated on a region-wide investigation of multifamily recycling supported by Metro Regional Government (Metro). *Barriers and Benefits* (ESA, 2007) identified perceptions of recycling among multifamily residents and property managers and provided specific strategies for local environmental planners to increase recycling practices among resident populations. Strategies include: distribution of clear and consistent educational materials in combination with a media campaign and ongoing evaluation of recycling areas to ensure clear and adequate eye-level labels with pictures for non-English speakers. The study also noted ethnic cohesion in some communities with low turnover rates, prompting the researchers to recommend culturally specific messaging and multicultural resources, particularly in "low-turnover communities due to the high probability of developing lasting, effective recycling participation" (ESA, 2007, p. 9).

Furthermore, "the message of such campaigns should focus at least as much on the "why do?" as the "how to?" in order to foster greater buy-in among residents and groups who may not be familiar with the "reduce, re-use, recycle, and rot" philosophy" (ESA, 2007, p. 9).

Following that study's conclusion, we proposed a multicultural study to learn more about the local Latino multifamily communities' environmental concerns, attitudes, and pro-environmental behaviors. Results would inform an outreach campaign. In recognition of both the region's changing demographics and the value of inclusive practices towards underserved communities, Metro saw the advantage of culturally specific outreach strategies as both an ethical practice and an opportunity to enhance the region's waste reduction goals. They agreed to support a region-wide study and with encouragement, other local governments agreed to participate at minimal cost to their own departments. Initially there was primary interest in simply obtaining appropriate translations of recyclable materials, but gradually all participating planners agreed to a deeper investigation into motivations, attitudes, and norms.

Thus, with Metro's support, a study was launched to gain insight into environmental behaviors, concerns, and attitudes among local Latino multifamily communities. The study aimed to foster better understanding of local Latino communities and inform environmental planning outreach efforts aimed at behavior change. The findings shaped outreach messages, strategies, and materials. Additionally, this study contributes to general practitioner knowledge about culturally targeted environmental efforts and contributes to the literature on the situated meaning of underlying concepts; in other words, context matters.

Background

As immigrants and diasporic communities permeate the urban makeup, culturally specific environmental planning strategies may help municipalities and local governments achieve environmental goals. Enactment of inclusive policies with culturally specific outreach campaigns supports ethical standards appropriate for public entities. Ongoing environmental social psychology research examines environmental concerns, attitudes, and the relationship between concerns, attitudes, and pro-environmental behaviors. Few studies evaluate these concepts cross-culturally. Although some research on environmental attitudes, concerns, and behavior identifies differences between Latino and other U.S. households, this research rarely seeks community input. Without serious consideration of the culturally constructed context of environmental attitudes and behaviors, environmental planning capacity for community outreach is limited. Thus, the discourse is enriched by exploration of environmental concerns, attitudes, and behavior within a region's Latino community. Ideally, public organizations should implement culturally specific environmental planning models, practice inclusivity, and support related research.

Environmental values are not greater among white households and by some assessments minority or immigrant populations have equal or stronger environmental concerns (Hunter, 2000). However research indicates recycling behaviors are higher among white households (Owens *et al.*, 2000). The disparity between environmental concerns and recycling behaviors indicates gaps in outreach to immigrant communities. Specifically, research on Latino populations has been particularly minimal and findings produce conflicting results.

Research which identifies environmental concerns and attitudes in a Latino immigrant community by giving voice to the community is needed. The discovery of connections between environmental concerns, attitudes, and behavior should encourage public sector practice of inclusivity, help planners identify culturally specific concerns and attitudes to guide environmental awareness campaigns, and contribute to discussions about culturally constructed environmental concerns, attitudes, and behavior.

Diversity and the environmental movement

The Latino population in the U.S. has grown steadily since the 1990s. In 2005, 14% of the population identified as Latino, with over half foreign born and almost half Spanish-preferred speakers (Fox and Livingston, 2007). In the metropolitan region of Portland, Oregon, Latinos represent the greatest percentage of new residents, who migrated directly from other countries or parts of the U.S., mostly of Mexican origin (Bermudez, 2007).

Generally, the environmental movement has not been historically inclusive of diversity. One study of 158 environmental institutions found no people of color in 33% of mainstream environmental organizations and 22% of environmental government agencies (Bonta and Jordan, 2007). This lack of diverse representation is inconsistent with evidence of environmental concerns among minority or immigrant populations. For example, a 2002 Public Policy Institute of California's environmental poll found Latinos are more concerned about urban sprawl and air and water pollution than non-Latinos (Pastor and Morello-Frosch, 2002).

Similarly, Max J. Pfeffer and J. Mayone Stycos (2002) cite studies which suggest environmental concerns among inhabitants of the Global South (or what the authors referred to as the "third-world") are high. They highlight debates which "question the *post-materialist thesis* that first-world environmental concerns emerge when a higher standard of living permits individuals to shift their attention from matters related to economic security to quality-of-life concerns" (Pfeffer and Stycos, 2002, pp. 64-65). They critique a past immigration discussion between Sierra Club members over about whether immigrants adopt U.S. resource consumption behaviors and eventually produce negative ecological impacts. To evaluate the credibility of this concern, Pfeffer and Stycos (2002) investigate the impact of environmental orientation, environmental knowledge, and acculturation on environmentally friendly behaviors (i.e., conservative resource usage, recycling) and conclude immigrants demonstrate high levels of environmental concerns but are less likely to engage in environmentally oriented political behaviors (i.e., signing petition for conservation legislation), a finding which indicates a general disconnection from the environmental movement. This finding potentially indicates the failure of environmental organizations to adequately address immigrant concerns. Moreover, Pfeffer and Stycos (2002, p. 64) determine that immigrants engage in non-politically oriented environmentally friendly behaviors, thus "fears of immigrants being less likely to engage in environmentally friendly behaviors are unfounded." They also posit "one might expect immigrants to be *less likely* to engage in environmentally friendly behaviors if such actions are an artifact of the post-materialist culture they have not yet assimilated" (p. 67). Specifically, they highlight recycling themes as U.S.-based environmentally friendly behaviors unfamiliar to recent immigrants. Their findings suggest immigrant communities demonstrate environmental concerns and pro-environmental behaviors, but have yet to adopt *unfamiliar* pro-environmental behaviors.

One purpose of our research is to challenge biases or perceptions of Latinos as indifferent to environmental concerns and behaviors and learn how environmental concerns and attitudes are framed differently from non-Latinos. We ask: Are concerns and attitudes rooted in different knowledge and awareness? What is the potential for either norm creation of pro-environmental behaviors at the community level or motivation of pro-environmental behavior at the individual level?

Immigrants and environmental research

Environmental psychology literature on immigrants is uncommon, but what exists suggests immigrants exhibit significant environmental values and concerns (Hunter, 2000; Deng *et al.*, 2006). The research identifies ethnic variation in environmental attitudes, concerns, and behaviors, primarily through measuring relationships between environmental concerns, beliefs, motivations, attitudes, and behavior through various preconceived scales (Johnson *et al.*, 2004). Some researchers find the role of concern differs culturally in predicting pro-environmental behaviors, thus recommend environmental education campaigns to "emphasize different aspects of environmental issues when working with different ethnic groups" (Milfont *et al.*, 2006, p. 763). Other research compares different measurement scales to demonstrate that either belief or environmental awareness may impact behavior (Stern *et al.*, 1995). While perhaps excellent tools for the Global North, we posit that preconceived measurement models, though meaningful, may reflect the cultural biases of their designers and thus be inefficient tools for some populations, particularly groups which haven't strongly voiced their own environmental views.

For example, an attempt to establish an environmental belief-behavior causal element and identify ethnic variation in environmental belief through the New Ecological Paradigm (NEP) scale was unsuccessful (Johnson *et al.*, 2004). The study found inconsistencies as "foreign-born Latinos were more likely to participate in nature-based outdoor recreation than whites" (Johnson *et al.*, 2004, p. 180) but less likely to report pro-environmental beliefs as measured by the NEP or to recycle. This inconsistency raises questions about whether the NEP measure adequately defines beliefs within a culturally inclusive framework, challenges the tool's cultural competency, and supports the need for further investigation. Furthermore, while few studies in industrialized countries demonstrate the relationship between beliefs and conservation behavior, they are more noticeably absent from poorer countries, such as Mexico (Obregón-Saudo and Corral-Verdugo, 1997, p. 215).

Some policy-driven research finds prevalent but varying types of environmentalism among different ethnic groups (EPA, 1997). Yet scales that measure these differences are not assuredly culturally competent, thus investigation into environmental behavior within a specific cultural framework is justified. The research highlights the need for further identification of the cultural context of environmental concerns, attitudes, and behavior. Given our region's growing Latino population, we recommended exploratory research to identify attitudes, concerns, and behaviors.

Reflection: praxis and research

Our research acknowledges the widespread prevalence of environmental concerns as posited by Pfeffer and Stycos (2002), yet debates continue about the general impact of attitude and concern on behavior versus models of norm creation (Bamberg and Schmidt, 2003). While various studies dispute the potential influences of social-psychological factors, we observe the impact of both circumstances to support norm creation and of concerns and attitudes as behavior motivators. Moreover, while research has been unable to confirm a direct relationship between environmental concerns and environmental behaviors, the cultural context of knowledge formation is potentially relevant to both norm creation and attitudinal impact on behavior. Given this assessment and our perception of biases in the NEP and other preconceived models, we attempt to identify specific concerns and attitudes as *potential* influences on behavior. Meanwhile, some research on environmental behavior (Vicente and Reis, 2007) highlights not only the impact of attitude on recycling behavior, but pragmatic necessities such as access to clear information about recycling, correct ways to recycle, and the benefits of recycling. Similarly, we also look at the *potential* normative impact of knowledge and awareness in addition to individual attitudes.

Moving beyond the relationship between attitudes and behavior, some pragmatic suggestions such as existence of on-site recycling facilities, access to information, appropriate education (Vincente and Reis, 2007), and supportive policies (Katzev *et al.*, 1993) improve recycling behaviors. To increase awareness of pro-environmental behaviors like recycling, we expect effective strategies to adapt environmental planning approaches within a culturally specific framework, in recognition of the cultural context of knowledge building, norm creation, and attitude formation.

Ultimately the goal of our research is to impact policies to reflect these strategies. Past policies exhibited by government environmental planning departments in the Portland area reflect biases unsubstantiated by research. The multifamily sector is a more challenging setting in which to identify pro-environmental behaviors because it is difficult to link behaviors with specific individual households.

While we don't dispute greater challenges persist for environmental planning efforts aimed at both types of communities—Latino and multifamily—especially in combination, it is important to illuminate ways in which a comprehensive, community-specific approach to outreach may be more effective than simple, routine outreach aimed at the general public. The latter may result in missed opportunities to introduce new norms or motivate behaviors by identifying existing concerns or attitudes. Moreover some Latino residents represent a new population, not yet inundated with community messaging and thus not indifferent; yet potentially more susceptible to learn new norms, adapt, and follow regulations. One purpose of our research is to challenge biases or perceptions of Latinos as indifferent to environmental concerns and behaviors. Increased knowledge about the practice and purpose of environmental behaviors like recycling should lead to improved performance.

A regional investigation into Latino environmental attitudes, concerns, and behaviors

Research design

Purpose of study

In collaboration with Metro, we launched an investigation into Latino environmental concerns, attitudes, and behavior with survey research of local Latino multifamily residents. We chose open-ended questions rather than administering a pre-existing measurement model of environmental concerns, awareness, belief, or attitudes. The research aimed to identify environmental concerns and attitudes and explore the impact of knowledge and awareness in Latino communities.

Methods

Snowball sampling techniques helped identify complexes as candidates for anonymous, door-to-door, in-person surveys with residents of Latino multifamily communities. Local government representatives from sustainability departments provided lists of communities with significant Latino populations and known recent recycling systems. From possible candidates, we chose 13 sites based on a range of factors including size of complex and location. We surveyed low, middle, and high income complexes to ensure varied representation, but as past research diminishes the importance of economic status (ESA, 2007), we did not control for individual income levels. We sampled a minimum of 10% of the households within 12 complexes, nearly 10% at an additional complex and interviewed the household member responsible for garbage disposal.

Multifamily complexes were chosen over single family residences because the adjacent or annexed structural component of multifamily buildings lends itself to a community setting; thus multifamily communities provide a good resource for the examination of community attitudes, knowledge, and behavior, particularly for diasporic communities that might be isolated into enclaves. We cannot assuredly claim that complexes function *socially*, yet given its *structural* semblance of community it is a good setting for norm identification and creation.

Surveys were approximately eight minutes long, contained both multiple choice and open-ended questions and had an option for a one-minute shorter survey. Respondents had a choice between English and Spanish. The two primary interviewers were bilingual and from bicultural families, with one (co-author Reyes García) of Latino heritage. We conducted 206 surveys and had few refusals. Of the 206 surveys, seven were rejected as invalid and another 14 were rejected because of a discrepancy in the way interviewers asked one question. Thus, a total of 185 were fully analyzed. The survey had a short or a full option, with a total of 5 two-part questions for the short and 19 mostly two-part questions for the full. Most respondents (169) opted for the full survey while 16 took the shorter survey.

When applicable, results were compared with the *Barriers and Benefits* (2007) study described previously. Telephone survey results from the *Barriers* study ($n = 316$) are compared with door-to-door, in-person surveys from our Latino study, thus comparisons are not perfect. However despite this design variation, comparisons are insightful and future research could assess statistically significant differences, a level of analysis not feasible for this type of exploratory research.

Through analysis of survey responses using qualitative coding and descriptive frequencies, we identified environmental concerns, attitudes, the pro-environmental behavior of recycling, related motivations, environmental knowledge, and environmental awareness, as well as the relationships between these traits.

Results

The findings reveal a prevalence of positive environmental concerns and attitudes within the local Latino community. Responses also indicate the potential impact of cultural context on some behaviors and attitudes rooted in the construction of knowledge, awareness, and concerns. Frequencies illustrate the most common themes and responses.

Demographics

Surveys were conducted at various times throughout the week and on Saturday to control for a varied representation of gender, age, and vocational bias. Of the 185 surveys a greater number of respondents were female (104 women compared to 73 men plus eight surveys with a male/female team). The higher proportion of women is likely because more women are home at all hours and because we asked for the person in charge of garbage and recycling which in many cases was the woman of the household. The majority of respondents (108) were aged 26–45 with few respondents (14) aged 18–25 and surprisingly few respondents (16) aged 46 or older. One hundred eighty-two respondents answered questions about length of time in the region: 40% of had been there three years or less, 17% between four and six years, and 43% over six years. When asked about time in the U.S., of 176 respondents, only 17% had been in the U.S. for three years or less, 6% between four and six years, while the majority (76%) has been in the U.S. for more than six years. This suggests many respondents may have migrated from other parts of the state or the U.S. rather than being recent immigrants.

Generally, interviewers noted the concept of "region" was not clearly understood by all interviewees and in some cases was interpreted as the state, city, town, or even individual apartment community or a local governing body. When asked by respondents, they clarified with the phrase "Portland Metropolitan area" but sometimes confusion continued. While this confusion indicated a potential language or cultural barrier to the concept or term, it also suggested a possible identity disconnect from the area. Some interviewees confessed to never leaving their apartment communities and thus being largely detached from any possible regional identity. Others may simply be so removed from the local culture they are unaware of the region's geographic identity. However, other respondents appeared to understand the term and communicated a general lack of familiarity with recycling until they moved to the region from other countries or other parts of the U.S.[1]

When asked "do your kids sometimes take out recycling or garbage?" approximately one-fourth of respondents (26%) responded affirmatively. The majority

---

[1] The study does not distinguish between countries of origin for three reasons: 1) The study examines U.S.-based Latino communities, which have their own identity characteristics including foreign-born or native-born and have unique characteristics, regardless of place of origin, simply as diasporic communities. 2) As previously mentioned, the majority of the region's immigrants or migrants are already known to be of Mexican descent. 3) Consideration of countries of origin would distract from the regional component of the study. Though considered, the question was determined as nonessential for our purposes, although certainly potentially relevant for future research. Ultimately, the term "Latino" was chosen for its descriptive purposes by government standards.

reported assistance from middle-school-aged children (42%), followed by an almost equal number in elementary (28%) and high school (27%). This finding justifies the case for inclusion of children-oriented outreach strategies potentially in collaboration with schools or at youth-oriented events.

Recycling behavior

Respondents were asked if they recycle always, often, rarely, or never. Over two-thirds (70%) were "recyclers" who recycle always (47%) or often (23%) while the remaining third (30%) recycle rarely (17%) or never (13%). Of the 30% who recycle rarely or never, about half (14%) reported (without prompts) lack of recycling options at their complex. When broken down further, of those who never recycle (13%), even more respondents (35%) don't because they lack opportunity at their complex. Thus, their behaviors may be more indicative of attitudes held by the property manager or hauler who prevents the opportunity to recycle rather than solely a reflection of respondents' personal attitudes.

Respondents were also asked how well they understood their recycling system or the labels on their recycling containers. Although many respondents (38.5%) reported a low understanding of their system, confusion about the system was not a common explanation of limited recycling behavior (only 5%). Limited recycling knowledge could be a subconscious motivator not to recycle and is certainly an impediment to the formation of recycling norms. Thus, as with the general public, communication about the system's process and its simplicity is important, but is even more so within the bicultural or bilingual Latino community. More *Barriers* respondents recycled always or often (89%) than the Latino respondents (70%). Limited recycling knowledge may be a factor since many more *Barriers* respondents (91.8%) than Latino respondents (61.5%) claim to understand their recycling system "mostly" or "fully."

In fact, interviewers frequently had to offer an interpretation of the term "recycling" because even the Spanish term *reciclar* was not regularly recognized. Interviewers offered an explanation: *separar la basura* ("to separate the garbage"). In some cases, respondents explained they separated garbage always or often but did not necessarily understand this as "recycling." We expected more familiarity with the concept, given the recent presence of recycling systems at all participant complexes and thus unfortunately did not systematically monitor the number of respondents unfamiliar with the term.

Knowledge and information

When asked if respondents understand their recycling system, over one-third (38.5%) reported a poor understanding. Many wanted more information on how or where to recycle (75%), what to recycle (53%), and recycling's benefits (52%), to indicate exposure to the recycling system does not equate with understanding.

Comparatively fewer Latino respondents understood their system "mostly" or "fully" (61.5%) than *Barriers* respondents (91.6%) who wanted more information on what to recycle (57.3%), less on how or where (41.1%) and relatively little on the benefits (29.4%). This discrepancy between the studies supports the importance of cultural context in recycling knowledge.

Attitudes

As previously stated, we posit recycling behavior can be affected by either individual attitude or community norm. We found that while valued at the individual level, recycling is not recognized as a norm. Personal attitudes differ from the perception about others' attitudes. When asked if recycling is important, responses were overwhelmingly affirmative (90%) with few claims of no importance (6%), some importance (1%), or uncertainty (3%). Yet relatively few respondents (35%) suggested recycling is important or somewhat important (19%) to others, while 33% were uncertain and some (13%) reported no importance to others. Respondents identified recycling as important, but did not expect their community members and neighbors to share that value. This finding suggests an opportunity to bridge the gap between personal attitude and community norms.

When asked if they changed their behavior for environmental reasons, roughly half of the respondents asked (51%) responded affirmatively. Ways behavior changed were most commonly described as recycling (64%), being clean or not littering (21%), driving less (12%), and using less (11%).

To gain insight into individual attitudes that impact behavior, we asked why respondents recycle. Over half (56%) of the "recyclers" gave environmental explanations for their recycling behavior. Most (37%) were general, not specific, reasons including "to help, take care of, protect, or save" *el medio ambiente* ("the environment"). When broken down further, most frequent responses included to keep the home, complex, garage area, or environment "clean" (6%), to limit "pollution" (5%), to reuse items or materials (5%), or because of a specific environmental reason (3%). A large group (16%) gave mainly functional explanations about sorting or separating garbage, such as "[recycling makes it] easier to separate the garbage," "[I recycle] so that the trash container doesn't overflow," or "[I recycle because] the containers are there." Another group (13%) recycles to follow the rules. Other less common responses include health, civic reasons (it's the right thing to do), concerns about family, or because of something seen on TV, while some (5%) don't know.

When asked "what are the benefits of recycling?" environmental reasons were the most common responses (58%) which when broken down include the reuse of items or materials (14%), specific environmental reasons (14%), to keep the home, complex, garage area, or environment "clean" (12%), to limit "pollution" (11%), and general environmental reasons (9%). Other responses included financial benefits (8%) such as bottle and can refunds, functional descriptions of sorting garbage (6%), health benefits (5%), and civic benefits (3%). This was a challenging question, with many "I don't know" responses (15%).

The generic environmental response suggests limited knowledge or uncertainty among respondents. Awareness about the environmental impact of recycling was not a consistent indicator of behavior, perhaps due to limited knowledge about recycling's *specific* benefits.

Generally, the functional responses described the process of sorting or separating garbage. Significantly, the large number of these responses lacked a value assessment of recycling.

One would expect culturally constructed values about pro-environmental behaviors to be found among populations with greater knowledge about recycling: recycling awareness. Low levels of recycling awareness prevent opportunity for recycling attitude construction. On the other hand, performing a behavior out of habit indicates norm creation but not necessarily value or attitude. Thus, there is an opportunity for education and norm creation if the population is receptive to following regulations or guidelines and receptivity to increased recycling awareness if knowledge about benefits is low.

Environmental concerns

When asked what environmental problem impacts interviewees or their families, many respondents mentioned *contaminación* (pollution) or specific forms of pollution (37%). The next common response was "I don't know" (23%). Some claimed no problems impacted them (12%). Others identified garbage or waste (9%), or specific environmental problems of climate or global warming (9%). Irritants, litter, factories, cars, or health were additional, though infrequent responses. The large number of "I don't know" and "no problem" responses suggests limited environmental awareness.

When asked what environmental problem impacts the region, the majority of responses (37%) were "I don't know." Some responses mentioned pollution (16%), garbage (9%), litter (5%), factories (5%), or cars (5%). Climate and global warming, irritants, and health were mentioned infrequently. A few respondents reported no problems or concerns (8%) because this region is "better off than where they came from." Respondents were significantly less likely to identify "pollution" as a problem with impacts on the *region* than on themselves or their families, thus many respondents appear unaware of regionally based problems. The large number of "I don't know" responses suggests limited knowledge of the area, but could also indicate confusion about the question. Some respondents were unsure whether "region" referred to a geographic location or a governance organization. This question highlights the potential gulf between a Latino (or other immigrant) cultural identity and a regional identity. Conversely, participation in local practices like recycling could foster greater environmental awareness of the region. These are important considerations as regional identity, whether its city, county, or state-based, is crucial to environmental planning.

If perception of regional environmental problems is low, environmental awareness may be limited. If concern is high, but awareness of region-specific concerns is low, motivation for environmental friendly behaviors may be low as well. Thus, outreach messages could better educate about local problems to increase awareness and stimulate motivation. Furthermore, given greater concern over problems that impact the self and family over the region, successful outreach strategies might frame regional issues in relation to personal and family issues. Notably, temporary residency status (among migrant workers) can further impact connection to a regional identity.

Discussion

Implications of findings

Environmental planners have an opportunity to foster greater recycling participation among Latinos. Reports of recycling behavior were higher than expected, but perceptions of others' behaviors substantially lower, suggesting an absence of a recognized norm yet potential for expansion. Culturally specific environmental outreach efforts could benefit any region.

Generally, the Latino respondents exhibited less recycling awareness and understanding of recycling systems than *Barriers* respondents. Recycling is not consistently recognized as separate from garbage or reuse, thus may be a new value and habit, whereas reuse is a more familiar concept (Obregón-Saudo and Corral-Verdugo, 1997). Lack of knowledge likely comes from less exposure to recycling infrastructure in other countries or regions. As respondents made tenuous connections between environmental concerns and recycling's benefits, increased recycling awareness could positively impact motivations and attitudes rooted partly in knowledge and understanding. Exposure alone, without a cultural context, will not necessarily foster understanding.

Although respondents largely perceive recycling as important, their behavior does not always reflect a strong environmental attitude towards recycling. Low levels of recycling awareness, individual knowledge, or understanding may hinder development of supportive attitudes or motivations. Alternatively, there may also be low norm recognition, rooted in insufficient levels of community knowledge or understanding.

Generally, confusion about regional culture or identity suggests isolation, a trend not uncommon among diasporic, migrant, or immigrant communities. Government institutions which practice inclusivity, conduct culturally specific outreach to Latino communities, and investigate strategies to access communities, may achieve greater cultural competency and outreach success.

Ultimately, increased understanding and knowledge about recycling's processes and benefits may foster environmental attitude formation and norm creation of pro-environmental behaviors. Inclusive outreach efforts could identify community leaders and respected sources of information and include more bicultural educators.

Recommendations: policy and practice

Given participants' concerns about the environment, we recommend clarification of the relationship between environmental concerns and recycling. Outreach campaigns can include culturally and linguistically familiar messages framed according to the population's environmental concerns with a local context. Planners can connect pro-environmental behaviors like recycling with already existing concerns about the environment, pollution, family, health and cleanliness, and culturally familiar knowledge about reuse, sorting garbage, and prioritization of cleanliness or clean spaces.

An effective messaging campaign has inclusive language and content, with a local context. Messages will alter misconceptions that "if it looks clean, there's little pollution." Encouragingly, Latinos are receptive to media and informational outreach (DMA, 2006). Moreover, cultural sensitivities to the authority of government or property management may create receptivity to their messages. Efforts strengthen, when also aimed at school-aged children. Ideally, outreach identifies local environmental concerns, fosters greater awareness of local environmental problems, and clarifies relationships between recycling and those concerns and problems.

Planners should also recognize how multifamily complexes with concentrated Latino communities operate as enclaves. Some respondents divulged they had never left their immediate town, neighborhood, or even complex. Moreover, Latino communities with less migratory populations often have low turnover rates (ESA, 2007), providing opportunities for comprehensive, focused outreach.

Additionally, as with all recycling systems, pragmatic factors in place such as access to information, understandability of systems, and leadership support help ensure successful programs. This requires some initial breakdown of biases among haulers and property managers with attitudes based on faulty perceptions of limited environmental concerns among Latino populations and among government departments whose pursuit of "low-hanging fruit" planning policies may be short-sighted.

Challenges

Although ideal, cultural competency is not always readily available for environmental planners as we experienced ourselves. Members of our research team anticipated greater familiarity with the term recycling, reflecting biased expectations. Moreover, respondents may be apprehensive of interviewers as government representatives.

Subsequently, some insider cultural representation is essential for planners to gain access to local Latino communities and reduce bias. Planners will be more inclusive and successful with Latino representation in outreach networks. However, cultural competency is not always easy or feasible given funding or staffing limitations. When possible, building relationships with recognized Latino community leaders, authorities (including property managers), or volunteers expands networks and supplements the limitations of environmental planning organizations.

Our study required collaboration between governments and a university program with researchers and students privileged to pursue new avenues. Through funding and time investments, our study helped expand region-wide recycling awareness among residents and recycling and property management professionals. Investment in culturally competent outreach contributes to long-term norm creation of pro-environmental recycling behaviors, a strategy applicable to environmental planners working on related pro-environmental campaigns.

Conclusion

We found culturally framed knowledge and concerns and identified opportunities to impact individual environmental attitudes and community norms through the development of culturally specific campaigns to raise recycling awareness. In terms of broader implications, the relationship between environmental concerns, attitudes, and behaviors is part of an ongoing debate and epistemological exploration.

Given the absence of any dominant and widely accepted theory, this initial research did not operate within preconceived measurement models but was more exploratory. Furthermore, we feel the predominance of environmental concerns globally diminishes the need to identify specific beliefs as evidence of these concerns. Thus, we gave greater emphasis to the opportunity for respondents to provide their own voice outside of any preconceived assessment models.

Although these assessment models are valuable, they may have embedded cultural biases. We suggest environmental attitudes are partly constructed within a cultural context of environmental knowledge and concerns.

While we do not suggest all environmental concepts are culturally constructed, we highlight the potential for cultural interpretation. Rather we encourage recognition that some concepts are culturally constructed and avoiding assumptions that absence of pro-environmental behaviors implies absence of environmental concerns. Rather identification of specific concerns framed within culturally specific outreach campaigns may help motivate the behavior both by fostering development of an environmental attitude through raising awareness and by fostering norm recognition.

Afterword

The work conducted for this study allowed CES to reinforce the value of its contributions when collaborating with the public sector. CES was able to adapt and build upon the previous years of experience in multifamily communities, and develop research practices that were culturally sensitive and inclusive, positively impacting the capacity of both students and staff. Ultimately, CES helped Metro to integrate perspectives of Latino multifamily communities into public education efforts, and thereby increase the impacts of Metro's environmental outreach. More inclusive multicultural outreach is now better integrated into recycling education campaigns. The findings also informed work with another local partner, the Oregon Museum of Science and Industry, on a five-year National Science Foundation Informal Science and Education (ISE) project to promote pro-environmental behavior among Latinos in the region. From influencing the public sector to ISE, CES continues to develop capacity to include perspectives of the growing multicultural communities in the region. Thus, in addition to CES's renowned wastestream analyses, the organization stays true to its roots and continually contributes to the public sector's recognition and inclusion of Portland's underserved communities, and to the expansion of culturally inclusive environmental planning.

References

Bamberg, S. & Schmidt, P. (2003). Incentives, morality, or habit? *Environment and Behavior,* 35, 264-285.

Bermudez, E. (2007, August 9). State's face is changing—Fast. *The Oregonian,* Local News, Sunrise edition.

Bonta, M. & Jordan, C. (2007). Diversifying the American environmental movement. In E. Enderle (Ed.), *Diversity and the Future of the U.S. Environmental Movement* (pp. 13-33). New Haven, CT: Yale School of Forestry & Environmental Studies.

Deng, J., Walker, G.J., & Swinnerton, G. (2006). A comparison of environmental values and attitudes between Chinese in Canada and Anglo-Canadians. *Environment and Behavior,* 38, 22-47.

DMA (Direct Marketing Association) (2006). *DMA Publishes 2006 "Reaching the US Hispanic market report."* Hispanic Trending. Retrieved from http://www.hispanictrending.net/2006/06/dma_publishes_2.html

EPA (Environment Protection Authority) (1997). *The Environment and New South Wales Ethnic Communities.* Sydney: EPA.

ESA (2007). *Identifying Barriers and Benefits to Effective Multifamily Waste Reduction and Recycling Behaviors.* Prepared for Metro Solid Waste and Recycling Department by ESA in association with Portland State University and Tabor Consulting. Los Angeles: ESA.

Fox, S. & Livingston, G. (2007). *Latinos Online: Hispanics with Lower Levels of Education and English Proficiency Remain Largely Disconnected from the Internet.* Washington, D.C.: Pew Hispanic Center and Pew Internet Project. Retrieved from http://pewhispanic.org/files/reports/73.pdf

Hunter, L.M. (2000). A comparison of the environmental attitudes, concern, and behaviors of native-born and foreign-born U.S. residents. *Population and Environment,* 21, 565-580.

Johnson, C.Y., Bowker, J.M., & Cordell, H.K. (2004). Ethnic variations in environmental belief and behavior: An examination of the new ecological paradigm in a social psychological context. *Environment and Behavior,* 36, 157-186.

Katzev, R., Blake, G., & Messer, B. (1993). Determinants of participation in multifamily recycling programs. *Journal of Applied Social Psychology,* 23, 375-385.

Milfont, T.L., Duckitt, J., & Cameron, L.D. (2006). A cross-cultural study of environmental motive concerns and their implications for proenvironmental behavior. *Environment and Behavior*, 38, 745-767.

Obregón-Saudo, F.J. & Corral-Verdugo, V. (1997). Systems of beliefs and environmental conservation behavior in a Mexican community. *Environment and Behavior*, 29, 213-235.

Owens, J., Dickerson, S., & Macintosh, D.L. (2000). Demographic covariates of residential recycling efficiency. *Environment and Behavior*, 32, 637-650.

Pastor, M. & Morello-Frosch, R. (2002, July 8). Assumption is wrong: Latinos care deeply about the environment. *San Jose Mercury News*. Retrieved from http://cjtc.ucsc.edu/docs/op-ed_AssumptionIsWrong.pdf

Pfeffer, M.J. & Stycos, J.M. (2002). Immigrant behaviors in New York City. *Social Science Quarterly*, 83, 64-81.

Stern, P.C., Dietz, T., & Guagnano, G.A. (1995). The new ecological paradigm in social-psychological context. *Environment and Behavior*, 27, 723-743.

Vincente, P. & Reis, E. (2007). Factors influencing households' participation in recycling. *Waste Management & Research*, 26, 140-146.

12

Decolonizing sustainability

Students, teachers, and indigenous–university partnerships

Katrine Barber and Donna Sinclair

The process may be a significant outcome of your project.

The weekend we spent with two of our students in remote Bay Center, Washington (population of 276 in 2010) was sunny but cool. The ocean air, which held the promise of spring, refreshed everything including our spirits at the end of winter term. Greta and Carolee had taken at least two courses apiece that included some community-based research with the Chinook Indian Nation and it wasn't the first time that they had been in Chinook territory. But this time we were all staying with Jane Pulliam, a tribal council member, as a guest in her house for several days of intense work on a website. Greta, an undergraduate, and Carolee, who was to enter the graduate program the following fall, volunteered to join us while our host supplied us with work tables, electrical outlets, feedback, and wonderful meals. This was an intimate form of community-based learning where on-the-ground research included ongoing, informal conversations with our host and other community members and partner feedback could be immediate.

Since 2009, Portland State University (PSU) faculty and students have collaborated with the Chinook Indian Nation on a series of interlinking public projects. These efforts will culminate in a website that documents the Nation's history through archaeological findings, the historical record, oral history interviews, and an iterative and ongoing partnership that seeks to dissipate colonial legacies. Project development has incorporated graduate and undergraduate students and interns, a state historical society, K-12 teachers, and the Chinook Culture Committee and community through an oral history project, multi-pronged public programs, educational workshops, and college-level courses. As colleagues and co-directors, we juggle many elements. But our goal is clear: create and maintain a collaborative process that aims toward a decolonizing public history practice and provides space for our students to collaborate in and improve upon our necessarily messy and imperfect process.

In this chapter, we argue that purposefully incorporating decolonizing practices in public history and pedagogy can enhance cultural sustainability. We use the Chinook Nation website to explore integrating students into community-based research in collaboration with Indigenous peoples in ways that do not replicate the colonial inequities of the past. We believe that process is as important as product, that a scholarly community can thrive with diverse partners and students, that together they can reshape historical narrative and methodology in critical ways, and that how we work as scholars in a settler society makes a difference. Our work is situated theoretically in community-based research and decolonizing research methodologies and has at its core cultural sustainability.[1]

For the purposes of this chapter, we define decolonizing public history methodologies as those that

- Abandon faith in the superiority of the dominant culture

- Acknowledge Indigenous communities and their histories

- Engage Indigenous experts identified by their communities

- Respect tribal protocols and governance

- Develop narratives that debunk and oppose those that naturalize the colonial past

Cultural sustainability emphasizes social foundations; that is, those aspects of culture that are carried forward with intergenerational solidarity as key to moving toward a sustainable future. For example, through direct engagement with the Chinook, we learned that continuously occupied sites along the Lower Columbia River connect and bind kin, community, and their political struggle for recognition. As anthropologist Keith Basso (1996) points out, what people make of place is often complex, intangible, and taken for granted until lost or removed. The Chinook Website explores several sites of loss and memory where U.S. government policies have significantly impacted community sustainability—economically, politically, and culturally.[2] By capturing stories of environmental and human relations in the distant and recent past, educational partnerships between students, teachers, and

---

1 We draw our methods from public history practices that emphasize "shared authority" and from the literature addressing indigenous research and methods. For "shared authority," see Frisch (2003) and Adair *et al.* (2011). For indigenous research and methods, see Denzin *et al.* (2008); Wilson and Yellow Bird (2005); and Tuhiwai Smith (1999).

2 Center for Columbia River History: www.ccrh.org/comm/chinook

the Chinook document cultural continuity, a critical component of sustainability (UNECE, 2004–2005; Parker, 2012).

These decolonizing practices suggest pedagogies for cultural and intercultural sustainability, which we will address below through three turning points in the project: 1) rethinking geographic and historic scope; 2) the loss of sustained project funding; and 3) student-generated critiques of our collaborative process. These moments reshaped our work by challenging how we thought about collaboration with our partners and our students. Most importantly, they led us to understand that purposefully incorporating decolonizing practices in public history and pedagogy can enhance cultural sustainability.

Project origins

What we now call the "Chinook Project," a website that invites visitors to re-vision the historic Chinookan landscape of the Lower Columbia River, has its roots in the work, partnerships, and mission of the Center for Columbia River History (CCRH), a public history educational organization. In 1999, with Department of Education funding, CCRH undertook a series of community history web "exhibits," a project that launched several collaborations over the years. These exhibits featured layered stories of change in Columbia Basin communities through historic images, documents, and oral histories. They also emphasized transformations in both land and people. Although we engaged in community-based public history through consultation, attempted to debunk celebratory narratives, consulted with local historical societies, and interviewed community members, the three-year, well-funded and staffed project included clear academic boundaries.

Our journey with the Chinook soon thrust us outside of these relatively comfortable and detached norms, incrementally shaping a more challenging, intellectually engaging, and relational process. That journey began with the partnerships that comprised CCRH, a consortium of two universities (Portland State University and Washington State University, Vancouver), and a historical society (the Washington State Historical Society). Consortium partners often drew from one another's expertise and networks, so that when the Chinook partnered with the Washington State Historical Society during the 2004–2005 Lewis and Clark Bicentennial, CCRH served as a research link to the universities. An initiative for the Lower Columbia River Chinookan Communities website developed from that initial contact.

At our first meeting with our Chinook liaisons, Samuel V. Robinson and Charles Funk, we began to glimpse some of the contradictions embodied by the Chinook. They lacked federal recognition, but carried distinctly Native experiences. Charlie's father had participated in the Indian Civilian Conservation Corps on the Yakama

Nation Reservation.[3] Sam spent several weeks each summer on the Columbia River and animatedly described the annual canoe journey[4] and its personal and community meanings. Both served as representatives for then-chairman Ray Gardner, with special attention to working with the National Park Service at *qilq'ayaqilxam*, the Middle Village site that helped to fund this project. We expanded our partnership to the Culture Committee, a body that needs to be consulted in any tribal–university partnership.[5]

Our next steps included creating an advisory board and seeking grant funding. Limited resources and the mission of CCRH prompted us to take a multi-pronged approach to creating the web exhibit. We hired out some of the research, recorded public programs put on by the Chinook for placement on the website, incorporated graduate students and volunteers, and used the project to further connect with PSU through a 400/500 level Public History Lab. With the help of our partners we began to understand the Chinookan world as a riverscape, rather than landscape, a series of waterways and landings. As we structured the website, we created categories to enhance public and community understanding of Chinook culture, federal treaty-making, and a "How Do We Know?" section for educational purposes and to make the level of scholarly work transparent. Envisioning the site as a digital repository, we included a resources section to enhance cultural connections for Chinook within and outside of their homelands.

Rethinking project scope

> *If this is going to be a true collaborative project, don't forget that it doesn't happen without both parties.*

A critique of our project's scope by our advisors upended the initial plans we had made and underscores the wisdom of Culture Committee chair Tony Johnson's (2014) advice: "Be prepared to be in a project you didn't expect or be asked to do something that stretches your boundaries. Be flexible (and learn to like it)!" We were game to broaden the project and began to face the very issues our institutional

3 The federal Civilian Conservation Corps (CCC) provided Depression-era employment to young men nationwide. In the Pacific Northwest, CCC "boys" cut forest trails, channelized streams, and aided in fire suppression. Several of the region's Indian reservations hosted Indian CCC camps that served tribal populations.

4 Revived in the late 1980s, tribal "canoe journeys" are important annual intertribal cultural events in which "canoe families" travel the region's rivers to visit one another, visit important cultural sites, and to celebrate Native heritage.

5 Tribal Culture Committees serve at the behest of elected tribal councils to interface with outside communities and maintain internal cultural integrity on multiple issues.

partners hoped to avoid, namely the way in which the history of the Indigenous past is politicized in the present.

The director of the Washington State Historical Society recommended a focus on the pre-1820 fur trade era and highlighted archaeology and Chinookan material culture at two well-studied archaeological sites. By limiting the chronological period and geographic scope, we could avoid contemporary conflicts over traditional territorial boundaries as well as the political issues around recognition that embroiled the Chinook Indian Nation. From the perspective of CCRH institutional partners, this tactic was justifiable: we could maintain scholarly integrity with a project broad enough to develop meaningful analysis while also avoiding pressing contemporary issues.

But it was not valid to our community partners whose engagement was political as well as scholarly. To limit geographic scope could suggest that the bands that comprise the contemporary Chinook Nation were historically limited in their territorial reach. At our inaugural meeting, the advisory board suggested a wider geographic focus. Pat Courtney Gold, the well-known Wasco Chinookan weaver, proposed a focus on Sunken Village, an ancient site on Sauvie Island near Portland. Kenneth Ames, the renowned archaeologist who led multiple excavations around the region, emphasized the more recent site at Cathlapotle, where a new Plankhouse had been opened to the public just a few years earlier. The plankhouse generated conflict between the federally unrecognized Chinook and the recently recognized Cowlitz.[6] Including these other locations forced us to face how territorial designations made by previous scholars indelibly shaped federal and intertribal relations. Those designations did not account for how Indigenous peoples understood their territories, rights to landscapes, or continued connection to place—significant elements in sustaining culture.

---

6 Both the Chinook and Cowlitz obtained federal recognition in 2001. Intertribal conflict with the Quinault led to the rescission of Chinook federal recognition 18 months later while the decision to recognize the Cowlitz was upheld. Federal agencies, like the U.S. Fish and Wildlife Service, which manages the Cathlapotle Plankhouse, are obligated to confer with federally recognized tribes but not with unrecognized groups. However, they continue to consult with the Chinook Nation based upon their analysis of archaeological evidence. They have also contributed to our work.

Rethinking periodization[7]

Eat! It's an Indian rule.

As we made the long drive home from Bay Center on Willapa Bay in January 2010, we realized that decolonizing our work would require more than changing geographic scope. We had just finished our second Culture Committee meeting at the tribal office, center of Chinook federal recognition efforts. At our first meeting, we had presented *our* project and turned down a meal. We later realized this had been a mistake. This time, we ate. This time we asked the Culture Committee to tell us what was important to *them*. How might they benefit from the project? The answer thrilled *and* intimidated us: oral history. Their primary goal was cultural sustainability in the 21st century. We should interview the elders. As we sped over dark country roads back to the city, we reevaluated the project. "If we do oral history, we'll have to focus on the 20th century," one of us said. By then, we understood the Chinook plight. Terminating the project at 1820 would not meet their needs. In fact, by focusing only on archaeological sites and the Chinookan past we would be replicating the very colonial processes we sought to avoid.

The Chinook Indian Nation had been formally working toward federal recognition since the turn of the 20th century. Federal recognition affirms government-to-government relationships. As Brian Klopotek (2011, p. 3) stated, "to lack status as a tribe within the meaning of federal law means to live without the limited protections and benefits available for tribes under that law." With the limited resources of a small community, tribal members were not willing to contribute to a history-based project that did not also address their current concerns or document the decades of political work in the more recent past. It became quickly apparent that the Chinook could put our research-based narrative to other purposes, and we welcomed that. In fact, we saw the project as a tool that we could develop collaboratively and then pass on to the community. They could then use it in any way they wanted, including advocating for recognition.

7 Historians grapple carefully with periodization because the scope of our research can shape our conclusions. For a critique of periodization in archaeology see, for example, Julien *et al.* (2008).

Rethinking methodology

Cite the elders. Recognize, respect, and attribute Indigenous knowledge and expertise.

We approached interviewing Chinook elders cautiously. Oral history can be a powerful way to contextualize otherwise partial records of government agencies. But the scholarly act of "collecting" stories from Indigenous peoples is historically fraught. In the late 19th and into the 20th century anthropologists collected life histories and other forms of intellectual property—traditional and ceremonial stories, songs, language, and names—from people who represented supposedly dying cultures. Such collections distorted the materials and benefited scholars whose careers rested on the labor of "informers," many of whom saw little advantage (see, for example, Coody Cooper, 2007; Sleeper-Smith, 2009). It was in this context that we accepted the charge to do oral history with the Chinook.

The committee also moved forward warily. They determined whom we would interview and provided initial contacts. Following the guidelines of the Oral History Association we developed a protocol for PSU Human Subjects review which the Chinook approved. We obtained funding from PSU and recruited graduate students to help with genealogical research and question preparation. Several accompanied us to the coast, sat in on interviews, and eventually transcribed and indexed them.

In addition to interviews, the Culture Committee asked that we help tribal members scan family photographs. Although the request would benefit the website and the tribe, it also presented additional labor and unexpected questions. How would we find the time? Who had preservation responsibility? What was our obligation to the tribe? This request taught us an important lesson. As Tony Johnson later noted, working with tribes requires offering something genuine. "Yes, token gifts are important, but bring something of substance."[8] We agreed to undertake the endeavor, which we soon realized made ours a true community-based project. We could expand our interviewing network while scanning photographs. And we'd have something to give back to the community at large. We could contribute to Chinook cultural sustainability. Culture Committee member Jane Pulliam advertised two days of scanning in the *Chinook Tilixam* newsletter, and we headed to Bay Center for our second overnight trip. We brought two scanners, multiple computers, our audio recorders, and two graduate students whose presence multiplied our achievements. That visit yielded ten interviews, dozens of scanned pictures, and ultimately generated trust and acceptance by the Chinook.

8 Personal communication with Tony Johnson via email, September 25, 2016.

Losing funding

Keep your project timelines flexible, as they may not match those of the tribe. Be flexible regarding expectations and outcomes.

By taking a community history approach and documenting 20th-century Chinook in their historic homelands, we also contributed to Chinook cultural sustainability. The interviews and the images traced lineage directly back to the 1851 treaty era,[9] with only a few generations in between. We learned of the grandmothers who stayed in place and raised their children as Chinook, teaching them to weave, to gather foods from the land, and to fight for recognition. We heard about the grandfathers and uncles who taught them to fish, carried government-issued "Indian blue cards," and participated in national wars, but still could not vote. We learned about the families determined to stay in place, whose children attended Chemawa Indian School and who held Indian Trust Land in Bay Center and South Bend. The interviews and images demonstrated continuous occupation on the Lower Columbia since the treaty era and before. They taught us about important places like Pillar Rock, Long Island, and Goose Point, where an Indian Village developed as the Chinook waited for treaty ratification and a reservation. They also taught us that the most important issue for the Chinook is federal recognition, a concern grounded in lived experience, in place, and in maintaining cultural ties to one another.

By 2011, we had developed major portions of the website, collected hundreds of images, video footage, and constructed dozens of web pages. Meanwhile, CCRH underwent a slow but steady death. For two years, as the economy ate away at state funding, Donna Sinclair's position as program manager decreased from full-time to four, three, two, and finally one day per week. With decreasing resources, we focused lectures, teacher workshops, and grants all on the Chinook project. As CCRH entered its final days, the Chinook arranged a public program in Bay Center, replete with salmon and crab, and we handed over digital copies of all the materials that had been gathered—our primary contribution. By then, we both felt personal responsibility for this important project, but how could we complete it without institutional support?

We reoriented the project to attend to bits and pieces within the courses we taught in PSU's History Department. Students in the introductory public history course analyzed interviews. In an oral history seminar students transcribed and conducted additional interviews. Students taking courses on the history of the American West and the Pacific Northwest sharpened our analysis. We developed new courses as well. Donna Sinclair taught an upper-division public history course, "Chinook History on the World Wide Web," and Katrine Barber taught a seminar, "Indigenous Histories in Public Places." At every opportunity we ticked off the many tasks outstanding on the project within the guise of our teaching

---

9 The unratified 1851 Tansey Point treaties provide the foundation for federal recognition efforts by the Chinook.

duties. Working with students also forced us to carefully articulate our methods, especially those that addressed sovereignty and cultural sustainability. What began as an emergency measure to substitute for lost funding turned into a way to enrich the project with student energy, time, and intellectual insight.

The loss of funding certainly slowed our progress and fostered anxiety about whether and how we would fulfill promises made to members of the Chinook Nation. But it also presented some surprising possibilities. Forced to become ever more resourceful, we turned toward students who nearly always met the high academic standards of the project and were eager to engage in partnership with the Chinook. As we considered how to teach our students about ethical and decolonizing partnerships, we engaged them in ongoing discussions about sovereignty and methodology that enriched the public history offerings at PSU and further inspired us to pursue a decolonizing practice. Students became integral to our work beyond their classroom participation by attending Culture Committee meetings, engaging in field work, meeting with elders, and volunteering for tasks long after classes had ended. They also had much to say about the project and how it had evolved.

Students evaluate the process

Be passionate about what you learn. This stuff is important. Treat it that way.

It was meant to be a short assignment in the course "Indigenous Histories in Public Places." Katrine Barber passed out copies of a comprehensive 12-page timeline generated in collaboration with elders of the Chinook Nation to students and asked for feedback. What kinds of themes emerged from the entries? How did the timeline reflect how members of the Chinook Nation made sense of their past? One student tentatively mentioned that entries identified tribal members by name. Another quietly noted how frequently women had been included. And then a third broke the ice by declaring that the timeline wasn't decolonizing *enough*. The very language of the entries described the Chinook as people to whom history happened rather than as historical agents in their own right. That sparked discussion and in quick succession students applied the course's methodological readings to the Chinook timeline. And then the assignment grew as they rewrote key entries.

That afternoon students could not know the care that had gone into crafting the timeline. They did not know that a graduate student wrote the first draft or that staff at CCRH further developed it before working closely with former Chinook chairman Gary Johnson, for additions and revisions. The copy given to students had also been vetted in a public gathering of Chinook members who made further revisions. We had faced similar challenges in shaping other portions of the website. In one case, a photo caption read: "Archaeologists identified this empty field as the site of the former *qiíq'ayaqilxam* (Middle Village)." When reviewed by the tribe, we were told that the Chinook had always known where Middle Village lay. This and many other instances taught us that making mistakes was inevitable, but our increased level of participation generated trust and acceptance. We changed the caption and continued our close consultation. It had taken a long time, but as Tony Johnson told us in 2014, "Once you are accepted expect to be treated as family. Be prepared for borderline abuse and lots of jokes (maybe at your expense). Have a thick skin throughout."[10]

What has developed in the multi-level collaboration between PSU students, ourselves, and members of the Chinook Indian Nation is a rich, if imperfect, relational process that strengthens our public history practice and contributes to Chinook cultural sustainability. The Chinook have connected their own website to ours. Our students have connected with the Chinook in powerfully personal and academic ways as evidenced by those who came to Bay Center on their own time. Moreover, several students spent a term weaving together the strands of their former coursework, field experience in Chinook country, and the scholarly foundation for ethical public history practice to describe what they identified as decolonizing protocols for working with tribes. We modified and revised their initial language into the "lessons learned" below, which we juxtapose here with those articulated by Tony Johnson, who is now the tribal chairman. These are the same students who accompanied us to Bay Center we described at the outset of this chapter. They are among the many former students whose experiences working directly with the tribe led to unexpected levels of commitment well beyond their contributions in the classroom. They bear witness to the Chinook's ongoing political struggles for recognition and by doing so contribute to the cultural sustainability of the tribe. We hope they also carry into future public history work decolonizing pedagogies that can sensitize others.

Public or applied history collaboration with Native peoples is grounded in unique historical, cultural, and political circumstances, which reverberate with cultural injury to Indigenous peoples. Indigenous–university partnerships require a relational process that attends to the past, generates reciprocity, and creates outcomes that benefit Native communities. Collaborative student and community-centered approaches in this project have contemporary and future implications for the Chinook Indian Nation and for public history as it is taught at Portland State University. They link past, present, and future through the work of students, teachers, and Indigenous community members, through which best practices for working with Native communities have emerged. By contributing to democratic thinking and genuine dialogue as key components of sustainability, students and Native and non-Native teachers play an important role in decolonizing Indigenous–university partnerships. Thus, our experiences lead us to believe that purposefully decolonizing public history pedagogy can enhance tribal cultural sustainability.

10 Personal communication with Tony Johnson, via email, September 25, 2014.

Lessons we are learning, suggestions for best practices[11]

Community-based research and teaching is always situational and these points are not meant to be prescriptive. See Table 12.1 for a summary of these learning points.

Table 12.1 **Lessons learned for best practices**

Katrine Barber, Donna Sinclair and students	Tony Johnson, Chair of the Chinook Indian Nation Culture Committee
Ask permission and gain consent. Understand that tribes are sovereign nations, politically and culturally. They decide what to share and what remains private.	Don't expect a short-term relationship or have expectations of a quick turnaround.
Explain your project clearly. Be prepared to discuss personal motivations, not just goals or methods.	Expect it to take a while (maybe a long while) until you are trusted and accepted. Once you are accepted expect to be treated as family. Be prepared for borderline abuse and lots of jokes (maybe at your expense). Have a thick skin throughout.
Do your homework. Native communities are not all the same; it is critical that you learn about issues specific to the community with which you work.	Don't think work will be 9–5. If you are invited to a ceremony, go. If a meeting is at 6 p.m. and runs until 10 that is the way it is. If that potlatch runs all night stick it out.
Find out what is important to the community and follow up. Determine outcomes collaboratively.	Eat! It's an Indian rule.
Identify appropriate cultural resource contacts. You may need to seek permission from cultural committee, tribal elders, and/or other tribal gatekeepers.	If this is going to be a true collaborative project don't forget that it doesn't happen without both parties.
Keep your project timelines flexible, as they may not match those of the tribe. Be flexible regarding expectations and outcomes.	If someone on your team isn't a good fit tell them so, don't let one personality ruin the project.
Tribes may have unique protocols regarding when, where, and how to transmit historical/oral narratives. There may not be consensus about sharing cultural information outside the tribe.	Come with something genuine to offer. Yes, token gifts are important, but bring something of substance.
Cite the elders. Recognize, respect, and attribute Indigenous knowledge and expertise.	Be prepared to be in a project you didn't expect or be asked to do something that stretches your boundaries. Be flexible (and learn to like it)!

→

---

11 Carolee Harrison, Joshua Ross, and Greta Smith drafted the initial version of the "lessons learned" for the website in 2014.

Katrine Barber, Donna Sinclair and students	Tony Johnson, Chair of the Chinook Indian Nation Culture Committee
Discuss and respectfully negotiate findings with community and tribal partners.	Be passionate about what you learn. This stuff is important. Treat it that way.
The process may be a significant outcome of your project.	Have an opinion and take a stand. Like the point above, this is important. Our histories are full of injustices. If the facts support a position, commit to it. The Tribe has to outrank the university. Its history is longer and its future more tenuous. Make it clear the Tribe is the expert. Be humble.

References

Adair, B., Filene, B., & Koloski, L. (Eds.) (2011). *Letting Go? Sharing Historical Authority in a User-Generated World*. Philadelphia: The Pew Center for Arts and Heritage.

Basso, K.H. (1996). *Wisdom Sits in Places: Landscape and Language among the Western Apache*. Albuquerque, NM: University of New Mexico Press.

Coody Cooper, K. (2007). *Spirited Encounters: American Indians Protest Museum Policies and Practices*. Walnut Creek, CA: AltaMira Press.

Denzin, N.K., Lincoln, Y.S., & Tuhiwai Smith, L. (Eds.) (2008). *Handbook of Critical and Indigenous Methodologies*. Los Angeles: Sage Press.

Frisch, M. (2003). Sharing authority: Oral history and the collaborative process. *Oral History Review*, 30(1), 111-113.

Johnson, T. (2014). Recommendations submitted by Tony Johnson for *Western Lands, Western Voices* Conference presentation, Salt Lake City, Utah, September 20, 2014.

Julien, D., Bernard, T., & Rosenmeier, L. with review by the Mi'kmawey Delbert Elders' Advisory Council (2008). Paleo is not our word: Protecting and growing a Mi'kmaw place. In P. Rubertone (Ed.), *Archaeologies of Placemaking: Monuments, Memories, and Engagement in Native North America* (pp. 35-58). Walnut Creek, CA: Left Coast.

Klopotek, B. (2011). *Recognition Odysseys: Indigeneity, Race, and Federal Tribal Recognition Policy in Three Louisiana Indian Communities*. Durham, NC: Duke University Press.

Parker, A. (2012). Interview with Rudolph C. Rÿser. In Z. Grossman & A. Parker (Eds.), *Asserting Native Resilience: Pacific Rim Indigenous Nations Face the Climate Crisis* (pp. 137-144). Corvallis, OR: Oregon State University Press.

Sleeper-Smith, S. (Ed.) (2009). *Contesting Knowledge: Museums and Indigenous Perspectives*. Lincoln: University of Nebraska Press.

Tuhiwai Smith, L. (1999). *Decolonizing Methodologies: Research and Indigenous Peoples*. London: Zed Books.

UNECE (United Nations Economic Commission for Europe) (2004–2005). Sustainable development—concept and action. Retrieved from http://www.unece.org/oes/nutshell/2004-2005/focus_sustainable_development.html

Wilson, W.A. & Yellow Bird, M. (2005). *For Indigenous Eyes Only: A Decolonization Handbook*. Santa Fe: School of American Research.

13

Critical Indigenous Pedagogy of Place

Bridging teaching, researching, and mentoring for social sustainability, equity, and change

Alma M.O. Trinidad, Keisha Mateo, Berenis Peregrino-Galvez, Kris Kelsang Lipman, Pablo Saldana, Mireaya Medina, and Imani Muhammad

The rise of a Pinay scholar warrior of aloha

For five years at Portland State University (PSU), I taught the Freshmen Inquiry course (FRINQ) on Race and Social Justice. As a tenure track professor in a shared line with the School of Social Work and University Studies, this course occupied a big portion of my livelihood. Having worked with youth and young adults and contextually based, culturally responsive programs as a social worker and scholar, the use of Critical Indigenous Pedagogy of Place (CIPP) became the foundation in my work as a *Pinay scholar warrior of aloha,* a stance I discovered within myself a couple of years ago in my journey. When I think back to my upbringing—a young, low-income Filipina, a child of Filipino immigrants living in pineapple plantation towns of Molokai and Oahu in Hawai'i—I never imagined occupying a space in the academy. When reflecting on my life journey leading up to my present work, my roles and responsibilities become clear. A *Pinay* warrior is rooted and grounded in Filipino and other Pacific, Indigenous island cultures. A woman warrior is one that fights for ideals and principles important to the community. Historically, *Pinay* warriors, such as Gabriela Silang, fought alongside Filipino men against the Spanish colonial regime. Their anti-colonial stance perpetuated an identity that I uphold today. It speaks to a social justice framework that embraces Filipino indigenous values of *barangay* or *barrio* (*small, town community*), *kaili* (*township*), and *pamilia* (*family*). It honors womanhood, sisterhood, and feminism in the context of community. *Aloha* (*love*) stems from my roots growing up in Hawai'i, specifically the island of Molokai. To *aloha* speaks to commitment to deeply love and fondly care for one's community or place that has been injured, oppressed, and in need of healing. These values are embodied in a Pinay scholar warrior of aloha stance. For me, it means passionately holding both beauty and fierceness in my work in teaching, mentoring, serving, and conducting research for collective empowerment and social change.

The academy is a space our people were not historically a part of. Despite the ongoing challenges and loneliness of being a tenure track woman of color professor in the academy, my becoming of a Pinay scholar warrior of aloha has granted me with such a privilege and opportunity to do the work I do in and at PSU, and *with* and *among* inspirational people every day. I am in awe every day of my students, mentees, colleagues, and community-based partners in service-learning activities and research. It is through our collectivity and collective impact I am grounded and have a clear sense of purpose. Hence, this work that we collectively present in this book chapter serves as a way to highlight such collaboration with students, mentees, fellow colleagues, and leaders in community-based partners.

We stand on the shoulders of our ancestors and many who came before us, and know that our presence here is not for personal prestige or gain, but one for a collective. People, places, and processes embedded in the academy and community have pulled us together. Our collective purpose is crystallized each time by the people, places, and processes rooted in Critical Indigenous Pedagogy of Place (CIPP). We strive for interdisciplinary teaching, mentoring, and research *with, in* collaboration, and *for* community-based organizations promoting social sustainability, equity, and change. We hope this book chapter highlights the collective work and impact of Dr. Trinidad's FRINQ Race and Social Justice.

Literature review on Critical Indigenous Pedagogy of Place

CIPP builds upon the literature on critical pedagogy, the concept of place, and indigenous and ethnic studies. CIPP is a facilitative learning tool to recognize and confront inequalities in a specific geographic community (Trinidad, 2011), and embraces indigenous identity and ways of knowing that are rooted in place (Johnston-Goodstar *et al.*, 2010). Educators may utilize CIPP as a possible tool to facilitate social change in communities of color by acknowledging unique histories of oppression and resistance, genealogies, and cultural values perpetuated and expressed in a specific geographic place. As indicated in Figure 13.1, there are three major CIPP processes rooted in geographic place: 1) analysis of power and oppressive forces; 2) indigenization; and 3) sociopolitical development through student–community engagement. These processes can be embedded in learning opportunities.

Figure 13.1 **Processes of Critical Indigenous Pedagogy of Place**

Source: author

Analysis of power and oppressive forces	• Recognize and confront inequities of a geographic place • Analysis of power and its manifestations in structures or systems and how people interface with them
Indigenization	• Centering Indigenous and cultural community epistemology and values • Reclaiming and retelling a community's histories, genealogies, languages, and social practices
Sociopolitical development through student–community engagement	• Access and engagement of critical ideas, social networks, and learning opportunities • Acquire commitment to serve community and responsibiity • Opportunity to participate in knowledge–action–reflection cycle of critical praxis

Critical pedagogy: Analysis of power and oppressive forces

Critical pedagogy can be translated to an approach that facilitates a process of critical consciousness. This process includes an analysis of power (who possesses and imposes it), and how it is manifested in the structures or systems and impacts people's lives. Four key dimensions of critical pedagogy are integrated in community learning:

- The elimination of hierarchy or equalizing a stance of the expert instructor
- Sharing and development of a body of knowledge based on lived experiences
- A process of critically reflecting on and then acting on acquired knowledge and information

- Creating a culturally responsive learning environment where culture, in this case, indigenous and/or racial/ethnic culture, serves as the collective bonding agent (Zullo and Gates, 2008)

This situates the role of the instructor in higher education as a facilitator of critical consciousness and an ally for social change.

Place embodying a process of indigenization

CIPP's approach is deeply contextually based with a focus on rootedness and spirituality, and makes individual and collective empowerment ecologically valid and credible to a specific cultural group, and its historical experiences and knowledge base. Focusing on indigenous and cultural epistemology, CIPP allows indigenization to occur by providing a space to retell and reclaim a community's history, languages, and social practices (Trinidad, 2011). The indigenization process and strategy can transform a place of marginalization, including its knowledge, culture, language, and social practice, to a place of resistance to victimization and oppression, empowerment, and hope (Grande, 2004; Smith, 1999; Trask, 2000; Trinidad, 2012a). Indigenous and cultural epistemology or knowledge production is central to CIPP, and is intertwined with community values (Trinidad, 2012a). Taking a critical-dialectical perspective on community values and epistemology, what emerges for a community through CIPP is a list of issues, concerns, and needs deemed important to address for people who are interested in being allies and change agents through social change. The central values and beliefs identified by a community are built upon meaningful connections, rooted in geographic place and interdependent social relationships. They exist as guideposts to prioritize issues and needs for the community. Community voices and healing can emerge from the process of indigenization (Trinidad, 2012b).

CIPP provides a venue for community members to explore the social, psychological, and cultural dimensions of what it means to live and be from a geographic place (Agnew, 1987; Cresswell, 2004; Trinidad, 2012b). The meaning making of a place serves as a way of understanding one's social context or environment, and makes critical consciousness relevant. Place provides sources of wisdom. For example, in Native Hawaiian communities, place is not just a mere geographic location, but holds a deeper relationship with the land itself which is strongly tied to structural oppression due to colonialism (e.g., loss of land, language, religious and spiritual practices, and self- and collective determination) (Trask, 1993; McMullin, 2005). As Trinidad (2012a) indicates, "Land as place and sources of wisdom (Basso, 1996), and rediscovering them *collectively* and *dialogically* restores a spiritual dimension (Ball, 2002) of well-being" (p. 5; emphasis in original). This can be applied to other cultural communities who have faced parallel oppressive forces by deeply acknowledging and validating its way of life in a given geographic place.

The cornerstone of community epistemology is its way of living in place, and its symbolic and embodied way of expressing its cultural values. To survive and thrive is to deeply know one's genealogies and histories, and having the ability to practice, experience, and live one's culture well. Utilizing all human senses—listening, witnessing, observing, smelling, and feeling—CIPP can foster dialogue across multiple generations of a community in restoring and reclaiming indigenous and cultural ways of knowing and reclaiming a place and culture that have been exploited, uncared for, and commodified. In turn, the community can identify sources of wisdom through purposeful connections to place, practices, and responsibilities nurtured through collective action (Trinidad, 2012a).

Indigenization puts Indigenous knowledge, worldviews, and concerns at the center of practice. It helps a community know and understand theory and research from its own perspectives and purposes (Smith, 1999). **Reinhabitation**, a parallel process to indigenization, is also vital to Indigenous epistemology. It focuses on contextual, ecological, place-based education (McGinnis, 1999; Sale, 1985; Traina and Darley-Hill, 1995). Reinhabitation results in learning to live well, socially and ecologically, in a place or area that has been disrupted and injured through past exploitation (Berg and Dasmann, 1990) and eco-colonization (Watson, 2008), and learning how to live well from where one is (Orr, 1992). The meaning of *living well* differs geographically and culturally. Reinhabitation consists of re-creating an intimate, organic, and mutually nurturing relationship with a place. It is the art of restoring detailed knowledge of a place and restoring a sense of care and rootedness (Orr, 1992; Sale, 1985). Reinhabitation means regaining ownership, control, and access to the natural resources that sustain living and spirituality. It also means interweaving, replacing, or speaking against Western narratives of place that have been oppressive with Indigenous narratives that instill hope and healing.

A community can take part in indigenizing its geographic place through relationship building, utilizing community epistemology and values, and practicing the human spirit of connection, radical love, and sense of family. How these relationships are sustained takes deliberate thought and action. Knowledge production occurs collaboratively (Trinidad, 2012a; Kanahele, 1986; Meyer, 2001). Through relationships and mutual learning, a sense of responsibility, accountability, and solidarity for and with one another and place can lead to making things right and just (Trinidad, 2011). This process enhances the power of community voice that pushes for accountability and ethics based on community needs (Trinidad, 2012b).

CIPP: sociopolitical development and student–community engagement

CIPP incorporates student organizing or participation and sociopolitical development (Watts and Flanagan, 2007; Watts *et al.*, 1999, 2003; Watts and Guessous, 2006). It facilitates a process of learning about the root problems of oppression and inequality, and promotes both individual and collective empowerment as students authentically engage and participate with a specific geographic community.

Results from a study of a youth organic farm indicate that processes facilitated by the use of CIPP can provide access and engagement of critical ideas, social networks, and critical learning experiences (Trinidad, 2011). Findings also demonstrate the potential of CIPP to help Native Hawaiian young adults achieve the following learning outcomes: 1) identify the disparities that exist in their community; 2) critically explore the complexity of oppression and systemic inequalities related to health; 3) acquire a commitment to serve the community while cultivating a sense of *kuleana* (responsibility); and 4) participate in a knowledge-action-reflection cycle of critical praxis. Data suggest that CIPP can serve as a conduit to sociopolitical development among Native Hawaiian youth. Through its emphasis on power relations, critical consciousness, native epistemology, and attachment to place, CIPP has promise to build social change agents among Native Hawaiian youth. In general, CIPP can be a facilitative tool for encouraging young adults to recognize and confront existing inequalities in their community. This study provided inspiration for the FRINQ Race and Social Justice course.

The case study: FRINQ Race and Social Justice course

As the instructor for FRINQ, I intentionally integrated CIPP to bridge community service-learning projects and facilitate university–community partnerships regarding social sustainability, equity, and social change in Portland. Past studies on CIPP served as models as they provided sample learning opportunities that could be replicated and translated to community-based or -engaged education in higher education. The utilization of CIPP includes place-based learning opportunities such as youth summits, leadership conferences, community photovoice, talking circles, asset mapping, and auto-ethnographic work. It is work facilitated by educators yet implemented with or for community-based organizations and their members. For university instructors, CIPP can serve as a tool and approach that makes value-based praxis more tangible, accessible, and inclusive for indigenous and other communities of color. Most importantly, it can move practice toward social action and social justice (Prilleltensky, 2001) as it challenges structural oppression and makes practice accountable to the community or target population served.

Figure 13.2 **FRINQ Race and Social Justice curriculum**

Source: author

Fall	Winter	Spring
• How race is created and constructed by examining human biology, social analysis, racial identity, and other identities, history of domination • Project focus on one's personal experiences of racism and other oppressions • Participate in "Freedom School" (anti-racism community-based curriculum with American Friends Service Committee)	• How social justice is theorized • Examine how law, policy, public opinion, and other systemic dynamics are influenced by race and other oppressive forces • Project focus on a structural-historical analysis of a social issue related to race and other oppression • Service-learning project include volunteering at Portland's Youth Summit (sponsored by Youth Organized United to Help)	• How social justice is organized and implemented (social movement) • Examine leadership development, techniques and strategies of organizing people and communities • Analyze how nonprofit, community-based organization or grassroots group frame social change • Project focus on a social movement implemented by a grassroots group or community-based, nonprofit organization • Organize and implement a student-led collective service-learning project

The FRINQ Race and Social Justice yearlong course is one of a dozen FRINQ themes a freshman student can choose from. In Figure 13.2, each academic quarter focused on specific aspects of oppression and social justice. The fall quarter focused on unpacking the concept of race and systems of oppression. Students participated in a process of identifying oppressive forces and power and privilege in their own lives through the writing of one's critical auto-ethnography. Students also participated in a community-based curriculum, "Freedom Schools: Undoing Racism," with a community-based partner, American Friends of Service Committee. This provided engagement with social justice community organizers and courageous dialogues with community members about race and other identities related to social locations. The winter quarter examined the array of theories and conceptual frameworks of social justice. Particularly, students analyzed how laws, public policies, public perceptions, and other systemic dynamics influenced oppression and/or justice. Additionally, students were provided the opportunity to conduct small-scale, community-based research projects on a social issue of their choice and analyze how systemic oppressive forces, including historical factors, play out. As part of a collective service-learning project, students were assigned specific roles and responsibilities in volunteering at a Youth Summit. This provided an opportunity to show students how a community-based organization frames social justice and implements a project. In the spring quarter, students examined characteristics and processes of social movements focused on addressing racism and other oppressive forces on local, national, and global levels. Additionally, students examined leadership development, techniques and strategies of organizing people and communities, and how nonprofit, community-based organizations or grassroots groups framed social change. Most importantly, students organized and implemented their own collective social movement project. The scaffolded student-led processes and a two-tiered (one done collectively and one self-selected based on the student's interest area) community-based service-learning component explicitly provided students the opportunity to authentically engage in social justice work within Portland, as a place with unique but parallel history of oppression, and its diverse people in deeply meaningful ways.

Figure 13.3 **University Studies learning outcomes**

Source: author

Communication	• Students will enhance their capacity to communicate in various ways—writing, graphics, numeracy, and visual and oral means—to collaborate with others in group work, and be competent in appropriate communication technologies.
Inquiry and critical thinking	• Students will learn various modes of inquiry through interdisciplinary curricula—problem-posing, investigating, conceptualizing—in order to become active, self-motivated, and empowered learners.
Diversity of human experience	• Students will enhance their appreciation for and understanding of the rich complexity of the human experience through the study of differences in ethnic and cultural perspectives, class, race, gender, sexual orientation, and ability.
Ethics and social responsibility	• Students will expand their understanding of the impact and value of individuals and their choices on society, both intellectually and socially, through group projects and collaboration in learning communities.

As part of the University Studies (UNST) program requirements, all FRINQ courses need to provide learning opportunities that focus on four learning outcomes, as indicated in Figure 13.3. This case study puts special focus on two learning outcomes: 1) diversity of human experience; and 2) ethics and social responsibility.

The teaching team: Facilitators of processes of CIPP

The unique structure of FRINQ consists of a teaching team that facilitated and implemented the processes of CIPP, as indicated in Figure 13.4. The team included the professor, a learning community advisor (LCA), and a peer mentor (PM). Because the FRINQ was part of the First Year Experience, a residential life program, students enrolled must be part of a learning community. This component required students enrolled in this FRINQ to live in the same residential hall, participate in *additional* community-based learning opportunities in collaboration with a LCA.

Figure 13.4 **FRINQ teaching team structure**
Source: author

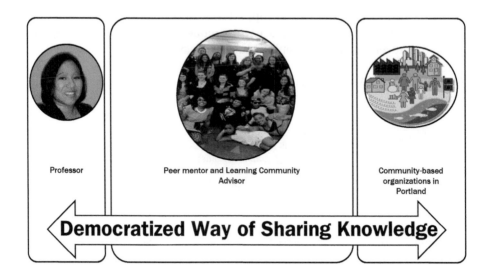

Professor   Peer mentor and Learning Community   Community-based
                   Advisor   organizations in
                                                               Portland

‹Democratized Way of Sharing Knowledge›

Scaffolded mentorship from both the LCA and the PM was an essential component. What emerged in the case study is how the integration of social and academic
support into the course created a deepened sense of community. Both the LCA and
PM shared their experiences from their stances and how their work helped promote student outcomes of diversity and social responsibilities. Additionally, they
highlighted key moments, processes of CIPP, and its impact.

Pablo's narrative as the LCA: living community

As a LCA, I had a very unique structure to work in. I attended the students' FRINQ
main sessions, and also lived on the same floor as these students in the residential
hall. This allowed for two things: a greater insight on each individual and also the
opportunity to take class content beyond the classroom. This structure and process provided me with the privilege to see each student in an academic setting, as
well as in a social environment. It led to greater insight and depth in understanding
their personal background and journey.

During our teaching team meetings, we would discuss each student's needs and
situation. I felt I was able to provide my evaluation or assessment of each person
based on their needs at a more cohesive level due to my knowledge of what was
going on in other courses and personal challenges they were facing.

This mentorship model provided an opportunity for race and social justice conversations that happened in the main sessions to be continued beyond. With a topic
such as race and social justice, every individual is impacted one way or the other.

More than once, the conversations held at the residential halls were emotional ones. These conversations ranged from feelings of internalized oppression to unmasking injustices in other parts of our communities. Additionally, many opportunities were available to apply course concepts into pop culture.

It was quite a journey filled with highs and lows being an LCA for a course such as this. Notably, I was the only LCA of color that particular academic year. Being part of the FRINQ, I was extremely in tune with the dynamics of race and power and any communication exchange I was a part of in my personal life. My radar for micro-aggressions and oppressive behaviors was very high.

As an LCA, I had an "open-door" policy, which meant that I was always available for critical discussions regarding media, or personal struggles through the lens of race and social justice. Within the teaching team, we had intentional outreach with community partners around the city, and different campus resource centers (e.g., Queer Resource Center, Diversity and Multicultural Student Services, and the Conflict Resolution Resource Center). We had two goals: linking or exposing students to different stories from members of different communities; and building networks of social justice advocates.

Kris's narrative as a PM: beyond bridging students and institution

For FRINQ students, a mentor can serve as a bridge between student and institution. Because mentor sessions occurred outside of the classroom and were provided in their own space and time, potential for relationship building was vast. Mentoring urges one to be critical about how to engage in the act of learning with people as a collective within the oppressive hierarchical structure that so many places of scholarly learning enforce. Race and racism are topics that invoke visceral reactions in people. Before I began my work with these students, I made sure to do research on some of the patterns and stages of learning that occur when people are urged to confront their political identities. I anticipated we would have difficult discussions; that the white students in the class would initially feel attacked and perhaps move into a place of understanding towards the end of the year. I hoped that the students of color present would feel a little more liberated and supported in their learning journeys because of our course.

It was not until mid-way through our year together that I realized how little I knew about the practice of, what bell hooks refers to as, **engaged pedagogy**. I was surprised to realize how deeply I had internalized that hierarchical learning structure, in spite of my acute awareness of its existence. As a mentor, enabling students to wholly engage in the classroom environment required humility and inquisitiveness. It required patience and sometimes the suspension of judgment. That is not to say that one cannot bring oneself authentically to the table when in a position of power. On the contrary, my work with these students led me to realize that the most effective way to help create an authentic learning environment was for me to be as transparent and vulnerable with them as I expected them to be with me.

In order to bring ourselves closer, we did a lot of community-building activities, and I tried to focus on creating opportunities for each student's unique voice to be heard whether in written or oral form. It was important to me to use multiple media platforms in order to stimulate various senses and informational process-ing systems. We explored hip-hop often, and shared song lyrics and videos with each other that we could analyze in the context of historical anti-Black racism and trauma. We did free-writes at the top of every mentor session to ground ourselves in that day's lesson and readings. We were very process-oriented. Upon reflec-tion, I realized that this was not as sensitive to those students who were more task-oriented in their learning styles. Because the readings and lessons were often packed with historical events and dense theories, we worked on making the infor-mation we were receiving relevant to current events and to our personal lives. I think this is where the students became most engaged in the material.

Our mentor sessions were sometimes very intellectually and practically driven. I realized quickly how important it was for me to assist the students with navigating the bureaucratic beast that is college. We brought our identities into even these conversations, especially when attempting to locate resources for those students who identified as disabled or as queer and/or transgender.

Some of our richest conversations began simply with sharing the highlights of our week with each other at the top of a mentor session. I witnessed trust develop between our small groups gradually. Because each mentor session consisted of only six to ten people, we were able to become quite intimate with one another. It became clear that we shared a mutual respect for these spaces we worked hard to maintain. As we closed in on the gap between student and teacher, we were also able to bridge the gap between personal and political, enabling us to internalize our academic content and to form well-rounded perspectives that were truly our own. Thus, a sense of personal and social responsibility developed genuinely. I am indebted to these students for challenging me to push my growing edge in my role as their mentor, and I am so grateful to them for their dedication and authenticity.

The impact of CIPP through student eportfolios

For the purpose of this case study, two former students who were active in Dr. Trinidad's recent community-based participatory action project at a school dis-trict share their insights on what emerged in their eportfolios to demonstrate the ongoing progress and growth of continuous engagement with social change. They were asked to pull out examples of student learning opportunities, including com-munity-based, service-learning projects (with community partners such as Youth Organized United to Help, American Friends of Community Service, Reaching and Empowering All People, and the Living Cully Eco-District Partnership), and their impact on student outcomes of diversity and social responsibility.

Keisha's story: The awakened Pinay/Filipina American from Hawai'i

As a college freshman going into FRINQ, I did not even know what social justice was. Surprisingly, it has been one of the most influential classes I have taken so far. My whole thought process and perceptions changed throughout the year and I am still applying what I learned. When I took Dr. Trinidad's FRINQ, I had very little knowledge and understanding of social justice. I did not understand the basic terminologies (e.g., privilege, power, and systems of oppression). Dr. Trinidad has successfully provided me the groundwork for my understanding of social justice, and it has affected me to such an extent that I am applying it in my daily life experiences, including how I move in this world.

The topic of race and social justice is extensive and complex. I struggled a lot. I could not wrap my head around it within such a short time. Luckily, Dr. Trinidad was very intentional with the lessons she shared by connecting them to real life examples, and providing history and readings from diverse authors to help us understand the course. With all the challenges I faced with the course, one day everything just clicked. I think the way Dr. Trinidad framed the class was essential in understanding social justice, because she first eased the students in by focusing on our own oppression and privilege, and I was able to critique my experiences from my childhood to the present. It helped me understand which systems were in play to keep that power. In looking at our own privilege and oppression, I was able to see where I have and do not have power in certain aspects of my identity. It also made me aware of what I can do to utilize my privilege to become an ally with groups of people who do not have that privilege.

In the second term, we focused on certain macro systematic oppressions that we were interested in. This project helped me understand the intersectionalities between other forms of oppression. I easily connected it to the media and understood the ways it was upholding Eurocentric standards of beauty and living, and how that perpetuated stereotypes of people of color. Being constantly bombarded by images of only fair-skinned people, I began to understand why diversity and representation is necessary in the media and critique positions of power. There are so many different types of people from different cultures and when they are represented accurately in larger systems, they could take part in the power structure and recreate a different system. Finally, we learned in order to have equity among oppressed groups of people, these systems need to be dismantled as a whole. As a class, we thought about our own roles to create change, and what ideals and models to use to create the needed change.

When the class finished, I was not able to stop thinking about the things I've learned, because it was so easy to apply them to any issues that were happening. Before taking on social responsibility, I think it is important for the individual to keep learning and to become conscious of any problems by dissecting the oppressive forces that play out in the issue. FRINQ was very helpful in improving my critical thinking skills, because we looked at social issues through a critical lens. It made me examine the macro systems and how power played out. In regards to being socially responsible, I made a goal for myself to speak out about things that are problematic (e.g., addressing racial slurs) or making a habit to call people out in offensive situations. These are little things that can make a difference. FRINQ has been very influential. To this day, I continue to unlearn the prejudices I have and strive to become socially conscious.

Berenis's story: Latina power

Having the opportunity to take the FRINQ course at PSU, I can honestly say that it has granted me with the gift of helping me better understand my social responsibility when it comes to equity-related issues. I gained an abundant amount of new information through the many assignments we had that consisted of writing papers, presenting the readings to the class, and getting to work personally with a diverse community. Although all the assignments were very beneficial to me, there were some that impacted me more than others and that really focused on understanding my social responsibility. Those assignments are Mini-Paper #4: My Commitment to Ending Racism, Mini-Paper #1: Sex Trafficking, and the assignments that were part of getting to work with the Cully community.

At the beginning of the term, our assignments really focused on our identities and our understanding of social issues. It was at this time when I had the chance to find out who I am, what I really cared about, and what led me to understanding my identities. The Mini-Paper #4: My Commitment to Ending Racism was a paper that highlighted what I learned about the different kinds of oppressions that many people of color face on a daily basis. This paper helped me clarify my commitment to what I wanted to see done. As a woman of color, I felt a social responsibility to stand up for my community. By identifying as a Mexican, I became aware that my race is not portrayed in a pretty picture, but I also became aware that it is my responsibility to my community to not be ashamed. I needed to show people that we are not the same as the media portrays us, and that we too deserve to have a voice.

The next assignment that helped me understand diversity and social responsibility was Mini-Paper #1: Sex Trafficking done during the winter term. It was an eye-opener for me. It allowed me to learn something new about my community that I was not aware of. We had to choose a system of our choice to research on. I chose sex trafficking, because I wanted to learn more about this topic and see if it existed in the Portland area. To my surprise, Portland was one of the top cities where sex trafficking occurred. I knew I had to do something to help diminish this problem. This assignment helped me clarify my responsibility by informing people how this social issue and the system affect many girls in our community. As a community, we have a social responsibility to be aware of what is happening, and not just ignore what is right in front of our eyes.

During spring term, we had the opportunity to work together with the Cully community. The Cully community is unfortunately experiencing gentrification which is negatively affecting many of the families of color that live there. With this assignment, I had the chance to apply what I learned from the readings, research, and critical reflections to working one-on-one with the Cully neighborhood. This is where I demonstrated my social responsibility to the Cully neighborhood. I knew what was happening to the community was not just or fair. They have the right to be heard and to voice how they felt about what was directly affecting them.

As you can see, all the assignments that I described helped me develop an understanding of what diversity and social responsibility mean to me. Social responsibility to me is knowing that no matter what the cause might be, I am obligated to take action in a way that I know will benefit the people and society as a whole. I am very much thankful for taking this course. Without it, I would not have seen the importance of knowing what responsibility means or how it looks in a positive manner, and how to apply it to life. Knowing this will most definitely help me both professionally and personally.

The impact of CIPP through community-based partnerships

Two long-term, community-based partners, American Friends for Service Committee (AFSC) with Mireaya Medina as our key person and Youth Organized United to Help (Y.O.U.th) with Imani Muhammad as our key person, provided their experiences as community partners in service-learning projects and research. They were asked to share how our partnerships promoted student outcomes on diversity and social responsibility and impacted the community.

Mireaya's narrative: Fostering peace through partnership

Dr. Trinidad has been a valuable partner in our social justice collaborative projects. The Portland Peace Program and the Seattle Healing Justice Program both strive to develop youth leadership through social justice skill building. By partnering with Dr. Trinidad's FRINQ classes, we have collectively worked with over 200 students to learn the roots of institutionalized racism and poverty by hosting interactive workshops that get youth to think critically and creatively find new ways to eradicate racism in their communities.

Our collaborative work in undoing institutionalized racism has been successful, mostly because of the partnership with Dr. Trinidad's classes. The mutual benefit, in my opinion, comes from the profound shift in the student participants' ideas around the subject of race. After the workshops, students expressed in their reflection assignments that they have made some internal changes. The reciprocity of our partnership is found in creating a new cultural awareness in youth.

Here are two quotes that speak truth to power from FRINQ participants last year.

> Many of the questions that we were given helped sharpen my critical inquiry, understanding of human diversity, social responsibility and ethical skills (Keisha Mateo).

> Human diversity is the acknowledgement of our differences and respecting them. In terms of race, there is clearly more oppression against people of color in the past and in the present. To ignore that is irresponsible (Cesar Ortiz).

Dr. Trinidad has made it her mission to inspire not only her students, but also our community to dig deeper and to change those things around us that are inequitable.

Imani's narrative: Building youth empowerment through hip-hop pedagogy

The journey of a grassroots project collaborating with PSU for several years has been an amazing opportunity for our nonprofit and its participants. The partnership between Y.O.U.th and PSU students through Dr. Trinidad's class has been an important and intentional experience. The Y.O.U.th Summit tends to push boundaries and promote social justice from a unique perspective. It has continued to enlighten and inspire many people especially the freshman in FRINQ. Over the years, we have seen and heard from students who stated they had never explored or felt like they were given the opportunity to embrace another culture outside of their own. The Y.O.U.th Summit provided the space for them to explore their own biases and prejudices.

One highlight comes from our second year in partnership. This FRINQ class was so inspired by the workshops and youth talent showcase that they organized their own spring service-learning project, which followed a similar approach and format to the Summit. The students also were able to invite back to Portland, Jasiri X, who was the Y.O.U.th Summit keynote speaker and guest performer. His music and lecture was so inspiring and motivating that the students brought him back to Portland.

The Y.O.U.th Summit in partnership with PSU students has been an opportunity for our local nonprofit and our partners to expose and showcase Portland-based organizers, workshop presenters, and local artists to a demographic that are preparing to be our next leaders and advocates for change in our world and local communities. The link between local nonprofits and college students is important to the growth and awareness of social justice and diversity. PSU students are preparing to be the next leaders, while the Y.O.U.th Summit is a networking and educational platform that allows those from various backgrounds to learn and join together in the name of youth, justice, inspiration, and change; this partnership is unique and has resulted in a multitude of change and impact in all the participants over the years.

As a true Oregonian, there have not been many long-lasting events of this kind that pulls together government, university, small businesses, and nonprofit sections in one place in the name of education, information, and knowledge to/for our youth. The Y.O.U.th Summit has remained consistent and will be celebrating ten years in 2016. Through the continued partnership over the last six years, PSU with Dr. Trinidad's assistance has helped stabilize and maintain the intended purpose of the Summit and its need in our community.

Most of the influential feedback came from PSU students who wrote reflections of their experience. Many of them had never been a part of a summit or conference of this kind. Countless students wrote reflections expressing their desire to continue to learn more about social justice and become more involved in their community or college career. A handful of reflections over the years existed where the students admitted to their own stereotypes and biases, and realized they were lies that had shaped their social construct. Something worth noting is how for the first time, students experienced being around Black culture, particularly hip-hop culture. They disclosed the stereotypes they had, and how the experience being involved in the Youth Summit removed barriers for engagement and lies they had been living. Most importantly, their personal understanding of hip-hop was completely changed. The students appreciated the Summit for opening their eyes to another world and reality, which challenged their worldviews. Simultaneously, some Black students expressed empowerment and enlightenment for being a part of such a transformative learning opportunity that integrates hip-hop culture and Black identity.

Without the partnership, the Y.O.U.th Summit would not have practical data and research to support the work that we have done over the years. This partnership has been remarkable and supportive in the work in bettering and changing our communities through social justice with youth as central.

Lessons learned as a community rises

The utilization of CIPP provides processes for social change. Centralizing Portland as a place provides learning opportunities for students to understand diversity and develop their sense of social responsibility and ethics in the work they do. From my work at PSU, specifically through FRINQ Race and Social Justice, I conclude with key lessons learned that implicate the role of higher education (Brandt, 2004) and the promise CIPP has for advancing social change relevant to communities of color.

CIPP's process of decolonization through power analysis requires learning how to recognize disruptions and injury and address colonial causes (Trinidad, 2011), and develop an act of resistance that rejects and transforms dominant, mainstream ideas (Bowers, 2001). It is a "process of cultural and historical liberation; act of confrontation with a dominant system of thought" (hooks, 1992, p. 1). Decolonization's main intent is to take apart the story, reveal underlying texts, and give voice to things that are often known intuitively (Smith, 1999). It is the process of "com[ing] to know the past" and to "hold alternative histories" and "knowledges" (Smith, 1999, p. 34). To us, it means to decolonize our minds and ways. I learned that this process takes time and patience. It's challenging to partake in because of shame or fear. Our role in higher education is to provide such process early on in a student's developmental trajectory.

CIPP's process of indigenization "brings out spatial and historical dimensions to reclaim one's own story or past—local and global, the present, communities, cultures, languages, and social practices" (Trinidad, 2011, p. 211), and foregrounds indigenous knowledge, worldviews, and concern at the center (Grande, 2004; Smith, 1999, Trask, 2000). I learned that at times histories of communities of color were kept silent through power and control. I learned that knowing our Indigenous histories have brought pain and trauma. Healing is not done overnight. It is a continuing process that needs to be done in community. Higher education needs to provide such a space of collective healing.

CIPP's process of sociopolitical development refers to "the psychological process that leads to and supports social and political action" (Watts *et al.*, 1999, p. 256). I learned that the socio-emotional aspect of social justice work requires great stamina to engage with deep feelings of rage, anger, hopelessness, and despair. I learned that places like student-run organizations and university—community partnerships can provide a circle of aloha to deal with such feelings. We need not cope with discovering the many oppressive forces that play out in our communities alone. We must lean forward or inward for support, including reaching out to our allies.

CIPP's last process, "aloha-ization," a term I will coin here, is the process of caring and loving a place and its people, and the desire to make a difference in making it a better place (Trinidad, 2011). I learned that this process leads to the engagement of social responsibility and ethics, individually and collectively. Such engagement encourages an ongoing discussion on accountability. I learned that scaffolded mentoring can assist in this process. Hence, reaching out to community members and those that came before us can provide guidance. I learned that we need allies outside of one's respective community to push for our shared agenda of social justice. I also learned it requires great amount of tending to grow our community.

Reflecting on my journey and role in the academy, it brings a sense of pride and vulnerability. We have a sense of social responsibility to make PSU a place where we can integrate CIPP processes. As demonstrated in this chapter, each can serve as mentors and role models that exude care for students' talents, strengths, and passions towards social change. I call for PSU to strive to provide places that embrace all identities and social locations, harness a sense of belonging and appreciating all of a person and community, and acknowledge its genealogy and spiritual dimensions, and make them matter. It is my hope that PSU can be a place that perpetuates aloha, and provides a place for emerging leaders to perform and practice the aloha ethics. Together, we can rise and become a community of warriors and protectors of peace, freedom, and aloha!

References

Agnew, J.A. (1987). *Place and Politics: The Geographical Mediation of State and Society.* Boston, MA: Allen & Unwin.

Ball, M.W. (2002). "People speaking silently to themselves": An examination of Keith Basso's philosophical speculations on "sense of place" in Apache cultures. *American Indian Quarterly*, 26(3), 460-478.

Basso, K.H. (1996). Wisdom sits in places: Notes on a Western Apache landscape. In S. Feld & K.H. Basso (Eds.), *Sense of Places* (pp. 53-90). Santa Fe, NM: School of American Research Press.

Berg, P., & Dasmann, R.F. (1990). Reinhabiting California. In V. Andruss, J. Plant, & E. Wright (Eds.), *Home! A Bioregional Reader*. Philadelphia, PA: New Society.

Brandt, C.B. (2004). A thirst for justice in the arid Southwest: The role of epistemology and place in higher education. *Educational Studies*, 36(1), 93-107.

Bowers, C.A. (2001). *Educating for Eco-justice and Community*. Athens, GA: The University of Georgia Press.

Cresswell, T. (2004). *Place: A Short Introduction*. Malden, MA: Blackwell Publishing Ltd.

Grande, S.M.A. (2004). *Red Pedagogy: Native American Social and Political Thought*. Lanham, MA: Rowman & Littlefield Publishers, Inc.

hooks, b. (1992). *Black Looks: Race and Representation*. Boston, MA: South End Press.

Johnston-Goodstar, K., Trinidad, A.M.O., & Tecle, A. (2010). Critical pedagogy through the reinvention of place: Two cases of youth resistance. In B.J. Porfilio & P.R. Carr (Eds.), *Youth Culture, Education and Resistance: Subverting the Commercial Ordering of Life* (pp. 197-216). Rotterdam, The Netherlands: Sense Publishers.

Kanahele, G. (1986). *Ku Kanaka Stand Tall: A Search for Hawaiian Values*. Honolulu, HI: University of Hawai'i Press.

McGinnis, V. (1999). *Bioregionalism*. New York, NY: Routledge.

McMullin, J. (2005). The call to life: Revitalizing a healthy Hawaiian identity. *Social Science & Medicine*, 61, 809-820. doi:10.1016/j.socscimed.2004.08.051

Meyer, M.A. (2001). Our own liberation: Reflections on Hawaiian epistemology. *The Contemporary Pacific*, 13(1), 124-148. doi:10.1353/cp.2001.0024.

Orr, D. (1992). *Ecological Literacy*. Albany, NY: State University of New York Press.

Prilleltensky, I. (2001). Value-based praxis in community psychology: Moving toward social justice and social action. *American Journal of Community Psychology*, 29(5), 747-778. doi:10.1023/A:1010417201918

Sale, K. (1985). *Dwellers in the Land: The bioregional Vision*. San Francisco, CA: Sierra Club Books.

Smith, L.T. (1999). *Decolonizing Methodologies: Research and Indigenous Peoples*. New York, NY: Zed Books.

Traina, F., & Darley-Hill, S. (1995). *Perspectives in Bioregional Education*. Troy, OH: North American Association for Environmental Education (NAAEE).

Trask, H. (1993). *From a Native Daughter: Colonialism and Sovereignty in Hawai'i*. Honolulu, HI: University of Hawai'i Press.

Trask, H. (2000). Native social capital: The case of Hawaiian sovereignty and Ka Lahui Hawaii. *Policy Sciences*, 33, 385-385. doi: 10.1023/A:1004870517612.

Trinidad, A.M.O. (2011). Sociopolitical development through Critical Indigenous Pedagogy of Place: Preparing Native Hawaiian young adults to become change agents. *Hulili: Multidisciplinary Research on Hawaiian Well-Being*, 7, 185-221.

Trinidad, A.M.O. (2012a). Critical Indigenous Pedagogy of Place: A framework to indigenize a youth food justice movement. *Journal of Indigenous Social Development*, 1(1), 1-17.

Trinidad, A.M.O. (2012b). Indigenising the sustainability movement through Critical Indigenous Pedagogy of Place: A case study of a youth farm. *The Journal of Pacific Studies*, 32, 45-58.

Watson, T.K. (2008). *Ho'i Hou ia Papahanaumoku: A history of ecocolonization in the Pu'uhonua of Wai'anae* (Unpublished dissertation). Honolulu, HI: University of Hawai'i.

Watts, R.J., & Flanagan, C. (2007). Pushing the envelope on youth civic engagement: A developmental and liberation psychology perspective. *Journal of Community Psychology*, 35, 779-792.

Watts, R.J., & Guessous, O. (2006). Sociopolitical development: The missing link in research and policy on adolescents. In S. Ginwright, P. Noguera, & J. Cammarota (Eds.), *Beyond Resistance! Youth Activism and Community Change: New Democratic Possibilities for Practice and Policy for America's Youth* (pp. 59-80). New York, NY: Routledge/Taylor & Francis Group.

Watts, R.J., Griffith, D.M., & Abdul-Adil, J. (1999). Sociopolitical development as an antidote for oppression: Theory and action. *American Journal of Community Psychology*, 27, 255-271.

Watts, R.J., Williams, N.C., & Jagers, R.J. (2003). Sociopolitical development. *American Journal of Community Psychology*, 31, 185-194.

Zullo, R., & Gates, A. (2008). Labor education in the time of dismay. *Labor Studies Journal*, 33(2), 179-202. doi: 10.1177/0160449X07303079

14

Building culture
Design thinking and architecture–community relationships

B.D. Wortham-Galvin

The perception of the architect as a genius artist whose buildings manifest mysteriously through an opaque creative process has been a fixture in both the mythologies and realities of real figures and fictions of the architect—Ayn Rand's Howard Roark remains the archetype despite the fact that most current architectural students and/or the public have never read *The Fountainhead*. Charles-Edouard Jennert changed his name to Le Corbusier in configuring himself as the revolutionary artiste-architect of modernism at the start of the 20th century. Frank Lloyd Wright infamously wanted not only to be the maestro of the design of his buildings, but also to control the furniture, place settings, décor, and even fashion of its occupants. The contemporary generation of star architects (whose father figure is Frank Gehry and whose most recent loss is Zaha Hadid) have fashioned themselves as design commodities whose artistic genius has become branded and consumed. The tenacity of this position of the architect and their work are the predominating contemporary cultural understandings (as well as aspiration of hundreds of North American (if not global) architects and architectural students).

This prevalent ethos of what it means to be an architect prompted a counter exhortation, in 1968, at the 99th national convening of the American Institute of Architects—in Portland (for the first and only time). Civil rights leader Whitney Young served as the keynote speaker to this gathering of architects. His lamentation to the group is now infamous in academic circles (whose focus is community-based architecture). Young admonished,

[…] you are not a profession that has distinguished itself by your social and civic contributions to the cause of civil rights, and I am sure this has not come to you as a shock. You are most distinguished by your thunderous silence and your complete irrelevance. […] That architects as a profession wouldn't as a group stand up and say something about this, is disturbing to me. You are employers, you are key people in the planning of our cities today. You share the responsibility for the mess we are in terms of the white noose around the central city. It didn't just happen. We didn't just suddenly get in this situation. It was carefully planned (Designing Activism, 2011).

If one takes Douglas Kelbaugh's (2004) assessment of architectural education at face value, then almost 40 years later the thunderous silence remains, leading most to believe there has been little movement in heeding Whitney Young's call. Kelbaugh critiques the education of the potential architect based on seven fallacies:

- The architect as individual artist whose sole (and highest) pursuit is personal expression

- The assertion of perpetual innovation and originality in all design work

- The embracing of extreme positions for the sake of provocation

- The focus on the building as singular object, rather than on context or relationships to that which already exists

- The selling of architecture (and architects) as a global commodity and/or brand

- The emphasis of architecture and architects as being in service only to those with power and/or wealth

- Architecture as an act of consumption

In many ways Kelbaugh's concerns about architectural education (and praxis) are still true today. Nevertheless, in the past decade there has been a move of, what is now termed, public interest design from the margins to a re-centering of architectural education and practice.

This chapter will first look at the distinction between design products and design process in architecture. Second, it will show how values-based design thinking has the opportunity to set up various partnerships between architectural education and communities in order to effect change in architectural practice. Finally, architecture–community relationships will be highlighted in a discussion of a relationship between Portland State University's School of Architecture and the nonprofit neighborhood organization, the Rosewood Initiative, as a way of rethinking the fallacies of architectural education.

Architecture as design product versus design process

It is clear that Frank Gehry's design for the Guggenheim Museum in the Spanish industrial port of Bilbao remains a watershed moment in the nexus of architecture and the commodification of culture and design. The ubiquitous phrase the "Bilbao effect" speaks to the power of this moment. It is notable that the phenomenon surrounding this museum in fact speaks more to the architecture and architect than it does to the client and the collection. Opening in 1997, Frank Gehry's tour de force of sculptural titanium generated about $500 million in economic activity and roughly $100 million in taxes during its first three years and approximately five million visitors in its first five years (Rybczynski, 2002, p. 138). As journalist Wayne Curtis (2006, p. 113) notes, "It's evidently no longer enough for a city to have a defining single icon or a richly textured and complex history. It must now have a brand". The "effect" that cities believe in is that star architect(ure)s will brand them and attract the same quantities of visitors and dollars that Bilbao Guggenheim did in its first decade of operation. The "effect" on the relationship between culture, neighborhoods, and architecture has been that (before Bilbao Guggenheim even opened) other cities began commissioning their own iconoclastic buildings, which supported the rise of the star architect, commodified the cultural impact of architecture, and made the collections and/or missions of these museums secondary to the consumption of the architectural spectacle.[1]

The fixation of architectural praxis with the commodification of aesthetic genius in the 20th and 21st centuries has been supported by an emphasis on the architect as reified author of the artistic object, rather than as facilitator of cultural practices.[2] Whether under the rubric of modernism or postmodernism, the everyday needs and experiences of people have been glossed over. In the former, the public as people are rendered generic and universal in their cultural praxis; in the latter, the public as people are defined as consumers of culture in the commodification of the container (architecture). In fact the conventional and ubiquitous global notion of architecture as practice concerned primarily with an aesthetic agenda is increasingly being challenged by heretofore fringe activities that have started to become mainstream under the monikers of public interest design, democratic design,

---

1 Rosalind Krauss (1990) provides a clear and early articulation of the commodification of the museum that later became known as the Bilbao effect. Paul Allen (cofounder of Microsoft) commissioned Frank Gehry to design the Experience Music Project in Seattle in 1996 prior to the opening of the Bilbao Guggenheim. In 1999 the Corcoran Gallery of Art held an invited competition (with just Gehry, Daniel Libeskind, and Santiago Calatrava competing) for the design of an addition to its Beaux Arts home; Gehry won the commission but through controversy and funding it was never built. Daniel Libeskind's Jewish Museum in Berlin attracted 350,000 visitors before it had any exhibits. For discussions of this museum phenomenon see: Rybczynski (2002); Curtis (2006); Yudell (2010); Greub and Greub (2006).

2 I have discussed this idea further relative to architectural praxis in two publications: Wortham-Galvin (2012, 2016).

and/or tactical urbanism. All of these activities place a focus on process first as a driver of the design product.

Towards a values-based (design thinking) process

In writing about principles that guide historic preservation activities in the United States, Randall Mason (2006, p. 26) notes that today's struggle with memory culture (the complex relationship between identity, community, and culture) is distinguishable from that of the early 20th century in at least three ways:

- The current memory culture is more grassroots and therefore less elitist (although these are matters of emphasis and degree, not absolute terms)

- It is more openly politicized, and the awareness of unequal power among agents in the memory culture is notable (witness the ubiquitous concern with "participation" and "access" these days)

- Contemporary memory culture is inseparable (or nearly so) from the market

While Mason's aim is to contextualize the emergence of a new model for preservation practice in the United States, both his characterization of the context and his proposition for a new methodology for preservation are relevant for the rethinking of architectural processes and how they are introduced into educational models via heretofore fringe activities operating under the previously mentioned names public interest design, democratic design, and/or tactical urbanism.

Public interest design, democratic design, and/or tactical urbanism share philosophical foundations that emphasize that the design of our built environment is socially and politically charged and, thus, design thinking should be a tool for furthering social justice issues.[3] These modes of creative action provide a means of addressing intractable human concerns (aka wicked problems). All three engage in socially oriented, civic practices that emphasize the role of the public in place making in an increasingly privatized society. All three also emphasize various levels of participatory action in the making of things and places, with a particular focus on extending architecture processes to those people and places left out, or behind, design-development decisions. These movements are now worldwide as they intertwine the cultural and physical and have created knowledge communities/networks that are informing local practice. Certainly in the case of public interest or democratic design current research demonstrates that more than 80% of students and young professionals demand more opportunities to engage and learn skills in this area (Feldman *et al.*, 2013). What these various practices suggest is the need for codifying and propagating value-based design processes.

---

3 Key texts for further reading on these topics include: Meron (2012) and Wortham-Galvin (2013).

The methodology used by Kounkuey Design Initiative (KDI) in the Kibera Space Project is an exemplar of value-based processes being implemented in design (Odbert and Mulligan, 2014). While working in Nairobi's informal settlements, KDI sought to transform marginal waste areas into "Productive Public Spaces." For KDI, productive public space:

1. transforms an environmental liability into usable public space;

2. is authored and operated by its end-users collaborating with outside groups;

3. integrated income-generating and socially empowering uses;

4. adds value to a space without alienating the original community;

5. meets expressed community priorities and links to larger improvement efforts; and, 6. uses strong design concepts to create beautiful places (Odbert and Mulligan, 2014, p. 179).

This certainly is what Mason suggests for memory culture work as well, as he notes that the shift is from a focus on the aesthetic object to its significance. Mason's (2006, p. 35) arguments for a values-centered preservation include: the ability for more holistic understanding of places that support a large range of values; the inclusion of more diversity of stakeholders and full recognition of whom they might be; comprehensive knowledge about a site's value; and revealing gaps in current knowledge. While Mason is talking about places and sites in terms of preservation, the same arguments could apply to architecture, the making of a sustainable city, and how those ideas are taught to architectural students so that they will carry them into practice.

What KDI and Mason represent is one part of a larger process model known as design thinking. Design thinking has a wide body of literature that began in the 1960s but has flourished in earnest in the 21st century and is proffered by a variety of disciples to include: architecture, design, engineering, business, computer science, and neuroscience. Published origins are often traced to Herbert Simon's *The Sciences of the Artificial* (1968), Victor Papanek's *Design for the Real World* (1972), Horst Rittel's *Dilemmas in a General Theory of Planning* (1973), Robert McKim's *Experiences in Visual Thinking* (1973), and Peter Rowe's *Design Thinking* (1987). Today design thinking is most oft characterized as a mode of creative action that provides a means of addressing intractable human concerns (aka wicked problems).[4] Design thinking is characterized by: the exploration of present and future conditions; simultaneous alternative scenarios; identifying both known and

4 Horst Rittel is credited with coining and conceptualizing "wicked problems" as first published in a response to Rittel by Churchman (1967). Rittel finally published his idea in Rittel and Webber (1973). Essentially a wicked problem is one difficult to solve (or recognize and define) because of the complex interdependencies involved. Others who characterized this effort include: Faste *et al.* (1993); Brown (2009); and Buchanan (1992).

ambiguous terrain to discover hidden and marginalized parameters or constraints; iteration; redefinition of the initial problem; embracing ambiguity; using divergent thinking to offer variant ideas; using convergent thinking to prefer, resolve, and realize solutions based on the divergent iterations; and/or seeing all design activity as social activity. In other words, design thinking is a process- not product- driven model.[5] Design thinking is, therefore, at odds with the late 20th-century models set up by the much-lauded "Bilbao effect" that commodifies the architecture and collections into a brand/product to be consumed.

The implications of a value-based process of design can translate to a community-based architectural education by allowing plural conceptions of place; and, designing capaciously from the points of view of experts *and* lay people so that values, priorities, and management are not determined a priori. Design education that emphasizes university–community relationships, thus, can be characterized by processes which: identify both known and ambiguous terrain to discover hidden and marginalized parameters or constraints; redefine the problem *with* the community; use divergent thinking to offer variant ideas; use convergent thinking to prefer, resolve, and realize solutions based on the divergent iterations; and see all design activity as social activity. In other words, architecture–community design is a process- not product- driven model.

Architecture–community relationships

Community-based architectural education is not a new phenomenon in the architectural academy (it just carries a new term—public interest design). Anna Goodman (2015a) traces the history of university–community relationships in architectural education in the United States, pointing to its initial emergence in the 1930s particularly through the New Deal programs (such as the Works Progress Administration) and at universities such as Black Mountain College in North Carolina. Architecture schools reinvigorated their orientation toward this work during the social and civic movements of the 1950s–1960s leading to the establishment of many university-based community design centers.

Thus, this type of activity has a history. But perhaps what it has lacked until its strong reemergence in the 21st century is a critical eye toward both processes and products of architecturally based university–community partnerships. On its surface it has seemed like a way to allow students to gain real world making experiences while also providing assistance to underserved communities and populations. But as Goodman (2015b, p. 15) notes, while "praised for promoting social responsibility, the practice has also been criticized for aestheticizing poverty." She

---

5 I discuss this critical distinction between design process and design product in Wortham-Galvin (2012).

also asserts that the academy needs to move beyond whether a program "does good" or "works" based on the delivered architectural product to addressing more structural assessments of "how does it work" and "what work does it do" in terms of social-cultural networks and needs, not just physical and/or aesthetic ones. This shift is one that can help to destabilize the traditional role of architect as expert. As Kenny Cupers (2014, p. 6) exhorts, "An analysis of the social project of architecture today can no longer remain within the realms of intent, form, or representation but needs to tie these to consequence and affect."

How do we assess the efficacy of these community-based, service-learning projects burgeoning in the architecture academy? Using Hugh Sockett's (1998) philosophical analysis of levels of trust within university–community partnerships provides a frame with which critical questions regarding community-based architectural education can be made transparent.

As mentioned in the introduction to this volume, Sockett uses the terms Service, Exchange, Cooperative, and Systematic and Transformative to describe the four types of university–community relationships. How can design thinking allow us to understand how to constructive effective partnerships which allow residents to manage change in achieving sustainable urban places? How do differing resources, expertise, power, and/or agendas affect the efficacy of design thinking processes and products? A discussion of the relationship between the School of Architecture at Portland State University and the Rosewood Initiative (within Sockett's schema) serves as a means to illuminate these issues.

The Rosewood Initiative

> Rosewood to me is a place where my dreams, goals and passion ignited. It is a lifeline or a heartbeat in the community. Where people young and old of all nationalities come together. Where community partners offer services to support the community. Three years ago Rosewood took me in with open arms and believed in me and became my family. I have had the privilege of being a part of various Rosewood projects. I will continue to be a petal in the Rosewood Initiative to serve and represent the community (Rosewood resident Valerie Salazar).[6]

Located at the easternmost edge of Portland, Oregon, Rosewood is a new neighborhood (in a city that historically defines itself via the neighborhood system). It is not newly constructed or incorporated, but rather newly compiled from bits of surrounding neighborhoods by the mayor of Portland in 2011 as part of his, then newly launched, Neighborhood Prosperity Initiative. Little pieces of several older areas that needed some rejuvenation were separated from the neighborhoods to which they had previously been adjoined, and were compiled to form Rosewood.

6 The Rosewood Initiative, www.rosewoodinitiative.org, accessed May 2014.

The Portland Bureau of Planning and Sustainability recognizes that the Rose-wood area has distressed Census (2010) tracts, defined as areas with higher than citywide poverty rates (16%) and/or lower than citywide median household income.[7] The area contains many large, multifamily dwellings (with 90% of the neighborhood population living therein), creating a density of 18 people per acre, as compared to the Portland average, which is just over seven people per acre. Portland Census (2010) tracts show a minority population of 47%, twice that of the Portland citywide average. There are no public spaces, parks, or libraries within the Rosewood boundaries and the neighborhood has also officially been declared a food desert.

In 2011 a makeshift community center, the Rosewood Initiative, was formed in an abandoned space in a strip mall that was once a dry cleaner. The community has banded together and begun a nonprofit organization of the same name whose mission is, in their own words, "dedicated to making the Rosewood area a desir-able place to live, work and play."[8] Challenged by high crime rates and some apa-thetic residents, they are trying to change the way the rest of the Portland-Metro area looks at their little corner of the city. In their original location (that came with no heat, a bullet hole in the storefront window, poorly lit, unfurnished, and walls stripped down to the studs), they held neighborhood meetings, youth nights, and other activities under the facilitation of Jenny Glass (then an AmeriCorps worker and now Executive Director of the Rosewood Initiative). In the summer of 2011, B.D. Wortham-Galvin (the author)—newly arrived to the city of Portland—went to a meeting of community leaders at the East Portland Neighborhood Associa-tion and met Jenny Glass. Glass and Wortham-Galvin have facilitated a variety of engagements between Rosewood residents and Portland State University students that fall across Sockett's spectrum between 2011 and the present day.

Having just met, Glass and Wortham-Galvin entered into a service relationship in the fall of 2011. This level of partnership served them well as it allowed a low risk and low time intensive way to build trust and learn the capacities not only between each other but also between the stakeholders of residents and students. As the Rosewood Initiative was beginning to self-identify its own needs as a community, Wortham-Galvin and her students attended a youth activities night. Two things came out of that night and the interaction with the young residents of Rosewood. First, one of the teenagers was working with an artist to develop a mural to be painted on the nearby Shell gas station—through a grant Glass had obtained. The mural design was almost complete, but they were concerned about having enough people to help paint in a community that had not yet built up its own capacities rela-tive to neighborhood action. Wortham-Galvin's students volunteered to help. Thus they were neither leading the design of the mural, nor managing the project; they were just showing up to help get it done on painting day. Like many architecture students of the millennial generation, these students had a (Global North-based)

---

7 US Census Bureau, www.census.gov, accessed fall 2011.
8 www.rosewoodinitiative.org

humanitarian value system and a set of design skills, but were unsure of how to link them without engaging in a form of architectural colonialism by imposing their expertise and values systems on Rosewood. A service relationship led by the needs and activities of the Rosewood Initiative allowed them to "get involved" but in way that clearly established the youth as experts of the content and design of the mural. This service relationship was critical in subverting the architecture students' naturalized assumptions of their role as (future) professional experts.

Second, at the youth night that the PSU cohort attended, people were huddled around a broken ping pong table that served as meeting table, snack table, *and* game table. There were a few folding chairs to sit on and most people's coats and bags were scattered around the floor. The youth made it clear they needed places to sit, places to hang their things, more games, and for Jenny a place to post announcements and to hand out pamphlets about newly established events or social service programs. Following youth activities night, Wortham-Galvin found wooden doors on craigslist for seven dollars each. The PSU group offered to address the list of needs by making things for the nascent community center by creatively reusing the doors. Calling them usable murals (in a wordplay on the mural that was being installed at the nearby gas station), the students built bench seating (with hooks for coats and bags on the back), a chess table, and a pamphlet stand (with chalkboard painted areas for leaving messages) for the kids of Rosewood to use during youth activities night. In this act of design-build, the relationship moved from what may seem like a service arrangement on the surface, to one of exchange. Yes, the students were making designed usable objects for the community space (based on residents' and the Initiative's stated needs), but they were also getting an opportunity to practice their (future) profession. More critically they were designing not based on their personal whims (as oft happens in the academic studio setting per Kelbaugh's fallacies or the Bilbao paradigm), but on the directed uses and identity desires of the youth. Thus resources were exchanged that benefited both groups. In the case of Rosewood, they received physical objects they wanted. In the case of the students, they received a new way of approaching design thinking that did not preference their authorial voice and sole expertise, but were learning to co-produce design work.

Exchange partnerships have manifest between Glass and Wortham-Galvin from fall 2011 through spring 2014 when Wortham-Galvin led students in design visualization and feasibility studies of vacant lots and structures in the Rosewood neighborhood in multiple classes. Over these multiple studios and seminars, students have applied their design thinking to:

- Transforming underutilized parking lots with infrastructure to support farmers' markets, swap meets, book markets, etc.

- Designing bus stops for the mass transit system that included other community infrastructures (access to Wi-Fi, potable water, community announcements) in a community that has lower rates of car ownership and greater need and yet mostly has ad hoc bus signs on existing poles without real transit infrastructure

- Envisioning a hip-hop youth center to provide an outlet for expression and safer after-school activity

- Looking at vacant extant buildings and providing design propositions that included: a hybrid transit–health clinic center, daycare, a dance studio, an international food market, a media center focusing on small business, English as a second language, and other immigrant services assistance

These design studies were based on articulating residents' needs and other research reports and visualizing them so that the Rosewood Initiative might advocate to the City of Portland and Mayor's office the opportunities and deficits in their neighborhood from a representation point of view, rather than just based on tables, statistics, and written reports. This design work was accomplished cyclically by leveraging the Initiative's existing activities and broadening the scope to include discussion of social needs and how the design of their physical environment might meet those needs prior to any aesthetic or programming assumptions. In other words, this research-based design started with Rosewood's assets and deficits not an a priori design vision. No single class was encouraged to find "the solution." Instead, classes over two and half years continued to listen to the community discussions of their design proposals and iterate them. The design thinking was meant to illustrate and highlight a clear set of opportunities imbedded within the existing physical environment rather than declaring definitive solutions. While parts of these activities might veer into a cooperative relationship, as planning happened together, the responsibilities for this actions were held by the university team.

The service-cum-cooperative relationships deepened in spring 2016, when Glass called Wortham-Galvin and asked if students could occupy the parking spaces in front of the Initiative with tactical action.[9] Glass's ask was spurred by unusually warm spring weather and a desire to create a safe place for public gathering surrounding the Initiative in a strip mall parking lot where traditional policing methods have not been effective against drugs, theft, gang violence, and human trafficking. Wortham-Galvin agreed to gather students initially for what would have been a service-based activity for a sunny Saturday afternoon. Wortham-Galvin's position as a Faculty Fellow with PSU's Center for Public Interest Design (CPID) meant she was assisting in another CPID project: Opera a la Cart. The Portland Opera had received a grant to make opera mobile and bring it to neighborhoods that have a paucity of arts activities, and had contracted a relationship with the CPID for design assistance. Wortham-Galvin suggested to the CPID project leader, Todd Ferry, that in order to effectively research how to design a mobile opera platform, CPID facilitate guerilla opera actions in a series of neighborhoods to understand the needs of both the performers and the potential audiences. When the Portland

---

9 At this point the Rosewood Initiative was still in the same strip mall, but occupying a different and larger space. They moved out of the vacant dry cleaner in fall 2013 and into the nearby newly vacant billiards space. The owner of the strip mall agreed to keep their rent the same even though this almost quadrupled their square footage.

Opera agreed to this tactical research moment, Wortham-Galvin approached Glass and asked if the Rosewood Initiative could be the final stop for the guerrilla opera action. Thus what was to be a service-based action became a cooperative one. Wortham-Galvin and students associated with CPID occupied and activated the Initiative's parking spaces first by painting murals on plywood room dividers (used by Rosewood when multiple groups were using the space) with the assistance of Glass's team and encouraging passersby to join them. Then, those murals became the temporary backdrop for the guerilla opera when it arrived. The Initiative would receive the benefit of having their location highlighted as a public resource. The CPID would receive the benefit of researching how the mobile opera might function in a more official capacity in summer 2016 on its mobile platform which will then become a significant element of the Initiative's planned National Night Out in August 2016.

Systematic and Transformative relationships were pursued by Glass and Wortham-Galvin surrounding the transformation of the ad hoc physical space occupied by the Rosewood Initiative—initially in an abandoned dry cleaner space and then by winter of 2013–2014 in the newly vacant space a few doors down. In early 2013, the Rosewood Initiative received grant money to pursue rejuvenating their headquarters from its stripped shell status into a finished space. Glass contacted Wortham-Galvin who ran a summer course focused on designing the interior space with resident and Initiative involvement in all aspects of the design process (from conceptual, to schematic, to design development, and detail work). Once the Initiative approved of the university–community-produced design schemes (which were continually presented and discussed with residents as they developed), Glass and Wortham-Galvin worked on a list of contractors to interview for construction. As the interviews began, Glass heard from the strip mall's owner that he was about to sell the property and there was no guarantee that a new owner would affirm the Initiative's lease. Not wanting to risk the $70,000 on a space that might no longer be theirs to use, the Initiative put the money into social service and programming initiatives and the designs were shelved. That winter, the sale of the strip mall fell through. In a conciliatory move, the owner asked Glass if she would like the much larger, newly vacant, former billiards space for the Initiative at the same rental cost. Glass leapt at the chance. Glass and Wortham-Galvin began the same integrated process again to design and adapt the new space. This time with no money for the project to be realized (as the original grant had already been spent); but with the hope some public or private donor might step forward. To date the designs have not been realized. Instead, the students have continued to develop smaller needed work with the community supportive of the Initiative.

Both institutions have benefited in the various levels of partnership experienced in the PSU–Rosewood Initiative collaboration. This is not a unilateral "gift" of architectural expertise and/or products to a neighborhood in need. Glass believes their social services mission is best served by creating a well-designed place for gathering that will empower the residents by providing a physical place where they can address their socioeconomic, safety, and wellness struggles. The community will, thus, be strengthened through their engagement with the design of a public space that will become part of daily life. Wortham-Galvin also asserts that the intersection of design thinking and community-based action can foster an engaging public realm for Rosewood; but that the service-learning benefits the students receive are sometimes greater than what the community receives. The students are learning a new model of architectural praxis by doing. Thus, PSU's School of Architecture has been transformed by sharing in Rosewood's vision and supporting its manifestation in a way that challenges the temporary practice by and education of architects through preferencing building cultural processes rather than architectural products. Thus the words of the youth artist in charge of the gas station mural apply not just to residents but also to the university participants,

> I believe Rosewood changed my life by its presence and being supportive to my goals. When I say I want to do something creative or inspiring in my life, I get nothing but praise that I can do it. Not only that I can, but if Rosewood can help they will help me do it.[10]

Architecture may have nominally helped Rosewood, but Rosewood has substantially helped rethink the praxis and education of the architect.

Conclusion

The Rosewood story is not important because the relationship led to:

- The design of a neighborhood graphic brand and signage
- Furniture made from creatively scavenged materials
- Ways of rethinking vacant sites and buildings being underutilized in the neighborhood
- A community mural
- Tactical urbanism stagings to lay claim to a safe civic realm
- Interior spaces for the vacant shells within which the Initiative operates

These products are certainly tangible and easily identifiable outcomes, but if they remain as such then they superficially support the notion of design "doing good" or that "design works." Instead, how these "products" were achieved and how they are being used for current and future sociocultural production is far more valuable to architectural praxis and education. The interrogation of the process is what might lead to more co-productions of livable, sustainable neighborhoods.

10 www.rosewoodinitiative.org

As architecture schools attempt to realize their theoretical objectives through constructing physical structures as well as sociocultural dialogues, the following questions remain critical to the mainstreaming of university–community partnerships within the architectural academy:

- How can architecture as cultural practice challenge architectural products to generate a design process about people, not about things?

- How do we honor inequalities in the design of the built environment?

- How can we increase deep participation that honors the values of a people and place in order to avoid engaging in architectural colonialism or aestheticizing poverty?

- How do we make social aims an inseparable part of the economics of architecture, emphasizing co-production, making transparent gaps in architectural productions, and making evident who is framing a process or product through clear demarcation of the partisan nature of authorship?

- How can university–community relationships facilitate architecture as something other than a bastion of patrimony, or a commercially consumed object?

The other critical aspect that architecture–community relationships bring to the table is an interrogation of: how spaces construct a particular worldview for ourselves; how the discipline of architecture has passed on that worldview; and how the profession has embedded that worldview within the built environment, and helped thus to promote and determine patterns of consumption, exclusion, and environmental impact. Thus, when the Cooper-Hewitt, Smithsonian Design Museum followed up the Design **for** the Other 90% exhibit and publication with Design **with** the Other 90%: Cities, the shift from designing *for* underserved communities to designing *with* underscores a change in the emphasis of the approach of designers toward a more inclusive process. A process that recognizes differing beliefs underlying decision-making and values all participants as experts. The issue of agency is at the heart of 21st century architectural education and praxis. Who should decide what to make, *and* how, where, and for whom it is made? Can emphasizing architecture–community relationships become a guiding methodology where today's wicked problems (poverty, displacement, access to water and infrastructure, empowering women and girls, etc.) enter into public discourse by using architecture as a means to generate new discussions with people at the margins as principal discussants?

References

Brown, T. (2009). The making of a design thinker. *Metropolis*, October, 60-62.

Buchanan, R. (1992). Wicked problems in design thinking. *Design Issues*, 8(2), 5-21.

Churchman, C.W. (1967). Wicked problems. *Management Science*, 14(4). doi: 10.1287/ mnsc.14.4.B141

Cupers, K. (2014). Where is the social project? *Journal of Architectural Education*, 68(1), 6-8.

Curtis, W. (2006). Brand-new cities. *The American Scholar*, 75(1), 113-116.

Designing Activism (2011, December 31). Whitney Young 1968 speech to the American Institute of Architects. Retrieved from www.designingactivism.com/2011/12/31/ whitney-young-1968-speech-to-the-aia/

Faste, R., Roth, B. & Wilde, D. (1993). Integrating creativity into the mechanical engineering curriculum. In C.A. Fisher (Ed.), *ASME Resource Guide to Innovation in Engineering Design*. New York: American Society of Mechanical Engineers.

Feldman, R., Palleroni, S., Perkes, D. & Bell, B. (2013). *Wisdom from the Field: Public Interest Architecture in Practice*. Public Interest Design. Retrieved from www.publicinterestdesign.com/wp-content/uploads/2013/07/Wisdom-from-the-Field.pdf

Goodman, A. (2015a). *Citizen architects: ethics, education and the construction of a profession, 1933-2013* (Ph.D. dissertation). University of California, Berkeley, CA.

Goodman, A. (2015b). From "does it work" to "how it works": critical reflections on community design-build. *Dialectic III*, Spring, 15-23.

Greub, S. & Greub, T. (Eds.) (2006). *Museums in the 21st Century: Concepts Projects Buildings*. Berlin: Prestel.

Kelbaugh, D. (2004). Seven fallacies in architectural culture. *Journal of Architectural Education*, 58(1), 66-68.

Krauss, R. (1990). The cultural logic of the late capitalist museum. *October*, 54, 3-17.

McKim, R. (1973). *Experiences in Visual Thinking*. Monterey, CA: Brooks/Cole Publishing.

Mason, R. (2006). Theoretical and practical arguments for values-centered preservation. *CRM: The Journal of Heritage Studies*, 3, 2.

Meron, G. (2012). *Public Interest Design: An Annotated Bibliography*. Austin, TX: Center for Sustainable Development, School of Architecture, University of Texas.

Odbert, C. & Mulligan, J. (2014). The Kibera space project: Participation, integration, and networked change. In J. Hou, B. Spencer, T. Way & K. Yocom (Eds.), *Now Urbanism: The Future City is Here* (pp. 177-192). London: Routledge.

Papanek, V. (1972). *Design for the Real World*. London: Thames & Hudson.

Rittel, H. & Webber, M. (1973). Dilemmas in a general theory of planning. *Policy Sciences*, 4, 155-169.

Rowe, P. (1987). *Design Thinking*. Cambridge, MA: MIT Press.

Rybczynski, W. (2002). The Bilbao effect. *The Atlantic Monthly*, September, 138-142.

Simon, H. (1968). *The Sciences of the Artificial*. Cambridge, MA: MIT Press.

Sockett, H. (1998). Levels of partnership. *Metropolitan Universities*, Spring, 75-81.

Wortham-Galvin, B.D. (2012). Making the familiar strange: Understanding design practice as cultural practice. In S. Hirt (Ed.), *The Urban Wisdom of Jane Jacobs* (pp. 229-244). New York: Routledge.

Wortham-Galvin, B.D. (2013). An anthropology of urbanism: How people make places (and what designers and planners might learn from it). *Footprint: Delft School of Design Journal*, 13(Autumn), 21-40.

Wortham-Galvin, B.D. (2016, forthcoming). Agency, action and pedagogy in the making of contemporary places. *Dialectic IV: Architecture at Service*, Fall.

Yudell, L. (2010). Bilbao effect at the ballet. *Architectural Record*, 198(9), 72.

About the contributors

Editors

B.D. Wortham-Galvin, Ph.D., teaches studio, history, and theory of architecture and urban design in the School of Architecture at Portland State University. Her research focuses on how theories of cultural sustainability and the everyday can be applied to the design and stewardship of an adaptable built environment. She is a Faculty Fellow with three PSU institutions: the Center for Public Interest Design, the Institute for Sustainable Solutions, and BUILT (Building Science Lab to Advance Teaching), and she works with local and national communities on issues of equity and resilience in managing change in rural, suburban, and urban places. The *Daily Journal of Commerce* named her one of Oregon's Women of Vision for 2015.

Jennifer H. Allen is an associate professor of public administration and a Fellow of the Institute for Sustainable Solutions at Portland State University. Her areas of research encompass environmental and natural resource policy and administration, collaborative governance, sustainable economic development, and strategies for incorporating sustainability into higher education. She served as the Director of the Institute for Sustainable Solutions from 2012 to 2015, where she supported the development of sustainability-related research and curricula across campus and fostered partnerships between PSU and other institutions in the region and beyond. Jennifer has previously worked at the World Bank, Ecotrust, and the Oregon Economic and Community Development Department. She currently serves on the Oregon State Parks and Recreation Commission and on the board of the World Forestry Center. Dr. Allen holds degrees from Yale University, Yale School of Forestry and Environmental Studies, and George Mason University.

Jacob Sherman is the Sustainability Curriculum Coordinator for the Institute for Sustainable Solutions at Portland State University. He leads academic and student programs that seek to unleash higher education's ability to address complex problems, including PSU's largest community-engagement program focused on advancing urban sustainability. Jacob previously worked for PSU's award-winning general education program, University Studies, to better integrate student research, engagement, and other creative activities into the undergraduate curriculum. In 2012, Jacob was recognized as both Portland State University's and the State of Oregon's "Student Employee of the Year." He currently serves on the board of the Brentwood-Darlington neighborhood association and on Portland Bureau of Transportation's Local Transportation Infrastructure Charge committee crafting new transportation policy for the city. He previously served on the PSU Alumni Association and as Board Chair for the Brentwood-Darlington Neighborhood Association. Jacob holds a Master's degree in Educational Leadership and Policy, and a Bachelor of Arts in English from Portland State University.

Contributors

Adriane Ackerman is an undergraduate student at Portland State University studying Political Science with an emphasis on Public Service, working towards a Minor in Civic Leadership. She participates in both the University Honors and Political Science Honors programs and was a member of the inaugural cohort of Student Fellows at the Institute for Sustainable Solutions in 2015. Building upon over a decade of grassroots community organizing, Adriane is dedicated to studying best practices in promoting the public's involvement in the political process and increasing civic engagement, especially among marginalized communities. She uses her time as a Student Ambassador at PSU's acclaimed program, First Stop Portland, to glean insight from experts in public place-making the world over, and to inform delegations of leaders from the global public and private sectors about the Portland story of sustainable innovation.

Deborah Smith Arthur, M.A., J.D., is an Assistant Professor in the University Studies interdisciplinary department at Portland State University, and has been teaching community-based learning courses in the area of juvenile justice for over 13 years. Prior to teaching at PSU, Deb practiced criminal and juvenile law for over a decade, primarily representing juveniles in adult criminal court. In 2011, she received a Civic Engagement Award for Excellence in Community-based Teaching and Learning. In 2012 her Juvenile Justice Capstone course was recognized with a Volunteer Award for Exemplary Service by Multnomah County. Deb is a volunteer with the Oregon Youth Authority and has also volunteered with the Oregon Department of Corrections.

Julia Babcock has worked as a project coordinator for Oregon Solutions since 2009 on a number of local and state policy issues including the Lloyd Green District, the Federal Forest Advisory Committee Implementation Working Group (FFAC IWG), and the Sage Grouse Conservation Partnership (SageCon). She co-facilitates the Vietnam Forum at PSU to host visiting delegations and build a research agenda between Oregon and Vietnam through the Center for Public Service. Prior to moving to Oregon, Julia was a planner for the Cities of Clearwater and West Palm Beach in Florida. She holds a B.A. in English with minors in Geography and Urban Planning from University of Florida and a Master's in Urban and Regional Planning from Portland State University.

Katrine Barber is an associate professor of history and affiliated faculty of the Indigenous Nations Studies program at PSU. Publications include "Shared authority in the context of tribal sovereignty: Building capacity for partnerships with Indigenous Nations," *The Public*

Historian (November 2013), and *Nature's Northwest: The North Pacific Slope in the Twenti-eth Century*, co-authored with William Robbins (University of Arizona Press, 2011). She also authored *Death of Celilo* (University of Washington Press, 2005), which documented the inundation of one of the nation's most important Indigenous fisheries by the Dalles Dam in 1957.

Jack Corbett is Professor of Public Administration, Portland State University. He has more than four decades of experience organizing and directing international programs and collaborative projects in Mexico and Canada. Recent relevant publications include: "Social research and reflective practice in binational contexts" (co-authored with Elsa Cruz Martinez), in O'Leary *et al.* (Eds.), *Uncharted Terrain: New Directions in Border Research Methodology, Ethics, and Practice* (University of Arizona Press, 2013); "Can organizations learn? Exploring a shift from conflict to collaboration" *George Wright Forum* (2013) (co-authored with Nelly Robles Garcia).

Renée Bogin Curtis, MUS, ABD, is a program manager and evaluator in PSU's Center for Urban Studies. Renée analyzes social and environmental impacts of sustainability programs for government agencies and investigates diverse environmental attitudes to develop inclusive outreach campaigns. Upcoming articles include an evaluation of urban food recovery systems for *Resource Recycling* and an article on ethical markets under revision for the *International Journal of Consumer Studies*. Recent publications include a chapter on artisans in Charles Heying's *Brew to Bikes*, an article on Latino environmental attitudes for *Resource Recycling* and evaluation reports for National Science Foundation studies posted on InformalScience.org.

Mandy Elder is a graduate student dual enrolled in Master of Public Administration and MA in Sociocultural Anthropology programs at Portland State University. Her interest in educational equity drove her Fulbright research with Universidad Tecnologica de los Valles Centrales de Oaxaca and has since led to facilitating international courses for Mexican students. She is co-founder of the Portland-based nonprofit organization, Women's International Leadership and Learning.

Erin Elliott is a doctoral student in Public Affairs and Policy at Portland State University. She teaches undergraduate courses in the Civic Leadership Minor and in the University Studies Department on civic engagement, leading social change, and the fundamentals of public service. She also has a Master's in Public Administration from the Evergreen State College where she focused on nonprofit administration, cultural competency education, critical theory, and poverty policy. She has held multiple positions in public service agencies including working as a direct service provider at the Community Action Council in Lacey, WA and as an educator with a domestic violence agency teaching primary prevention to teens in Gainesville, FL. She is dedicated to serving her community via the nonprofit sector merging theory and practice to make meaningful connections in civic life. Recently she presented an original co-authored paper entitled "Toward a care-centered approach for nonprofit management in a neoliberal era" at the Association for Research on Nonprofit and Voluntary Action conference, and is currently working on a paper entitled "Rethinking mapping in the nonprofit sector: Dark matter as autonomous geographies" which will be presented at the Public Administration Theory and Praxis conference in 2015.

Shpresa Halimi is the Program Director of Vietnam-USA Professional Fellows Program at Portland State University. She has over a decade of experience working with Vietnamese institutions of higher education, central and local government organizations, and community groups on sustainable development, community-based learning and community-based environmental management initiatives in Vietnam. She holds a doctorate degree in Public Administration and Policy from Portland State University and a Master's degree in Environmental Policy and Natural Resource Management from Indiana University.

Per Henningsgaard is an assistant professor of English and director of the graduate program in book publishing at Portland State University. His research interests include editing and publishing, book history and print culture studies, Australian studies, postcolonial literature, and regional literature. Among his most recent publications are "The editing and publishing of Tim Winton in the United States" in the anthology *Tim Winton: Critical Essays* (2014), and "A pedagogical tool for studying the history of the book: Thirty-five years of bibliographical presses in Australia and New Zealand, 1977–2012" in the journal *Script & Print* (2014).

Charles Heying is associate professor of urban studies and planning at Portland State University. He has co-authored a book and numerous articles on the politics and development of Olympic cities. Professor Heying's current research combines his interest in the arts with his passion for community-based economic development. His book, *Brew to Bikes: Portland's Artisan Economy*, describes how the transformation from an industrial to a post-industrial economy is being articulated in the trend-setting edges of Portland's artisan production.

Marcus Ingle is Professor of Public Administration in the Mark O. Hatfield School of Government at Portland State University and Director of Vietnam Programs at the Center for Public Service. He has over 30 years of experience in international public service working in more than 80 countries. His career spans local to multinational assignments in the government, nonprofit, and corporate sectors. He has worked for the US Agency for International Development (USAID), The World Bank Group, and the University of Maryland. From 1997 to 2003 he served as Senior Associate to Booz Allen Hamilton, the worldwide strategy and technology consulting firm, in Colombia, Vietnam, Hungary, and the Balkans. Professor Ingle obtained his Ph.D. in social science from the Maxwell School of Public Affairs, Syracuse University.

Kevin Kecskes, Ph.D., is Associate Professor of Public Administration in the Mark O. Hatfield School of Government at Portland State University. He teaches in the Master's of Public Administration program on the global roles of NGOs, strategic planning, and ethics as well as undergraduate courses focused on community engagement. For over a decade, Dr. Kecskes provided university-wide leadership in various positions at PSU including Associate Vice Provost for Engagement and Director for Community–University Partnerships. From 1997 to 2002, he was Regional Program Director of the Western Region Campus Compact Consortium. Dr. Kecskes is on the editorial board of the *Journal of Public Scholarship in Higher Education* and has advised numerous college and university campuses in the United States and globally for over 15 years. He edited *Engaging Departments: Moving Faculty Culture from Private to Public, Individual to Collective Focus for the Common Good* (2006).

Kris Kelsang Lipman was born and raised in Elmhurst, Queens, uses she/her pronouns, and identifies as bicultural, Bhutanese, Jewish, and mixed. She received her MSW from NYU's

Silver School of Social Work and her BSW from Portland State University. Much of her clinical experience is in delivering individual and group therapy to women living with substance dependence and co-occurring mental health diagnoses. She currently works as a case manager at the Guardianship Project of the Vera Institute of Justice, where she advocates for people who are in need of a court-appointed legal guardian. Kris also serves on the steering committee of the Undoing Racism Internship Project (URIP), an organizing collective that aims to collectively unite the NY-based schools of social work to organize for a stronger anti-racist, anti-oppressive lens in their curriculum. She is an avid critic of the institutionalization of social work practice and its roots in white supremacy, imperialism, and capitalism. She could not be more appreciative or proud of her work with URIP.

Thea Kindschuh is a graduate of Portland State's Environmental Studies B.S. program and a former employee of the Campus Sustainability Office. During her time as Reuse Coordinator and Visual Communications Developer she facilitated both the Waste Reduction Task Force and Sustainable Drinking Water Task Force while growing the reuse program by rebranding and increasing community engagement to promote a culture of reuse. Thea studied at Seattle University and Uppsala University, Sweden before returning home to Portland State to continue her exploration of sustainable communities and quality of life. She is currently living in Montana pursuing her passions for the outdoors and wilderness conservation, and plans to return to Portland for graduate work in urban planning.

Margarette Leite teaches building tectonics, material sustainability, and community-engaged design at Portland State University's School of Architecture in Portland, Oregon, and is a Fellow of the Center for Public Interest Design there. She is known for her work with local schools and in disaster relief communities. These initiatives have garnered awards for civic engagement and have been the subjects of numerous publications and documentaries. Her work on the SAGE green modular classroom received a 2013 SEED award for social, economic, and environmental design. She has written about the SAGE project in *Architecture in An Age of Uncertainty* (Ashgate Press, 2014.)

Gwyneth Manser holds degrees in anthropology and environmental studies from Emory University, and is currently working towards a Master's in geography at Portland State University. Her thesis work focuses on the lived experience of "food deserts," and her broader academic interests include food justice, equity, and sustainability.

Stephen Marotta is a doctoral student and research assistant at Portland State University. He has a Bachelor of Arts in Integrative Studies and Master of Arts in Social Justice and Human Rights from Arizona State University. Past research includes environmental justice topics in Ciudad Juarez, Mexico and New Orleans, LA, and more recently the intersection between the creative economy and urban revitalization in Detroit, MI. Currently he conducts research for the Artisan Economy Initiative at Portland State University in Portland, OR.

Keisha Mateo, as a first year generation student, moved to Portland from Maui Hawai'i to pursue a Bachelors of Fine Arts at Portland State University. In taking Dr. Alma Trinidad's Freshman Inquiry Race and Social Justice, she has greatly developed an interest in social justice. She is passionate in wanting to help and understand people of color and communities facing racial and economic inequalities and wants to continue on her journey of social-awareness. In pursuing a BFA she wants to tie both her own aesthetic style and cri-tique systems of oppression she feels passionate about. She was also a research assistant with Dr. Trinidad's project on building parent-youth empowerment leadership to address edu-cational equity.

Catherine McNeur is an assistant professor of environmental and public history in Portland State University's History Department. Her publications include *Taming Manhattan: Environmental Battles in the Antebellum City* (Harvard University Press, 2014) and "The 'swinish multitude': Controversies over hogs in Antebellum New York City," *Journal of Urban History* (September 2011). Her writing has won several prizes including the American Society for Environmental History's George Perkins Marsh Prize, the Society for Historians of the Early Republic's James H. Broussard Prize, the New York Society Library's Hornblower Award, and the Victorian Society of America Metropolitan Chapter Book Prize, among others.

Mireaya Medina is an African American, "art-ivist" born and raised in Portland, Oregon. She is a first generation college graduate, a mother, a community organizer, a program director, and a musician who has worked extensively with youth for over a decade with Americans Friends Service Committee and other youth movements both locally and nationally. She also is a contributing writer for the *Rock N' Roll Camp For Girls* book, as well as instructing young girls on using samplers, keys, and beat machines in the Hip-Hop Elements program for nine years. She has dedicated her life to the intersectionalities of social justice and art.

Brad Melaugh is a graduate of the Leadership for Sustainability Education Master's program at Portland State University, and a former employee of the Campus Sustainability Office (CSO). As the food diversion coordinator at CSO, Brad worked to increase the university's capacity to collect and process food waste while engaging the campus community in pro-grams around waste. As an educator, farmer, student, and musician, he is dedicated to creat-ing just and sustainable communities through work in educational equity, sustainable food production, and food justice. Brad has a B.Ed. and B.Mus. from McGill University, and has experience in teaching, educational program development, and farming in South Korea, Rwanda, and Canada.

Imani Muhammad has been working with communities locally and throughout the country for close to a decade. She graduated with a BS in Psychology, Sociology and Bible studies from Cascade College (branch of Oklahoma Christian University) in 2003. Imani credits her unique upbringing from her parents for laying the foundation for her level of activism and commitment to always striving to better herself and in turn humanity as a whole. Both her black mother and her white father instilled the immense value of living a life of integrity, hard work, and reaching whatever goal was imaginable. Imani's interest in youth work was uncovered while working with the Boys and Girls Clubs in 1999, and in 2004 she became the lead teacher of a 7th grade class at Victory MS (housed inside Boys and Girls Clubs). It was this work that affirmed her life work with youth. Imani participated in the Millions More Movement, which deepened her commitment and dedication to the teachings of the Honor-able Elijah Muhammad taught by the Honorable Minister Louis Farrakhan and the work of the Nation of Islam.

Berenis Peregrino-Galvez was born and raised in Hood River, OR, identifies as Mexican-American, and is a first generation student. She is currently at Portland State University pursuing a bachelor of social work degree. Berenis has always had an interest in adversity and social justice, along with advocating the rights of those that are underrepresented.

Nelda Reyes García, MA, is a bicultural, Spanish/English bilingual consultant who specializes in culturally specific program and exhibit evaluation in Mexico and the United States. Nelda has developed and managed responsive methods for conducting studies in two languages, including for PSU and OMSI. Nelda led and advised on culturally appropriate evaluation and oversaw analysis for multilingual multinational Abbott Fund Science Education-Outreach Programs. Nelda is also an access and inclusivity consultant for several prestigious education and culture programs and foundations currently targeting minority communities. Publications include evaluation reports for Oregon Museum of Science and Industry and National Aeronautics and Space Administration posted on InformalScience.org.

Pablo Saldana is a first generation student who migrated to the United States at age ten with his immediate family in search of opportunities. He was born in Jalisco, Mexico. Living as an undocumented immigrant prevented him from feeling acknowledged by the system. Being involved with the Race and Social Justice discipline, he truly understands the sense of privilege and lack thereof. Pablo is now very close to graduating with his Bachelor's degree with honors, and is in a pursuit of a Master's degree in music and business.

Nydia Mata-Sánchez is Director of Outreach and External Programs at the Universidad Tecnologica de los Valles Centrales de Oaxaca and coordinator of UT initiatives with Portland State University.

Hunter Shobe is a cultural geographer and Assistant Professor in the Geography Department at Portland State University. He holds a PhD in Geography from the University of Oregon. His research explores the cultural, political, and economic dimensions of how people connect to places and environments. His work articulates the on-the-ground ways in which people experience and develop senses of place. Much of his work concerns how popular culture is implicated in how place is understood. Dr. Shobe's work appears in academic journals including *Urban Geography, National Identities, The Journal of Geography*, and *The Journal of Cultural Geography*.

Donna Sinclair is a practicing public historian and adjunct assistant professor of history at PSU. She teaches "Chinook History on the World Wide Web," has directed several large-scale oral history programs, and has worked with Native communities through the Confluence Project and the Center for Columbia River History. Publications include "They did not go to war: Chief Red Heart's band and Native American incarceration" *Columbia Magazine* (Fall 1998), interpretive social histories for the National Park Service at Fort Vancouver National Historic Site, and community history websites at ccrh.org.

Rita Sumner received both an M.P.H. in Health Administration and Policy and a Ph.D. in Public Administration and Policy at Portland State University. In addition, she previously completed a Master of Science degree in Health and Safety Administration at Oregon State

University focused on organizational performance, building internal capacity, and managing risk to institutional resources. Her PSU teaching experience has included undergraduate courses in both the health and civic engagement domains as well as graduate courses in the OMPH program. She is currently the Leading Social Change cluster coordinator for University Studies. Dr. Sumner's professional practice history in the public service sector has included work in the environmental and occupation health fields, and military service. She recently co-presented at the International Association for Research on Servicelearning and Community Engagement (IARSLCE) conference entitled *Creating Evidence of Institutional Engagement: Why Haven't We Figured It Out Yet?* Currently, she is co-writing a book on women veterans.

Alma M.O. Trinidad, PhD, MSW, is an assistant professor in the School of Social Work at PSU, and has served in a shared position with University Studies. Dr. Trinidad was born and raised on the island of Molokai, Hawai'i and has presumed a stance as a Pinay scholar warrior of aloha in her life work. She is a macro social worker and scholar activist. Her scholarly work focuses on Critical Indigenous Pedagogy of Place, youth empowerment, social determinants of health, multicultural education, youth participatory action research, social movements, and leadership for social change. Other research and teaching interests include critical humanist-centered designs, innovation, and social entrepreneurship, and culturally responsible research methods. She strives to encourage interdisciplinary scholars and practitioners to continuously critique and re-envision their roles and responsibilities in creating processes and places for such work on equity and change. She has published her work in *Polymath, Journal of Ethnic and Cultural Diversity in Social Work, Journal of Pacific Studies, Journal of Indigenous Social Development*, and *Hulili: Multidisciplinary Research on Hawaiian Well-Being*.

An environmentally friendly book printed and bound in England by www.printondemand-worldwide.com

PEFC Certified

This product is
from sustainably
managed forests
and controlled
sources

www.pefc.org

PEFC/16-33-415

This book is made of chain-of-custody materials; FSC materials for the cover and PEFC materials for the text pages.